Turkey Men

Volume 2

Turkey
Volume 2 Men

Thomas R. Pero

Illustration by Jack Paluh

WILD RIVER PRESS

www.turkeymen.com

Library of Congress Cataloging-in-Publication Data
Pero, Thomas R.
    Turkey men volume 2./Thomas R. Pero.—1st edition
    p. cm.
    ISBN 9780989523660
    1. Wild turkey. 2. Hunting. 3. I. Title.

    Library of Congress Control Number: 2016915404

Book and cover design by Gregory Smith Design
Front cover photograph of hunters by Chris Ellis for Nomad
Front and rear cover photographs and throughout book of live wild turkeys by Timothy C. Flanigan of Nature Exposure

Published by Wild River Press, Post Office Box 13360, Mill Creek, Washington 98082 USA

Wild River Press website address: www.wildriverpress.com

Book series website address: www.turkeymen.com

Printed in the United States of America by Jostens

10 9 8 7 6 5 4 3 2 1

DEDICATION

Again, this book is for all the young hunters,
teenagers and younger, boys and girls,
who will pull the trigger on their first wild turkey this year.
May you always be as thrilled.

ABOUT THE AUTHOR

Thomas R. Pero is a lifelong fly fisher and bird hunter. He a full-time professional writer, editor, photographer and publisher, and has been an active member of the Outdoor Writers Association of America since 1981. He is the owner of Wild River Press, publisher of quality fishing and hunting books. Many of these titles have won international awards for graphic and editorial excellence, including multiple gold and silver Benjamin Franklin Awards from the world's largest association of independent publishers.

Pero was just 18 when he started the Southeastern Massachusetts Chapter of Trout Unlimited, the youngest chapter president in the organization's history. In 1977, at age 23, he was named editor of *Trout* magazine. During his 16-year tenure, *Trout* was twice named Conservation Magazine of the Year by the Natural Resources Council of America. In 1992 Pero co-founded the non-profit Wild Salmon Center. In 2010 he was awarded the prestigious Starker Leopold Wild Trout Medal at the Wild Trout Symposium in Yellowstone for a lifetime of influential writing about coldwater fisheries conservation.

Pero is the author of *Till Death or Fly Fishing Do Us Part* (2008), editor of *A Passion for Grouse* (2013), author of *Gettysburg 1863—Seething Hell* (2016), and author of *Turkey Men* Volume 1 (2017).

CONTENTS

PREFACE

Two years ago I set out to capture the personal stories—in their own words and pictures—of 12 exceptional hunters who have successfully killed a wild turkey in each of the 49 states in America where the birds live.

My first book, *Turkey Men* Volume 1, published at the start of the 2017 spring turkey season, featured the adventures of Jeff Budz, David J. Ellis, Tony Hudak, Rob Keck, Clyde F. Neely and Randy Stafford.

Now, *Turkey Men* Volume 2, published in the middle of the spring 2018 season, features the U. S. Super Slam quests of Tom "Doc" Weddle of Bloomington, Indiana; Dave Owens of Acworth, Georgia; James F. Hascup of Ringwood, New Jersey; Daniel Rorrer of Pulaski, Virginia; James Wilhelm of Eagle Rock, Virginia; and Jon D. Pries of Trout Run, Pennsylvania. Each of their stories is extraordinary and engaging.

One of the things that makes this second collection of bright, full, unvarnished conversations with these accomplished turkey hunters different from the first collection is the complimentary compact disk audio recording that comes with your book. It was made at a noted professional recording studio called Postal Recording in Indianapolis, where I met Doc Weddle, who drove up from his home in Bloomington, and Dave Owens, who flew up from Georgia for the session. Once the musicians cleared out, I sat down with Doc and Dave among the Fenders and Gibsons, and listened to them talk turkey. It was all very casual and unscripted: I wanted the feeling of sitting around the campfire with the boys and eavesdropping on their banter.

The remarkable turn of events is that, a year and a half later, just before this volume was scheduled to go to press, Dave Owens was named Grand National Turkey Calling Champion, Senior Division Open, at the 2018 National Wild Turkey Convention in Nashville.

When I heard the news, I picked up the phone to congratulate Dave on his spectacular win. He characteristically accepted my congratulations with the modesty of the small-town Georgia boy he is. And he reminded me of what both he and his friend Doc had stressed during our long interview: that calling is only a small part of the hunting puzzle.

At Nashville, the young man had been up against the best: 45 individuals from around the country who had won local calling competitions or were past champions.

In listening to Dave explain what the judges asked him to do, I immediately grasped that the new calling scenarios, recently developed and adopted by the N.W.T.F., put a spotlight on his talent and allowed him to shine.

In Scenario 1, the callers were asked create the sounds of a hen waking up, flying down from the roost, and beginning to feed in a field:

- tree call
- fly-down cackle
- plain yelp
- clucking and purring

In Scenario 2, the callers were asked to reenact a fall flock that breaks up and scatters, reassembles, and two jakes begin fighting:

- kee-kee run
- assembling yelp of boss hen
- jake yelps
- fighting purr

Thus, the judges based their scores not only on the ability of a caller to expertly mimic the discrete vocals of a particular bird, but on a caller's visceral understanding of the natural scene, and his or her artful proficiency in reproducing the nuanced audio of the unfolding narrative.

Dave was in his element. Because Dave Owens hadn't merely studied the best turkey callers—Dave Owens had studied wild turkeys. He could sing their song.

THOMAS R. PERO

Dave Owens

HOME:
Acworth, Georgia

OCCUPATION:
Pest exterminator

FIRST WILD TURKEY:
1999, Georgia

COMPLETED U.S. SUPER SLAM:
2016, New Hampshire

Tom "Doc" Weddle

HOME:
Bloomington, Indiana

OCCUPATION:
Carpenter

FIRST WILD TURKEY:
1983, Indiana

COMPLETED U.S. SUPER SLAM:
2006, Kansas

COMPLETED SECOND U.S. SUPER SLAM:
2011, Missouri

HIS GRANDFATHER CALLED HIM "DOC." The youngster had never seen a turkey in the wild—how could he have? There weren't any. At least not until he was 16, when he heard that the Indiana Department of Natural Resources had released some wild birds near a 10,000-acre reservoir called Lake Monroe. It was the state's largest man-made lake. He knew the water and the woods around it well. His father, Tommy Lee Weddle, was the D.N.R. property manager.

David and Marie Caudill with Tom "Doc" Weddle in Florida, 2014. Caudill was a heavy equipment operator for the then-Florida Game and Fresh Water Fish Commission. He worked closely with the biologists restoring the native Osceola subspecies to Florida, playing a key role as lead turkey trapper at Fisheating Creek. From 1949 to 1970 some 6,000 wild birds were live-trapped and released throughout the peninsula.

Young Tommy wasn't a doctor—of medicine or philosophy or anything else. He was a kid who trapped muskrats (1,600 of them in one season!) and mink. Sometimes beavers. He can't remember a time when Grandfather Shine didn't call him "Doc," the way someone would be affectionately dubbed "Buddy" or "Pal" or "Bubba." Years later he realized that he was not the only "Doc" around. Granddad called nearly everyone that.

When, several years later, the state opened a legal turkey season, Doc was locked and loaded. His first try was disappointing. In three days he heard nothing but silence. On the second day he missed a ghostly jake. That only fueled his ambition. If the turkeys wouldn't come to him, he would go to them. He lifted a metal-frame pack on his back, crammed with sleeping bag and grub and shotgun shells, and hiked three miles into the Hoosier National Forest. He wasn't going to leave until he at least heard a turkey. At daybreak, in the pouring rain, he smeared his face with green and black grease paint. Later that morning, 23-year-old Doc Weddle pulled the worn trigger on his father's beat-up Herter's 12-gauge over-under. He was the only one of 93 permitted turkey hunters in Indiana in the spring of 1983 to kill a bird.

That was the start of his lifetime marathon. In the decades since, Tom "Doc" Weddle had devoted his life to the pursuit of wild turkeys. Completely and fully devoted his life, to the extent that he has refused to tie himself to a paying job that doesn't allow him three full months off each spring. (Think you're passionate about turkey hunting? Try that one one on for size at home.)

He drives around, state after state, hunting public land exclusively, sleeping and living out of a fully equipped, self-contained "super van." First, there was a ramshackle 1968 Ford Econoline. And before his current 2016 Fort, Doc's home away from home was a 2005 Sprinter, plastered with 310,00 miles before it limped into the trade-in lot. No word on what the new owner did with the window decal: IN LOVING MEMORY OF ALL THE GOBBLERS I'VE KILLED.

Along the winding way, Weddle has killed a wild turkey in all 49 states—not once but twice. No one else has done that; no one else has come close. And he is within grasp of doing it a third time within the next few years.

One spring day in 2016, a 31-year-old young man named Dave Owens, from Georgia, wandered into Doc Weddle's campsite in Vermont. Dave had just killed a wild turkey over in New Hampshire, across the Connecticut River. It was his 49th state bird. He was ecstatic.

Owens had never met Weddle face to face, but knew him by reputation and by chatter. The two had communicated online and shared information. They also shared a basic minimalist philosophy of the hunt: not too fancy, do-it-yourself, make things happen, the road is your home. Above all, when you step into the woods, keep things simple.

Dave admires Doc and considers him a mentor. Owens is already a Georgia state champion turkey caller. He was born in 1985 and raised in a small town, Cedartown, right on the Alabama line up in the northwest corner of Georgia.

ABOVE: It took some convincing by master caller Dave Owens to draw this Montana Merriam's out of its cottonwood river bottom in May 2105. **FACING PAGE:** Dave was manning the video camera and helped his friend Marc Heffron kill this Georgia gobbler that flew down to a pasture and starting strutting with several jakes.

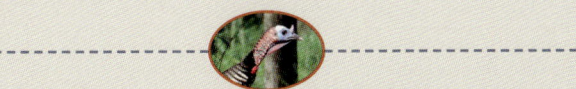

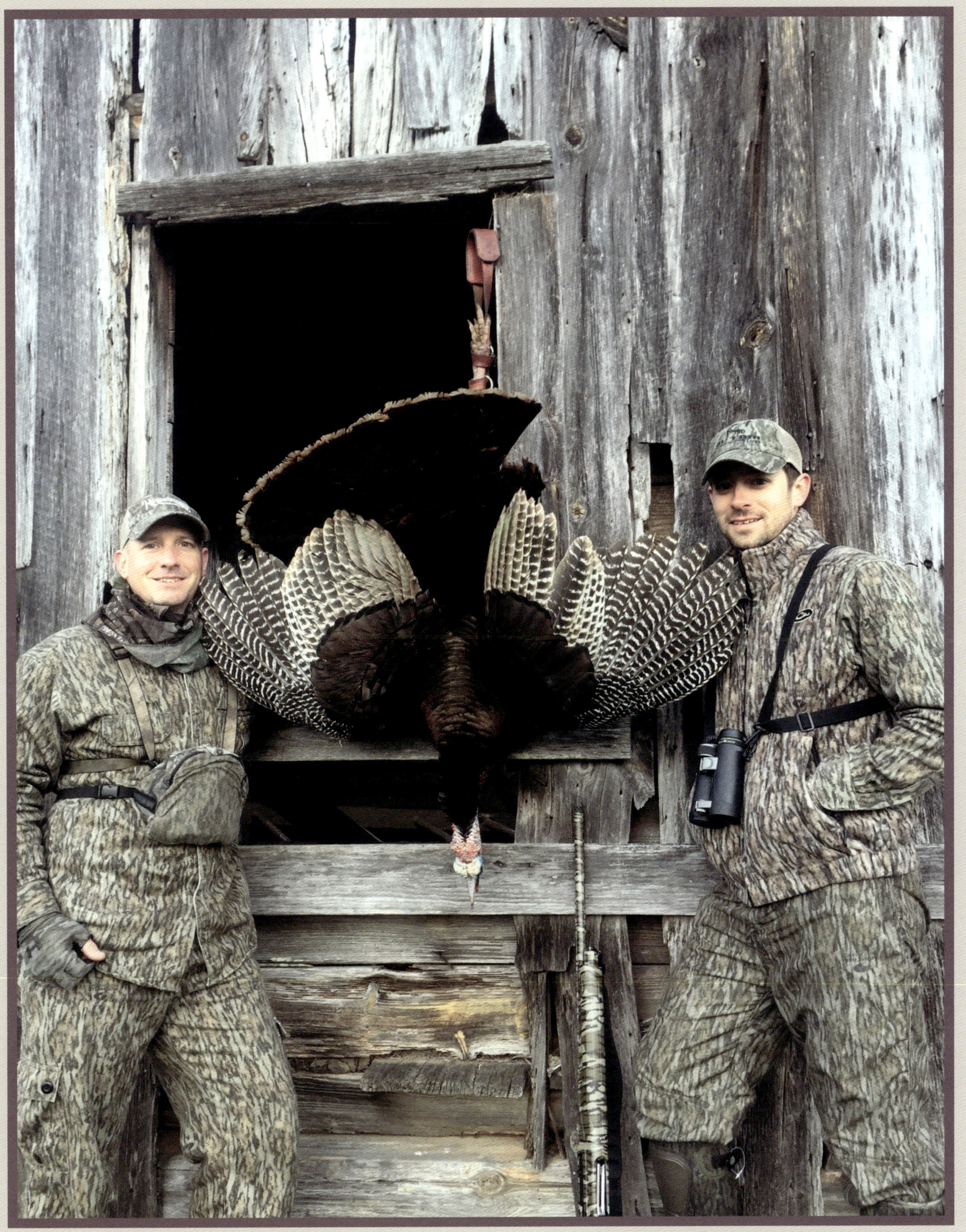

Dave Owens and Tom "Doc" Weddle

IN LOVING MEMORY OF

ALL THE GOBBLERS
I'VE KILLED

Did you grow up in the mountains or farmland?
DAVE OWENS: We're down towards kinda the foothills of the mountains. We're not in the big Blue Ridge Mountains like you would see in northeast Georgia. But yeah, that's where I was born and raised. Small town, Cedartown, not a huge metropolitan area for sure. I was fortunate enough to be in and around the woods my whole life. My dad is a fanatical deer hunter, which is probably what planted the seed with outdoors and wildlife and hunting and everything. And he was a deer hunter at heart, kinda all he did. We did have some rabbit beagles and such. But that's where the hunting bug started. Ever since I can remember, I was just eaten up with the outdoors and wanted to be out there. It caused some issues with schooling and that kind of stuff. I say issues, but it really kept me on the straight and narrow with schooling. Because my mother was very strict: "You go do your books and your studies first and then you get playtime." And she would always dangle what she called a hooky day: "You get to play a day of hooky if your grades are good." Which meant I always got to go with my dad on a deer hunt and skip a day of school, usually like a long weekend or something. So she would always dangle that carrot out in front of us. And that's the way they kind of kept me motivated about anything.

Do you have brothers and sisters?
OWENS: I have a brother, yeah, and a much younger sister. My brother is two years younger than myself and he was eaten up with outdoors about as much as I am. He's just a little bit more of a family man, to where I've kinda thrown that all to the wayside given this whole turkey fascination and obsession. But that's where I started as a young boy. Me and little Drew, my brother, we stayed outside. We tormented the song bird population and squirrels and rabbits and anything else that would be in the wrath of our pellet guns and BB guns.

I was gonna ask if a pellet gun was your choice of weapon.
OWENS: Yeah, absolutely, pellet guns. And we lived at the end of a little dead-end road, a cul-de-sac. And who only knows who all owned all that property behind us, but we treated it like it was our own. You know, we were young kids and would ramble out through there for hours and plinking—whatever we felt like.

What about your schooling?
OWENS: Graduated from high school, and then I was accepted at the University of Georgia. Went and finished in the University of Georgia a little over four years it took me there. Never really had a problem. I was never one of these people that are just smart without trying. And everybody thought I was that type of person. I really did have to work a lot harder than I feel like a lot of other people do. But I was disciplined in wanting to do well in everything that I ever took part in. And school was one of those things that I took part in. So I studied and I did well and graduated.

What did you go to school for?
OWENS: Went to school as a biology major and pre-dental intentions.

Owens played chess with a flock of roosted toms for a couple days in the wine country of Walla Walla, Washington, in May 2015. Dave finally took this one when he flew down at first light, before he got to his hens.

Why didn't you pursue that?
OWENS: Cuz it got in the way—turkey hunting got in the way.

Or it was gonna get in the way of the turkey hunting!
OWENS: Exactly. So that hit a rock wall real quick, and sent me down the path to where I have fallen now.

Did you ever get any shit for that from your family?
OWENS: Daily. [laughing]

Still?
OWENS: Still do, every family reunion somebody's gonna come up and slap me on the back and say, "Do you ever consider going back to dental school?" That's completely gone now and it's, like, "No, that's not ever gonna happen."

Owens took this eastern wild turkey in the rugged 708,000-acre Daniel Boone National Forest during the last week of the Kentucky season in 2014. "He lived in a nasty canyon," Dave said. "It was the second time we met."

Plus you're supposed to have a bunch of kids.
OWENS: Yeah, yeah, you're supposed to—when you're from Cedartown—you're supposed to, you know, be married by 24, 25, and have babies. And if that's what they had decided they wanted to do with their lives, great.

Kind of a Mayberry R.F.D. place?
OWENS: A situation like that, and I just didn't fit, especially when turkeys entered the scene. And I will say I was disciplined enough to realize that this turkey thing was gonna be a problem with that way of life. I didn't want anybody else to suffer. Because if I brought somebody else in who's gonna depend on me, unfortunately, due to my obsession with turkeys and being gone and moving

during the spring—basically throwing everything else to the wayside—everything was gonna suffer. And it's kind of hard to do something for only nine months out of the year, whether it's a spouse or raise children.

Dave, what do you do for a living during those non-hunting nine months?
OWENS: I graduated from college during the summer semester. Well, I have a cousin that had started his own termite and pest control business and it had gotten to a point to where my brother actually worked for him during the summer. He was just basically like grunt labor, helping him dig trenches for termite work and whatnot. And when I graduated from college, I thought, *Hey, I'll go*

and help him make some money, give me something to do and make some cash. Straight out of college and then I did that while I was applying for dental school. But when you graduate during the summer, you can't apply, I think, until the next October. So I had to wait almost a full year to apply. And then, I applied, got interviewed—blah blah blah—and didn't get accepted. Next year, I applied again—didn't get accepted. So, now we're talking three years after I had graduated from college and I've been working with him. And my traveling for turkeys had increased quite a bit given the freedom that I now hadn't been tied up with college work and stuff.

not going to give me the flexibility that I was wanting, to be gone for a month or more just during the spring and eventually, hopefully, three months.

You must have a pretty understanding boss.
OWENS: He's flying around the world, drinking fine wine. [laughing] Basically, yeah. He's still a big part of getting everything paid, but I've been with him long enough to learn how everything in the company functions.

What exactly do you do?
OWENS: Essentially, I operate a termite and pest control company. We have a base of customers

> Because if I brought somebody else in who's gonna depend on me, unfortunately, due to my obsession with turkeys and being gone and moving during the spring—basically throwing everything else to the wayside—everything was gonna suffer.

When did you first hunt other states?
OWENS: I started traveling for turkey hunting during college. I had always turkey hunted during my spring breaks from high school, but college spring break is several weeks earlier. And Georgia turkey season wasn't in. That's when I said, "Hey, I've gotta turkey hunt!" Figured out the only place to turkey hunt that was open was south Florida. So that's what kind of jump-started my whole traveling for turkeys. Well, anyways, I graduated from college and started working pest control. The dental school thing was kinda a thorn in my side. By the time I was thinking about applying a third time, you know, you get to wondering what is it that you really want out of life. And what I figured out quickly that made me happy was having the freedom to do what I wanted. I was afraid that my big plan to become a dentist, own a private practice, was that people expect you to be there. They expect to come in and see their dentist. That was

that need services and it's on a continuous basis like, for instance, a quarterly pest control service where I go out there four times a year. Somebody has to coordinate all that—let them know we are coming out, make sure that work is done and gets completed, as well as dealing with new customers.

So keeps you busy. . . .
OWENS: God, there's tons of stuff. From ants and roaches, millipedes, centipedes, scorpions, silverfish, there is just a ton of crawling insects. And not to mention termites—they cause millions of dollars of damage here in the Southeast.

How many years have you been doing this now?
OWENS: I've been doing it for almost 10 years now.

You must have seen some crazy stuff.
OWENS: Yeah, you don't really recognize how crazy people are, how odd people can be. I love all

my customers, but some people you don't realize how they can—you question how they get up every morning and put their shoes on. I had a customer, who wasn't a customer very long, came to the door stark naked.

Beautiful.
OWENS: Buck naked, I'm opening the door. . . .

A woman, I presume?
OWENS: No, it was a man, unfortunately. [laughing] He just came to the door *stark naked*.

With evil intent or because he was clueless?
OWENS: With evil intent, I'm pretty sure. Yeah, and then there's these reality TV shows out there now, "Bug Man." That stuff's real. Now, granted,

daily. And there's still really rough parts of that area, and we go down there usually doing rental properties for somebody. Some places can get really, really rough. You really have to watch over your back. Some of the stuff you see on the news, those people are really out there.

So you literally see the underside of living.
OWENS: You see a lot of very interesting, very outside-the-circle of what you realize is even out there. Cuz you're invited into people's houses. Of course, you have these immaculate houses, you knock on the door and the lady that invites you in and she's apologetic: "I'm so sorry, I haven't had time to clean this week" and whatever. And you go in there and you would be comfortable eating off the floor, it seems like it's so clean. And she's

> Yeah, and then there's these reality TV shows out there now, "Bug Man." That stuff's real. Now, granted, some of the stuff I think it's a put on, but there are houses that we've walked into and every step crunches, because you're stepping on roaches.

some of the stuff I think it's a put on, but there are houses that we've walked into and every step *crunches*, because you're stepping on roaches.

Yikes. And people live there?
OWENS: And people live there—and they have children in those type situations, which is really, really sad. You have people that are living in houses that you don't even realize, you don't even think that it's possible. But there are people that still live in houses that you have to watch what part of the floor you step on. And they have rodents that are just living in the house with them. Parts of Atlanta, I work in and around Atlanta,

apologetic the whole time you're there, talking about how dirty her house is.

We don't find those people interesting.
OWENS: [laughing] And then you go in a place and they don't care: "Yeah, we need the inside sprayed. We want the inside sprayed. And you walk in there and you can't even reach inside into any of the baseboards of the house, because there's junk piled up all along the floors.

You're not married?
OWENS: I'm not married.

FACING PAGE: On day four of a difficult, snowy hunt in the Blue Mountains of eastern Oregon in May 2014, Dave heard what he thought were two very vocal turkeys fighting. Then he watched a golden eagle chase this Rio Grande gobbler across three Ponderosa pine mountaintops. The bird lived—until Dave returned the next morning.

Never have been?

OWENS: Never have been married, never really have been close.

Because of the turkeys.

OWENS: Cuz of the turkeys. Like I said, I'm sure a lot of people have gotten into situations that they've had things blow up in their face or they've had to make some extravagant measures to get out of a situation or turkeys causes them divorces. I mean, I have friends whose hunting caused divorces. Maybe not turkey hunting specifically, but hunting in general. Not getting to do what they wanna do—I saw enough of that early on to realize that I really had to be careful when it come to that. So I approach everything relationship-wise as an open book. Look, this is how it is: if you think you're gonna change me, unfortunately, I'm gonna tell you you're not. There's been women ahead of you that thought they were gonna change me." I just let them know I'm one of those type people. I'm comfortable being alone. If that's the way it is 30 years from now, I will be comfortable being alone, knowing that I have the freedom to come and go during the spring season.

Your current girlfriend comes from a hunting family.

OWENS: Yeah, Courtney comes from a hunting family, which is probably why she's very passionate about things. And I think it really helps when someone has a hobby that's consuming to them.

Well, it's more than a hobby—she's an expert.

OWENS: Yeah, she is a wildlife biologist. She's got multiple wildlife biology degrees and wildlife management degrees and she's passionate about that.

Sandhill cranes, isn't it?

OWENS: Sandhill cranes is what she did her masters project on, basically the well-beings of their populations. Granted, this is me speaking in my

In May 2015, Dave Owens and his hunting partner, Kenny Mount, were successful in Minnesota and Wisconsin. On a bit of a lark they headed to Michigan and started knocking on the doors of dairy farms.

terms—she's got much more technical terms—but she essentially is tracking the birds from their wintering grounds to their breeding grounds. And trying to figure out there's several different isolated populations and there's some people call those population different things. And I think there's a question of whether it's the same population and so she's tracking them to see if they go to the same wintering grounds and whatnot.

Is Courtney also from Georgia?

OWENS: She is from Georgia. She's actually from the town that neighbors me, but now she's traveled all over. She's probably worked in 10 or more states doing internships and masters stuff.

Where did she go to school?

OWENS: She went to University of Georgia. She graduated from there, Warnell School of Forestry, there at the University of Georgia. Then she went to Knoxville, Tennessee for a little bit and then she went to Lubbock to Texas Tech for her masters.

FACING PAGE: One of four eastern gobblers that came to fight in the Iowa spring wild flowers in 2016. Owens got between two pair and picked off the closest one in the bluebells.

Now there's a long-distance relationship!
OWENS: Sixteen hours away.

That's a car drive.
OWENS: Yeah, 16½. And that's wide open—pissing on the exit ramps. [laughing]

And how long did that go on?
OWENS: Two and a half years, I think she was there. Yes. I tried to get out there as much as I could and she came back here quite a bit, cuz her family's still here.

How did that work during the turkey season?
OWENS: She had to come here to see me. That was the roughest spell, because when you got a limited

OWENS: She just took a permanent position and the end deal is her wanting to be closer to work—north, northwest Georgia, northeast Alabama, somewhere around those area. She specializes in migratory birds. She wants to be a migratory bird biologist for a state agency, a private entity, whatever it may be, but that's the end goal. And this is just another step. So in the same way that she's kind of cooperative and accepts what I do and me going during the spring—and how completely detached I am from her and everything to do with life during the springtime—I'm the same way about her and her desires to accomplish her end goal of getting her dream job. And like I tell her, there's not a lot of boyfriends that are gonna deal with their girlfriend in Knoxville, four and a half

> Not intentionally, but, yeah, anybody that's part of my life during the springtime is gonna be tested. Friendships, family relationships, and, obviously, any type of relationship, girlfriend-related, is gonna be tested during the spring.

amount of time, you don't ever get to see them, period. And they fly in for a long weekend and it's during turkey season. I obviously wasn't there.

What did Courtney think about that?
OWENS: Not happy about it. But she was able to grasp it and understand it. I've had other girls attempt to but never been able to handle it. And that eventually is what sent everybody on their separate ways.

So you tested her?
OWENS: Not intentionally, but, yeah, anybody that's part of my life during the springtime is gonna be tested. Friendships, family relationships, and, obviously, any type of relationship, girlfriend-related, is gonna be tested during the spring.

You just moved her down to Florida.

hours away, and then Texas, 16 hours away! Now she's in Panama City, which is five hours away. So there's not a lot of boyfriends who are gonna deal with what she does. And's there are not a lot of girlfriends who are going to deal with what I do.

So it's the perfect standoff.
OWENS: Maybe that's what it is, yeah. [laughing] A counterbalance. You're gonna have to deal with me—I'm gonna have to deal with you. [Note: Since this interview was conducted in the summer of 2016, Courtney moved to Hollywood, Alabama, where she is now the area waterfowl biologist.]

How's all this working?
OWENS: It's working.

Really?
OWENS: It's worked for over four years now.

In May 2015 Owens found this late-season eastern on public land in a remote creek bottom in Georgia.

And you brought Courtney turkey hunting for the first time.
OWENS: I did take her—she had never been turkey hunting. She has an uncle who's famous for making rifles. He was a military sniper, and then he started building his own rifles. She's shot deer and everything. She's got some enormous deer, much bigger than anything I've ever killed. But she had never shot a turkey before. I'm not even sure she had ever been turkey hunting. They were more into big-game hunting, and I don't wanna get in

a "shooting match" with her when it comes to rifles, you know?

Right.
OWENS: With me it's all turkey hunting.

So you brought her out and showed her the ropes.
OWENS: I took her out turkey hunting and showed her the ropes—and tried to show her without handing her things. But eventually she became frustrated. She wanted to kill a turkey like

Dave took this bird in New York State's Catskills during the first week of the 2013 season.

everybody does, and we got her a turkey year before last, and she enjoyed it. It was exciting. She went right over to Texas and killed one on her own, so I think she thought she had it figured out a little bit.

But you don't think she had wild turkeys figured out?
OWENS: Well, in this past year, and she's gonna hate me for this. . . .
DOC WEDDLE: I don't know if any of us ever do.
OWENS: Yeah, nobody has it figured out in that sense. But she feels like I have it figured out. And so this year was a big standoff: "I'm not taking you, and putting you on another turkey. I'll help you along the way."

You said that to her?
OWENS: Point blank.

How did that go over?
OWENS: She called me an asshole and a few other words, but it's essentially like everything else with the whole turkey hunting society—and this is probably gonna start getting to where I'm digging myself a hole. I don't want to cripple someone. Someone approaches me for information on turkeys, I'll be glad to send them to an area, but I don't wanna give them. . . .

But this is your girlfriend!
OWENS: It's different with turkeys with me.

[Laughing]
OWENS: I don't care if you're my mother. Even with my girlfriend, I would be glad to help. I pointed her in the right direction many times, and I even told her, "You locate a turkey, I'll be glad to go help you with him once you locate him." But I wanted her to do some of the leg work.

So you expected Courtney to roll out of bed in the morning at 4 o'clock and go scouting on her own.
OWENS: Yeah, that's what I wanted her to do. Basically, I wanted her to want it. I wanted her to feel that desire that I have.

Right.
OWENS: It's in my chest. It gets me up every morning. That passion won't let me miss a morning.

Did she get out there?
OWENS: She did quite a bit—more than most men that call themselves turkey hunters, I guarantee! But here again I put everything in comparison to what I do.
Yeah, but that's not fair. You are a wild turkey maniac.

FACING PAGE: Another gorgeous Merriam's gobbler he took in Montana in 2015, after phoning around to find open land that the state leased from ranchers for public hunting.

On opening day of the April, 2015 season in North Carolina, Owens listened as two feisty gobblers sounded back and forth across steep hardwood ridges. He coaxed one of them squiring two hens down an old woods road.

OWENS: Exactly what she keeps telling me—"You are a maniac!" She is, like, "You are comparing me to you and I am not gonna do that. [laughing] I don't have that type of desire."

WEDDLE: You've got what many would consider a mental illness when it comes to this.

How did it all work out—did she get one?

OWENS: She did not kill a turkey this year. She did miss one.

You were relinquished.

OWENS: She did have the opportunity to kill one and she missed one. Which is almost a little bit of salt in the wound as well. She did work this year and she probably put many miles on her boots,

like I said, compared to what a guy that would consider himself a turkey hunter. She probably did just as much work—if not more—than they did. But there's no substitute for experience. No matter how much you teach somebody, or tell somebody, or give them tips and strategies and whatever, there's no substitute for experience. And she doesn't have that yet. She just doesn't have the experience.

Right.

OWENS: It'll come. But, yeah, she did not kill a turkey this year. And after the season. I did feel a little bit bad about it. But over the years just coming up—and I'm sure Doc can relate—you give so many turkeys away. You take people turkey hunting. And they do nothing more than sit down in

front of a tree and shoot the turkey.

WEDDLE: Yeah.

OWENS: And then, not speaking specifically about Courtney, because she was very appreciative. She understands the high regard I hold even for an individual turkey. She appreciates that. You give a certain amount of them away, and then you watch the people that just shot the turkey, and they don't care.

WEDDLE: Yeah.

OWENS: And I guess it was about two or three years ago, four years ago, I kind of got to a point where I refused to do that. I used to turkey hunt with a dozen or more people, obviously doing what I do, and I'm known for being a turkey hunter. There's people who are known for killing. Big Boone and Crockett bucks everywhere. I'm

essentially a hotel on wheels. I'm not a white-collar worker. I don't make tons of money. I don't have the ability to buy anything I want. But I needed a truck long enough for me to be able to lay down in. I settled on a Toyota Tacoma long bed, four door, six-foot bed. I put a cap on it, first thing I did, so that it's a nice dry area. I've got a camp cot, six-foot cot that's in the back, so it fits perfectly in there. I'm able to keep it up all year long. Got a shelf built in there with my little box. I'm very organized when it comes to turkey hunting. I want everything to be fluid.

You're self-contained.

OWENS: Yeah. I don't like getting frustrated, cuz I can't find something. I've got lanterns. I've got a heater. I've got a fan. I've got anything that I could

> Everything in my life revolves around turkeys, so if I make a purchase, it's probably in some weird dark way related to turkeys. My vehicle is the same way. . . I wanted it to be essentially a hotel on wheels. I'm not a white-collar worker. I don't make tons of money.

just known as a turkey hunter—which I'm completely okay with. So, I'm approached with, "Man, let's go turkey hunting this year." And I've gone with a lot of people and taken a lot of people. Then they kill a turkey and it was a fantastic hunt and then the next morning they don't want to get out of bed. I'm like: "How did you just do that? You just had *that experience* and you don't want to get up and do it again?" That just shows me that they don't appreciate it as much as I do.

Describe your truck—you described it when we were driving over here.

OWENS: Everything in my life revolves around turkeys, so if I make a purchase, it's probably in some weird dark way related to turkeys. My vehicle is the same way. I wanted to buy a truck that got reasonably good gas mileage; I wanted it to be

need to survive for a week or 10 days, or two weeks, or whatever, just living out of the back of that truck. I've got it all in the back of that truck.

You drive all over.

OWENS: I drive all over and essentially stay wherever I get tired. It's pretty convenient, actually. I climb in the back of that truck and I lock myself in there. Climb on that cot—I sleep better on that cot than I do on my Tempur-Pedic mattress at home.

How do you take a shower, or don't you?

OWENS: Well, showers can be scarce at times. I'm one of those guys, as long as I can throw some water on my head and wash my head, I'll be well, and just wipe it down. So I take just spring water, just gallon jugs of spring water, and then keep that

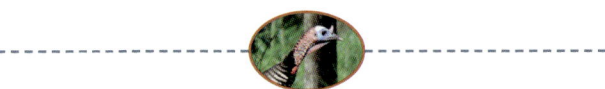

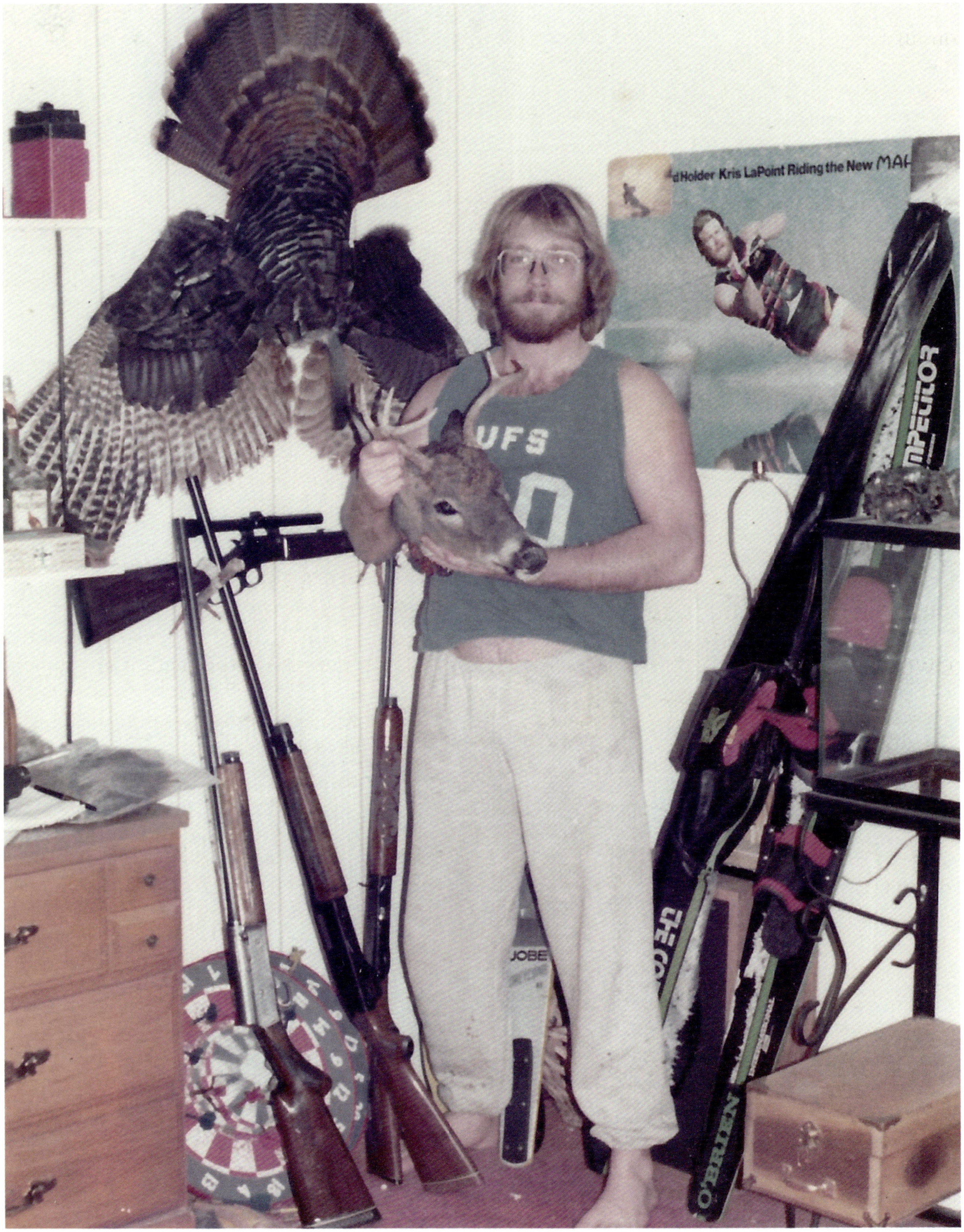
Holder Kris LaPoint Riding the New
UFS
O'BRIEN

with me. I found numerous truck stops that I use on my trips. And those are always welcomed. A nice hot shower. Just this past year, I was in Vermont and stumbled right into an awesome little truck stop. It had great food and for five bucks they'll let you get a shower, too. Became a thing. I just came in and dropped five bucks and they knew what I was wanting. And I got back there and got a good hot shower before I went and climbed in my bed. That's always a welcome surprise.

All right, let's give our host a chance to get a word in edgewise. Doc has been weeding.

trucks, stuff like that. They're nice because there's six feet of head room.

And you drive this for your work, as well?
WEDDLE: Yes, I'm a carpenter so I have all my stuff in there. Then, when it's turkey season, all my work stuff goes out and all my camping stuff and turkey stuff goes in.

If this were turkey season what would we see?
WEDDLE: You'd see a bunch of plastic tubs. All my stuff is very organized and compartmentalized. I know what's where and in which tub. Then

> Yes, I'm a carpenter so I have all my stuff in there.
> Then, when it's turkey season, all my work stuff goes out
> and all my camping stuff and turkey stuff goes in.

WEDDLE: And watering! [laugh] I'm gonna get my paint brush out.
OWENS: Yeah, looks like he's gonna start painting.

After our interview.
WEDDLE: All right.
Doc, why don't we take off where we just left off with Dave? Describe your rather unusual set of wheels.
WEDDLE: Well, he's got young knees, so he doesn't mind crawling in the back of a truck with a pop-up. No way, man. I need some place I can walk around. [laughs] So I got a Ford Transit and before that I had a Sprinter, and before that I had a Dodge with a raised roof—something I could get in.

So what are these vehicle made for?
WEDDLE: Service vehicles of one form or another. They're really popular in Europe—delivery

I've got a blow-up mattress that doesn't take any room—it's more comfortable than the bed that I've got at the house. And that's it. A couple of coolers, cuz I'm living out of my coolers. When it's raining or whatever, I can get in that van and stand up and walk around and stretch out while Dave's over there cramped in his little truck, being miserable.

[Laughing] And what's that sticker around the back there, the decal on the back?
WEDDLE: It says, IN LOVING MEMORY OF ALL THE GOBBLERS I'VE KILLED.

Perfect!
WEDDLE: I got that from the Gobbler Nation turkey hunting forum. It kind of says it all. [laughing]

One wonders, when you're stopped at a traffic light, what certain people think.
WEDDLE: Well, it got me out of a speeding ticket

FACING PAGE: With time out for a youthful fling with water-skiing, hunting was in Tommy Weddle's blood from the start. Here he is in 1983 with his first whitetail deer and his first wild turkey.

last spring—the cop who pulled me over was a turkey hunter.

No kidding? [laughing]
WEDDLE: The first thing he did, he walked up and said, is that right, you killed a lot of turkeys? "Yeah," I said. "I killed a few." I was just coming in off a month on the road. And he goes, "You know how fast you were going?" I said: "Well, I know I am in a hurry to get home to see if there are any turkeys gobbling." He said, "You were going 36 miles an hour over the speed limit." [laughing] But he said: "Let's get back to turkeys. I've been chasing this gobbler all spring, and I haven't been able to do a thing with him." And so we started

What happened with the situation with the woman you dropped off at the bus station?
WEDDLE: Oh, *that* one. . . .

No name.
WEDDLE: She'll know when she reads the book. [laughing]

How many years ago was this?
WEDDLE: It's been 15 years ago—or more. She came with me for the season. We started in Florida and we were working our way up the East Coast. We made about five or six states, which I thought

> I think what precipitated it was when she missed a big gobbler
> that I called in for her. She wasn't happy about that
> and we got into some silly argument that escalated.
> We had left her truck in another state,
> so I took her to the bus station and sent her back to get it.

talking about turkeys. He took my license and my registration and he went and checked me out. And he comes back and he goes, "I'm gonna do you a favor today and just gonna write you a warning ticket—but slow that thing down." [laughing]

And you weren't even blonde and good looking.
WEDDLE: Neither. [laughing]

So tell me about how turkeys have, shall we say, influenced your personal relationships?
WEDDLE: Man, that's a rough one! I'm just coming off a breakup because she couldn't take me being gone for two and a half months straight. I'll admit that. It takes a special kind of woman to put up with turkeys like us. That's what we do. That's who we are. Turkey hunting is where we're gonna be all spring long. Not being able to deal with that is a real deal-breaker. I ain't gonna change or

was remarkable. She drove her own truck so we had our own space. But we were traveling together. And we finally got into a little tiff. I think what precipitated it was when she missed a big gobbler that I called in for her. She wasn't happy about that and we got into some silly argument that escalated. We had left her truck in another state, so I took her to the bus station and sent her back to get it.

It was definitely your fault.
WEDDLE: I told her to get her shit and get out. [laughing]

And how was that received?
WEDDLE: We're back to being friends again, but it took a few years. It didn't work out very well at the time. I believe I was called a self-righteous pompous ass.

Rains in the spring of 1984 had raised Lake Monroe in Indiana to record levels. Doc picked up his friend Tom Skirvin at the boat ramp and they motored to a remote campsite. The next morning Doc shot his second tom dead—until he grabbed the bird by the neck and it sprung to life, beating its wings wildly against this larger predator, who hung on with a death grip. The happy hunter stumbled into camp bruised, bloodied, tattered and torn.

Well, that's good—I like that. We've all gotten that before.

WEDDLE: Yeah. Yeah, I was.

Let's turn to *Turkey Tails and Tales From Across the USA*, your book published in 2013. I thoroughly enjoyed reading it, Doc. Your book has great heart and great spirit, and I congratulate you for that. It's what everybody needs to strive for—everybody who has aspirations for writing any kind of memoir of this sort. I loved your "Final Say" chapter. As an incorrigible editor, I would have taken that sucker and moved it right up front. I thought it was terrific. I'm gonna read your opening line back to you: "I knew that I was hopelessly hooked on the sport of turkey hunting from the very first time I stepped into the spring woods wearing camo, but no attempt was ever made to cure myself of the addiction." That's pure. That says it all.

WEDDLE: Yeah.

OVERLEAF: This old abandoned farm house surrounded by native hemp plants served as the 2011 backdrop for an unforgettable Kansas bird called to the gun by Doc Weddle from a mile and a half away.

In 1988, Weddle had already filled his in-state Indiana tags. He had hoped to help his hunting partner, Ron Ronk, kill a bird by setting up 40 yards apart. The strategy didn't go according to plan, however, when a flock of toms appeared yards in front of Doc and began a fierce beak-and-claw donnybrook. It all worked out when Ron pulled the trigger on this 23½-pound limb-hanger, which they promptly nicknamed "Captain Hook."

You shot your first one in when, 1983?
WEDDLE: Yeah, 1983.

So what's kept you going all these years? What's kept the fire going?
WEDDLE: Turkeys captivated my soul from the very first time I heard one gobble. I was squirrel hunting in August. And then, when I finally saw my first one, I thought to myself: *Oh, my God! I've spent my whole life in the woods, but I've never seen anything so beautiful!* I love hunting of all kinds, but there is nothing else like turkey hunting. It's intriguing and exciting beyond measure. You get to communicate with the birds in their own language. I enjoy the unique aspect of taking on these individual birds one-on-one, in their own domain, and the contemplative chess-match way that most hunts unfold. The sport just fits me.

And Dave, what is it specifically about turkeys that captivates you? They are your sole focus as a hunter in the field, in the woods.
OWENS: It's one of those things that I struggle to put into words—what is it about turkeys themselves? Obviously, it's about the fact that they're different than hunting anything else. You have the dialogue, and you have what I feel is more of a one-on-one conversation. A lot of people call ducks, they call geese, and that kind of thing. But there's always decoys involved. When you're talking with turkeys, it's really a one-on-one game— just you and him involved. There's no other

Doc Weddle tagged his first double-beard tom turkey in 1987 in Orange County, Indiana.

trickery, so to speak. You're stepping into his life, you're stepping right into his world. And going nose-to-nose with him. I think it's that one-on-one approach.

WEDDLE: And then it's like it turns into a chess game of moves and counter-moves and positioning, and all the things that make turkey hunting so unique.

OWENS: With other hunting—deer camps and stuff—there's a big crowd that's involved. But with real turkey hunters, like ourselves and like all the guys that I'm sure that you've interviewed along this whole trail, I'd almost bet that all of those guys are more of a solitary kind of people.

It's a more solitary pursuit, no question about it.
WEDDLE: It's more contemplative. It's intellectual.
OWENS: Yeah, there's no need for those large

groups. And while I have hunted and shared hunts with many people, that's not the way I prefer it.

The stories are shared afterward.
WEDDLE: Exactly. It's more intimate than any other hunting, in my experience.

Doc killed his first bird in 1983—when did you kill your first turkey?
OWENS: Nineteen ninety-nine.

And you were?
OWENS: Fourteen years old.

You remember that scene?
OWENS: Absolutely. It's burned in my memory.

Let's hear it.

OWENS: I see these young guys, eight years old, killing a turkey, just cuz they had somebody helping them along the way. I'm a self-taught turkey hunter. My dad, he was a fanatical deer hunter, still is to this day. He never expressed any interest in turkeys. I have no idea why I did. But, like Doc was saying, as soon as I just learned their vocabulary, and learned the dialogue, it just kind of captivated me. That's all I cared about.

Tell me about the first bird you killed.

OWENS: Well, I was lucky enough to have a family friend and they owned a little piece of property. I'm just gonna throw a figure out there—maybe 20 acres. Had a lot of turkeys on the place. It was a really good property. And they gave me permis-

hear myself call. I was still young and a little bit naive when it came to the whole thing. Ended up getting up there finding me a big tree on top of that little old knob and got my calls out and played on every one of them.

You were all geared up, you had the camo outfit, etc.

OWENS: I was all geared up. I'd played all the calls and essentially laid back and scooted down the tree. Next thing you know, I was laying on my back sound asleep by this tree. I'm not sure how long from the time period, I don't know if they were coming to my calling or if it just happened that they wandered up on me. But I remember laying there on my back and in a daze and hearing a [makes clucking noise]. Just a cluck. I knew what it was and here I go trying to squirm my way back

> And my dear mother, God bless her, this is gonna blow everybody's mind away. We lived about 25 minutes away from this property and she would get up during the spring . . . hours before daylight and drive me over there to their property and drop me off, as a 13- and 14-year-old kid. . . .

sion. And my dear mother, God bless her, this is gonna blow everybody's mind away. We lived about 25 minutes away from this property and she would get up during the spring on our weekends when I didn't have school, Saturday and Sunday. She would get up hours before daylight and drive me over there to their property and drop me off, as a 13- and 14-year-old kid, and leave me and come pick me up at lunch. So it was one of those times. I had wrestled those turkeys for a season. And it was that second season—here again, I'd screwed up so much—but they had a lot of turkeys and we ended up at the back of their property at the top of the hill. They owned the property right across the top. And basically I liked to

up the trunk of that tree. And somehow I got up there and I could hear him right over the hill just walking [makes leaves rustle]. And they poked their heads up and they were red-headed and he poked up and had a little beard that pokes straight out like a little bitty, like a shotgun shell, just poking straight out like three inches. Pow! I shot him and that was my first turkey, a little bitty jake, and you couldn't have told me shit, buddy.

What did you feel?

OWENS: I was king of the mountain! [laughing] I remember walking down there to those people's house at the foot of the hill and sitting there by their driveway waiting on my mom and had him

OVERLEAF: Doc Weddle in 1989 with a fine central New York bird in a colorful spring dandelion field in Chenango County.

laid out there beside me. Buddy, I was the king—and all on my own. It's kind of how I kicked the snowball down the hill.

And you had no real mentor?
OWENS: No mentor. It's what speared that whole I-want-to-be-a-dentist approach at life. The only the guy I knew that turkey-hunted was my step-mother's boss. He was a dentist. He owned a private practice in Cedartown and he called himself a turkey hunter, so he apparently hunted turkeys. He was kind of a closed-off character, never offered to take me turkey hunting and whatnot, but I knew he was a turkey hunter. So I wanted to be a turkey

I've probably done just as much wrong as they have just because I never had anybody to get out there and show me the ropes.

Doc, in contrast, as you've written about so warmly in your book, you certainly did have a mentor, somebody who inspired you.
WEDDLE: I did. We never actually hunted to-gether, but Bill Madden was an inspiration to me. He was a wildlife biologist. He was one of my dad's colleagues in the Indiana Department of Natural Resources. He was turkey hunting in Arkansas and Missouri before my home state even *had* turkeys.

> I've probably done as much stuff wrong as anybody—regardless of whether my turkey-hunting career is much shorter than a lot of guys. I've probably done just as much wrong as they have just because I never had anybody to get out there and show me the ropes.

hunter. He was a dentist, made enough money to go turkey hunting and, by God, I wanted to be a dentist.

Well, at least you stuck with one pursuit. [laughs]
OWENS: Exactly. So, yeah, no mentors. Never knew anybody that ever turkey-hunted. I was for-tunate enough, being a little younger than Doc—I'll go ahead and poke a rib now—I had the ability to get on these hunting forums. Some receive a lot of flak nowadays for just being boastful folks, but I was able to get involved in those venues, maga-zines, all that kind of stuff and just kind of get some, maybe you call it groundwork, maybe some pointers and stuff. And the rest of it was just flat out getting out there and doing a bunch of stuff wrong.

You seem to remember that more than one would imagine.
OWENS: I've probably done as much stuff wrong as anybody—regardless of whether my turkey-hunting career is much shorter than a lot of guys.

How did Bill inspire you?
WEDDLE: Listening to his stories. They kind of lit a fire in my belly to want to be a turkey hunter, too. Then I ran into another biologist closer to my age who also turkey hunted, although, in talking with him, I found out that he had yet to actually kill a bird after seven years trying. But he invited me to come along.

What happened?
WEDDLE: I missed a jake on my second day ever of turkey hunting!

Wow. . . .
WEDDLE: That *really* stoked the flames. There was no stopping me now, so I decided to hike deep into the Hoosier National Forest and stay there until I figured this sport out. The very next morn-ing I experienced one of those absolutely magical hunts. I wrapped a tag around the scaly leg of my first wild turkey.

When Weddle approached this Oklahoma bird in 1990, he saw that it was banded—one of 10 birds he took in six states that season, including a double grand slam, his first.

You were hooked.
WEDDLE: For life!

Looking back all those years, how do you see that experience—no cellphone, no G.P.S., only the most rudimentary camo and loads? Do you ever wonder how you even did what you did?
WEDDLE: There wasn't any way to imagine how easy hunters today would have it. I just did what had to be done at the time, which was to write a lot of letters to game departments and wildlife biologists, and then wait for the information to come trickling in before analyzing and evaluating what it meant and figuring out where to go. Then, go there and put boots on the ground.

Same follow through.
WEDDLE: Yeah, that part of it is still the same, even though technology has certainly shortened the information gathering. It's a lot easier to prepare for the hunt.

Technology always advances.
WEDDLE: I suppose—flintlock rifle versus a stone.

But the difference between 1983 and today?
WEDDLE: If you even *heard* a turkey in 1983, you'd had a good season! Today, if I don't hear at least one gobbling tom daily, it's almost depressing. You inevitably start hearing people say, "they're already done—bred-out," or "coyotes have eaten them all." People *expect* to easily fill all

their tags. Anyone who doesn't is viewed as some kind of moron.

So expectations are vastly different.
WEDDLE: Man, in 1983, if you were lucky enough to see a turkey at some point of the season, people would come up to you with wonder and admiration in their eyes, hanging on your every word like you were some sort of guru of something.

You found your way around with topographic maps.
WEDDLE: Most young hunters today don't even know they exist. Or even what they are. And they wouldn't have any idea how to read a topo map if every turkey in the area was marked with a big red X.

You must have quite the collection.
WEDDLE: I must have about a bazillion of them for all 49 states that I've hunted. I am perfectly content on any given evening to sit and study the area where I'm hunting on these maps for hours. Everything you need to know about the land is all right there: creeks, fields, ravines, points, elevations, contours, slope, roads, trails, etc. Today you can of course go to Google Earth or some such site and be looking at recent satellite pictures, but you can only learn so much that way. Topos are still in my arsenal.

You are in a unique position—or at least highly unusual position—in that your turkey-hunting experience spans that entire period.
WEDDLE: Right, right.

And during that period you achieved two U. S. Super Slams. You have twice shot wild turkeys in all 49 states and you're on the verge of a third. You have seen it all, not only the geography and the changes in where turkeys live—their expanded range—but also all these changes in navigation technology and guns and shotshells and

so on. **How easily have you incorporated change into how you approach the sport today?**
WEDDLE: Well. . . .
OWENS: He's still a dinosaur. [laughing]
WEDDLE: Yeah, I'm still a dinosaur. I still carry a flip-phone. But I have been carrying a G.P.S. for many years. I don't do much with it other than marking roosts or kill sites. Sometimes it comes in handy. Just last spring Dave texted me the coordinates of a hidden field on public land in a small state where he'd heard a couple birds gobbling earlier in the year. I was able to plus them into the G.P.S. and go right there in the dark.

How did that work out?
WEDDLE: I ended up killing a bird. So I have Dave to thank—Dave and technology! Still, I like to poke fun at him and say how easy he's got it today. Dave's hard-core drive is enough that he'd do just fine without the technology, although I don't know if he'd admit how much easier it's made accomplishing the U. S. Slam.
OWENS: [Laughing]
WEDDLE: It's wonderful. But I'm still a dinosaur. I still do a lot of the same stuff that I always did as far as research and looking for places to hunt. I still write some letters, although today it's usually an email.

Sure.
WEDDLE: I don't have to wait the weeks in between to get responses. "Back in the day" I'd have to as for information like countywide kill sheets and hunter density maps or whatever else I could think of that might point me in the right direction, and then I'd have to corroborate all the data and overlay this with that and the other before picking areas to try. And today, just a few strokes of the mouse pad and boom! You've got all that at your fingertips. It's amazing. It's amazing.

What were you looking for?

FACING PAGE: Doc's first Rio Grande, from Oklahoma's Canton Lake Wildlife Management Area, in 1989. He was expecting cactus and tumbleweed; instead he was greeted by green wheat fields, inviting food plots and flowering redbud.

WEDDLE: My main goal was always to find places with a decent turkey population but not too many other hunters. I'd rather spend my time in second-tier habitat rather than the highest turkey-dense areas, if it means that I would have less of a chance of encountering "hunter interference."

And of course there have been tremendous advances in equipment and clothing and all of that.
WEDDLE: Yeah, to some degree. I mean, Dave and I both are sort of minimalist in that regard. I still carry a few basic things that haven't changed very much over the years. If you've got a gun, camo, calls and some toilet paper—that's all you really need when you come down to it. Anything else is extra weight. I don't carry a lot of things I didn't carry in the early days. Maybe a Thermacell. It's a wonderful tool. If you're hunting anywhere there's mosquitoes, it's the very best invention since turkey hunting began.

How about you, Dave: what's in your pack?
OWENS: Same stuff.

Pack or vest?
OWENS: It's a vest. I do prefer a vest. There's a few out there that would rather not have a vest. But my vest is—like I said, when you turkey hunt every single day all I have to do is pick up my gun and my vest. I know I've got everything that I could possibly need. But, yeah, basic essentials. The calls are there. Couple extra shells and then you got some things that I feel essential that will always be in my vest, like little pruning shears. Like he said, a Thermacell.

You've got your cellphone now, come on!
OWENS: Yeah, I've got my cellphone in my pocket. I've got my G.P.S. That always stays in my turkey vest. I wouldn't leave the backyard without my G.P.S. Which has become a little less used with the age of the accuracy of cellphones. I still like to

pull out a topographic map and look at that. That is one thing my friends have said: "I do not understand your fascination with topo maps." I love them. I love having that waxy weather-proofed map in my hands.
WEDDLE: Yeah.
OWENS: Because that's my material that I—usually wherever I'm at, whatever that area is—usually have that tucked away as well. I carry a little leather strap that a good buddy of mine made for me, like a leather turkey tote. That's one of those little sentimental things that is in my vest and will always be there. He's got my whole nickname punched in it and stuff. It's a pretty cool little deal.

Anything else?
OWENS: A range finder. That's one of those modern things that I use. I won't say I use a lot. But, yeah, when I sit down on a turkey, especially if I'm in open terrain, I've got a range finder that I can zap on a few things to give me some perception of distance. Essentially, the last thing I ever want to do is wound a bird. I wanna make sure I don't shoot too far. So I have a range finder in my vest. Then it's just your normal gloves and maps.

Do you remember the first time that you thought that you might like to kill a turkey in all states?
OWENS: It was as soon as I completed a single-season Grand Slam. I turkey-hunted then I killed a few. I went to Oklahoma and killed a Rio and I had traveled to south Florida and killed an Osceola or a couple by that point. So I had three of them. I was, like, *Hey—Grand Slam!* So we went next year to South Dakota and I killed a Merriam's, completed my Grand Slam. Next year, of course, I said, *Hey, I want to do it in one year.* And next year, we did it in one year, a buddy that I used to travel a lot with and I did it. Did it in one year and, as soon as I finished that, it was Doc I kept up with. Like I said, he and I met through these Internet forums. It sounds a little funny—you always have

FACING PAGE: Doc Weddle's philosophy of calling is that he aims to pick at a gobbler's curiosity "and get him to come look for me—always *him* looking for *me*. That's crucial to the ruse."

Doc with good friend Tracy Deckard (right) in Indiana's Hoosier National Forest, 1991. The hunt was a marathon cat-and-mouse game played out in rain and thunder among tangled and twisted timber, knocked down by a tornado.

to second guess people.

Well, it's either that or sex—turkeys or sex, I mean. [laughing] Seriously, where do you meet this guy?
OWENS: A chat forum or chat room or something.

Does that come with a blow-up turkey doll?
OWENS: That's extra. [laughing] I was keeping up with Doc's travels and then saw that he had done this U. S. Slam—I didn't even really know what it was. But I was keeping up with him taking turkeys in all 49 states and just knowing my desire to have those experiences in unfamiliar terrain.

At that point, how many states had you racked up?
OWENS: Just four. I had hunted in my home state

of Georgia for the eastern, went to Florida for the Osceola during spring breaks in college, went to Oklahoma on a spring break later on to kill a Rio. And then we got together for that trip to South Dakota.

That's interesting, because most of the guys I've interviewed didn't really start thinking about the goal of 49 states until they realized they were halfway there. So you thought about it early on. What about you, Doc?
WEDDLE: I was halfway. I'd already killed a bird in 25 states. It followed sort of a natural progression. First, I just wanted to kill a turkey. Then I wanted to kill another. Next I wanted to hunt in another state—I struck out on my first trip but

was back the following year. It was addictive. And then I thought it would be kinda cool to kill another subspecies of turkey. After doing that, things progressed to killing a Grand Slam, and then a double Grand Slam. After several of those I decided that I got more of a thrill from easterns and Osceolas, so I confined my trips to states supporting these two subspecies for a while, with only occasional forays for Rios' and Merriam's habitats.

Did you have a goal?
WEDDLE: My main goal was simply to get in as many days as possible and add new states that interested me, places where I'd never been. Then my good buddy Larry Sharp went and planted the U. S. Super Slam bug in my head. At first I thought, *Why would I ever want to do something so stupid?* But then I started thinking that it might be fun. Gosh, that sounds pretty interesting.

ground was very important to me. It became a huge extra incentive. Everything just snowballed from that point.

When you completed your first Super Slam, what was your last state?
WEDDLE: Kansas. I killed a bird in Kansas on my last hunt.

And what year was that?
WEDDLE: 2006.

You remember that last bird?
WEDDLE: Yeah, yeah.

What did you feel when you pulled the trigger?
WEDDLE: When I killed that bird, it really didn't feel any different than any other. It was just the culmination of another successful hunt, in my

> My main goal was simply to get in as many days as possible
> and add new states that interested me, places where I'd never been.
> Then my good buddy Larry Sharp went and planted the U. S.
> Super Slam bug in my head. At first I thought,
> *Why would I ever want to do something so stupid?*

What better way to see the whole country?
WEDDLE: Yeah, before that I never had any desire to go to Rhode Island or Delaware. Why not? Or Nevada—why would I ever want to go *there*? Some of these places didn't hardly have turkeys at all. But I figured there couldn't be too many people who'd ever done such a thing, so that became part of my motivation. I'm also a public-land hunter above and beyond anything else. I hardly ever hunt private land and actually hate the thought of knocking on a door and bothering someone by asking for permission.

Was that important to you?
WEDDLE: Yeah, doing a U. S. Slam on public

eyes. I had the same types of feelings and emotions running through my brain as I did in any other place. It was a complex mix of joy, relief, satisfaction, euphoria, sadness, sorrow. . . . I always sit for a while, reliving the hunt, and all the moves and countermoves and decisions that led to this victory. That was no different on that morning in Kansas. No bells and whistles went off. It was only later that the reality of what I had just accomplished sunk in.

Surely, you must have thought about it going into the hunt.
WEDDLE: I did to some degree, but not a bunch. I mean, I knew that it was inevitably gonna happen.

On his first hunt in New York State in 1988, Weddle heard this bird drumming before it responded to his Primos True Double mouth call. He watched the bird jump atop a hemlock root wad, neck stretched in fatal curiosity. An incredulous Doc rolled him over to see three beards!

I had a number of states lined up that spring anyway; I was just progressing on down the road. That's what I do. That's my lifestyle. But then afterwards, as I was filling out my hunting journal—which I do after every hunt—it hit me that this was it. The bird at my feet was *number 49!*

Big deal—real milestone for you.
WEDDLE: And then I start thinking about all the time and effort and money and energy that I'd poured into all those trips, and it hit me kind of hard. But at the moment, it was just like, *Wow, now what?*

And, Dave, you just completed your Super Slam.
OWENS: This past May. And it was an experience that was unlike what I thought it was gonna be.

Because I thought about it and I guess I hold turkeys in such high regard. I appreciate them so much—every single one, regardless of its notch on the gun stock, so to speak. When it happened nothing was really that different. I just finished this goal that I set for myself. It's exactly what I expected. Like that relief, that, *man, I finally finished it,* and it was almost quite the opposite.

Any remorse?
OWENS: Obviously, for me there's always remorse every time I kill a turkey. I don't fish much, but that's where I wish hunting was more like fishing, because I could catch and release it to be caught again. And that's not possible with turkeys.

Well, there's always that paradox, isn't there, with

those of us who hunt? We kill the things we love.
OWENS: Yeah, yeah. There's a Finn Aagaard [writer on the philosophy and ethics of modern hunting who lived from 1932 to 2000] quote. I'm not gonna try to quote that word for word, but he said the kill is essential in a successful hunt. It's the undeniable proof that there was success. But you don't take any pleasure in the act itself. And you're not sure why you hunt. It's just something that you do, and there's a desire there that's hard to explain. It's most likely because many generations before me have hunted. That's just something that you do. But, anyways, getting back to the bird. I just went up and appreciated the bird. Did my lit-

see him, I thought, *Is that him? Is that the one that's gonna finish it? Is this fixing to happen?* And then it did, and it was just, like, in my head everything was silent. I thought there would be a bunch of....

A band playing?
OWENS: Yeah, I thought there would be a bunch of things running through my head. And almost like I was supposed to be laying there, a sobbing mess. But then I was thinking, *You know, this bird's not any more important than No. 47 or No. 29 because without killing that state—the 29th state or killing a bird wherever—then I wouldn't be here doing this.*

> And I thought, *Is this the last time I'm gonna get up off this cot without having accomplished a U. S. Slam? Is this the last time I'm gonna lace these boots?* I remember, vividly thinking all that, loading my gun.

tle ritual I do every time I kill a turkey: pick him up. We sat down together next to the tree, re-live the hunt—the only thing that was really different that I did sitting there.

Did you think about it leading up to the kill—that this would be your 49th?
OWENS: I did more than I thought I was going to. I woke up out of the back of that truck and picked myself up off that cot, getting ready. And I thought, *Is this the last time I'm gonna get up off this cot without having accomplished a U. S. Slam? Is this the last time I'm gonna lace these boots?* I remember, vividly thinking all that, loading my gun. I remember slipping that little shell in that chamber and going, *is this the shell that's gonna kill my 49th state?* I remember everything about that. That turkey gobbled. I thought, *Is that the 49th state—is that my bird?* I said, "I'm damn well gonna try to make it the last one." But I didn't know. I heard him fly down—here he comes. As I

Now, if you could just start thinking this way about a potential wife, there may be hope for you.
OWENS: She'd get in the way! [laughing] The bird comes into this sunlit glade—is this the one? I do remember that I almost felt a sigh of relief and thinking, *Now I can go back to just hunting where I wanna go hunting.* Instead of hunting where the schedule's dictating where I go. That's exactly what I said. When I finished, I thought, *It's gonna be nice to hunt without an itinerary.* If I wanna go here and hunt for 10 days straight, 12 days straight, I don't have somewhere else to be. In a hurry to get a bird on the ground. Enjoy the hunt.

Now that you have accomplished the Super Slam, can you slow down and appreciate the hunt, allow yourself to be more in the moment?
OWENS: I'm always trying to slow down and appreciate it. But when you have an itinerary, there's always going to be a sense of urgency. And I'm glad I'm not going to have that anymore. I've

already said that I'm not going to. Not gonna do it. If it happens again, fine, but I'm not gonna forcefully attempt it.

So—and this is a question for both of you—I don't sense, in your conversation, any sense of competitiveness in achieving the Super Slam, that it was a hunting goal you set for yourself, but you weren't competing with anyone else.
OWENS: Absolutely.
WEDDLE: It's a self-made goal. The people you've interviewed have all accomplished the same feat,

And yet you've said that you think it makes up maybe 10 to 20 percent of the sport, in the big picture.
OWENS: If somebody comes in off the street and learns to be an "expert" caller, which is kind of ironic to even say that, without knowing that they spent time with turkeys, listening to turkeys. But if somebody perhaps could become what was labeled as an expert caller, if for some reason they could be an expert caller and expects to walk out of the calling room and walk out into the woods and kill a turkey, they're in for a shocking experi-

> If somebody comes in off the street and learns to be an "expert" caller . . . and expects to walk out of the calling room and walk out into the woods and kill a turkey, they're in for a shocking experience. Because the calling by itself is a very, very small piece of the whole puzzle.

but we're all brothers in arms. It's not the least bit competitive. The only competition I've ever felt in the woods is between me and the bird I'm trying to beat.
OWENS: Me and the bird, yeah. This is the one place that competition is not allowed. I'm a competitive person by nature. We play backyard basketball or we play a game of wiffleball. But not in hunting. Which is, I think, another reason it's more of a one-on-one thing. It's me and him. I don't want there to be somebody else there on my shoulder questioning my moves. It's *my* moves, it's *my* bad, it's *my* heart, it's for *me* to formulate the way I want it to happen.

I guess you get enough competition in your turkey calling, as distinct from hunting.
OWENS: As different as baseball and soccer! Turkey calling competitively and turkey hunting—completely different.

Let's talk about calling. Modesty aside, you are by any objective measure an expert turkey caller.

ence. Because the calling by itself is a very, very small piece of the whole puzzle.

What's more important?
OWENS: The ability to read maps, the ability to understand where you need to be. It's location, location, location we kept saying, because the closer you can get to the bird, the fewer obstacles he's gonna have to cross to get to you and to put him in shotgun range. Quite a few turkeys die without ever hearing a turkey call, or hear one just to bring his head up for a clean kill. In that situation, yes. Let's try to come up with an analogy here: being an expert baseball player, slugger so to speak, if every time you get to the plate you're phenomenal at hitting. But just being able to hit the ball a mile or whatever doesn't make you a good baseball player. You've gotta understand the game. You've gotta be able to do all the other aspects at least reasonably well to be a successful professional baseball player. Turkey hunting's no different. Just because you can be a professional caller, or an expert caller, or really good on a turkey call, in no

Doc in 1995 with an impressive bird on the steps of Mountain Tea Lodge, a cozy private log cabin smack in the middle of 1,400 acres of steeply wooded hills with no roads in southern Indiana's Brown County. Turkeys were gobbling everywhere. This one weighed 25½ pounds with spurs just shy of one and a half inches long.

shape, form or fashion makes you automatically a very successful turkey hunter.

Doc, where does calling fit into your game, and how has it changed over the years?

WEDDLE: I don't think it's changed a whole lot other than I've obviously gotten better as a caller throughout the years. But I'm kind of a minimalist in my calling. I'm kind of conservative in my approaches, generally speaking. Now, there are times when calling has pretty good importance. And we all really enjoy it. Like you said, calling is a huge part of turkey hunting because that's where we get the communication with the birds. But I'm more inclined to rank position as number one. Getting in the right spot. And then saying the right thing at the right time—rather than just sitting down

and calling, and calling, and calling.

Calling just to get a response.

WEDDLE: If anything, throughout the years, I've gotten much more confident that I *don't* have to make that turkey gobble. I can approach him in a different way. I can be more coy in that I can let him gobble and I can answer *him*. I can get inside his head rather than him getting inside mine. If you're out there in the woods and you call, and you don't get a gobble, first of all, you don't know where that turkey's at. You don't know whether he's coming in or running the other way. And you're left with doubt and worry in your head. So that turkey is living rent-free in your head! But if you can sneak in tight on him and then cut into the tail end of his gobble.

Like a hen.
WEDDLE: Like a real hen that's excited might do, now you've turned the tables on that tom. You've gotten into *his* head. Now, he's the one worrying about whether you are coming in or going out, and whether he needs to come look for you. You've switched things around. You've become the hunted rather than the hunter.

During the course of a typical day, how often do you call?
WEDDLE: There are days when I don't call a half-dozen times from dawn to dusk. But then there are days when you have to match or exceed the calling going on around you. Every day is different. You need to feel the pulse of the local birds. But I've never been one to walk around calling a lot to force the action. I'm much more content to spend more time scouting to find the places where the toms hang out. And then, like I said, getting in position—location, location, location—before calling at the proper time and saying the right thing. In most situations, less is more.

What about your general strategy? And I know that all situations are different to some degree, but what's your general approach?
WEDDLE: All of it is dependent on terrain. But my general approach to this turkey hunting game is to get to where he wants to go, especially on public land late in the season. You never know if you're hunting gobblers or ghosts until you have current intel, so the most important part is finding a tom. This can be done by scouting until you find tracks and droppings. Of course, the best and the most exciting way is to either see a tom or hear one gobble.

Then what?
WEDDLE: Then the chess match starts. You're trying to figure out where he wants to go, how he is going to get there, whether you can reach that spot before he does—and, if not, whether you might be able to sneak in close enough to alter his path with calling. You must also take into consideration the company he's keeping.

Hens?
WEDDLE: Yeah. And how they'll react to you trying to steal their boyfriend. Call a lot? Call tentatively? Don't call at all? You are trying to put all the pieces of the puzzle together, on a board that's always changing. Often the best strategy is to simply get in his way and shut up. Some people look down on that as unethical and look down their nose at it.
OWENS: Bushwhacking! They don't like it. They hate that term.
WEDDLE: They *hate* it. But I think there's a certain skill to do that well. It's all part of the hunt. There's a damn fine line between bushwhacking and "re-positioning."
OWENS: Yeah.
WEDDLE: But, of course, calling in the bird is what this game is really all about. That's how we would all like the hunt to transpire. It's when you slip into the tom's world and announce your presence. That's when the chess game really starts—when you announce your presence. And he starts approaching you for making a move on your location and then that's when the shifts begin—just like war.
OWENS: Or he doesn't.
WEDDLE: Or he doesn't. That's all part of the game, too. You're constantly trying to figure out the turkey and how he uses his habitat. That's when the real strategy starts. So, basically, my overall strategy doesn't change. Little bitty things may change, but overall it's just learning where the turkey is at. First off, finding his area, figuring out what he's gonna do in his area. And then a lot of times what happens, if you're successful, and you're standing over him and looking at the area he called home, that's when it all comes together. The pieces of the puzzle fit and you're, like, this gobbler calls this home. This has got good sun. He

FACING PAGE: This Osceola turkey taken by Weddle in 1993 was banded, sported wing tags, and carried a radio on its back.

can gobble from here and everybody down in this whole area hears him.

OWENS: I should've been sitting over there. [laughing]

WEDDLE: Yeah, if I would've been over there, this would have happened an hour ago. Everything makes sense after the fact. How many times I've asked myself, "If only!"

Both of you, employ what seems to me a surprisingly discrete approach compared with the flamboyance I've seen in turkey hunting adventures on television, for example. I've heard lots of animation, lots of raucous calling. So that's not what you guys do.

hunting. I think it's what makes it different from sitting in a deer stand and whacking a deer or whatever. And it is the most fun way.

Do you ever tire of it?

OWENS: If I had it my way, of course, every turkey that you would kill would be with me against the tree and yelp him down the gun barrel! Some people say, "I wish it wasn't that way, it would get boring." Not for me, because no two turkeys are gonna react the same. I think nearly every turkey hunter's favorite way of killing a turkey is gonna be calling him in. It's gonna be that conversation, that dialogue and knowing that you told him the right things. And he's expecting

> It's gonna be that conversation, that dialogue and knowing that you told him the right things. And he's expecting to walk in and find a fluffy or a feathery little eight-pound hen waiting for him when he's walking in there. And it's you with a shotgun.

OWENS: That's not what we do because we're out there to be realistic. Not to say that turkeys aren't crazy and loud. It's just that when you take into account the amount of days in a turkey's life and the amount of days that they're making that kind of racket, I'm sure that's a very, very small amount. So to be realistic, in my opinion, is to do what a turkey does. Only call as much as a turkey would normally call. And use volumes that they're used to hearing. That's just kind of what goes into that approach. Now, I love the calling aspect of turkeys, obviously. I've spent hours and hours and hours and hours trying to perfect it—and nobody will ever perfect it. And some of these guys are "professionals." They know turkey vocabulary as well as anybody, and they deserve all the respect in the world for knowing and having that experience. But we'll never perfect it. It's something that we have a long way to go, but the calling part of the whole hunt is a huge part of what makes turkey

to walk in and find a fluffy or a feathery little eight-pound hen waiting for him when he's walking in there. And it's you with a shotgun.

Doc, you also regard it as dialogue.

WEDDLE: I do, highly. I think a lot of this is that we sort of project our own personalities into the turkey hunt too. Some people are loud and boisterous and call attention to themselves—those are the kind of people who are going to be out there calling loud and drawing attention to themselves. Some people are more subtle and quiet and contemplative, or whatever. I think that's probably the way I am in life, so it's the way I am in my approach to calling turkeys. As Dave said, realism is what we most strive for. Trying to sound like a real hen is paramount. That's what's I am always trying to do: sound like a real hen and say something, as opposed to just making turkey noises.

You're entering another world.
WEDDLE: I think there's a certain sense of accomplishment in stepping out through your back door in the morning and going to your hardwood ridge or field—or wherever you happen to be—and stepping into the turkey's world. And him not ever realizing you were there. I think there's something to be said about somebody being able to slip into nature without disrupting the natural order of things. You know what I'm saying?

You're becoming a part of it.
WEDDLE: Exactly.
OWENS: That's huge. Instead of being in there and being disruptive and trying to force something to happen.

It's like being a hiker wandering through nature as opposed to a hunter *participating* in it.
WEDDLE: Exactly.
OWENS: You can walk through the woods and look at the scenery. Or you can become a hunter, and step in the woods and become a part of the woods.
WEDDLE: Just that ability to just step in there—I can walk in and turkey hunt, and slip through, and spend my morning trying to locate a gobbler, and I can leave and feel like I haven't disrupted anything. I feel like nothing's on edge. Maybe I'm mistaken, but I feel like I have the ability to slip in there, and I think that may be the difference in somebody that's experienced versus somebody that doesn't have the experience.
OWENS: Absolutely.
WEDDLE: I get the satisfaction, whether I killed a turkey or not, that I slipped in there, I got inside his world, and I did so in a way to where I don't think I interfered with his daily activities. Being able to step into the turkey's world without forcing anything, I think that's the biggest thing. That gives me the biggest sense of accomplishment, especially when I step into his world. He never knew I was there. Either kill him quickly, successfully, whatever label you and I put on it, I feel like I meshed with everything that was around, meshing into nature.

By the 1993 turkey season in Weddle's home state of Indiana, hunting wild turkeys had become an all-consuming obsession. The next year he made a life-changing decision: he took a carpentry job that gave him the income to expand his travel, while allowing him the freedom to continue leaving home for three months every spring.

Given this fundamental philosophy of what you're doing out there, how does your calling fit in?
OWENS: You call what nature is ready to accept, what nature already has accepted, whether you were there or not. So, for example, I'm visualizing a hen in the woods. She has no reason—she's not just gonna blurt everything out. So what I try to accomplish is stepping in, trying to become that little eight-pound turkey.

Become the hen.
OWENS: Become the hen.
WEDDLE: She's not gonna disrupt anything.

This Alabama eastern tom didn't come easy for Doc in 1998—as no bird on public land in the Yellowhammer State has.

You're not belligerent, you're less predatory, less boisterous. You're not becoming the tom.
WEDDLE: Absolutely not.

Hunters reading this need to grasp that.
OWENS: With my approach—and I think what Doc was saying earlier—a minimalist approach, I enjoy stepping into nature, becoming a part. I visualize myself almost sneaking in. I wanna walk through the woods and the squirrel sees me and he is not alarmed.

Stealth.
OWENS: Try to get in there and, like I said, disrupt as little as possible. Become a hen turkey. Do exactly what a hen turkey would do. Be in the locations that a hen turkey would be. That's what's going to put you in the right spot to kill a turkey, kill a gobbler. That's where they wanna be. They wanna be in the same location as a hen turkey is gonna be. And when you're able to slip through those woods, making subtle sounds, doing just enough to provoke a response from him, without disrupting what was already gonna happen. I want—when he hears my calls—I want him to think it's something that he's heard yesterday.

Explain.
OWENS: It's something he heard last week. It's something that he was really desiring to hear, something that he really wanted to hear. But it's almost something he didn't expect to hear. You wanna be coming in there and do what a hen would do, but something happened and you make that call and he heard you and it didn't provoke a response. I wanna be able to go on about my business

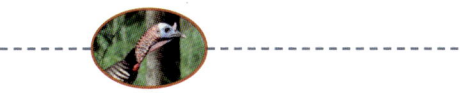

as if I never knew he was there. But tomorrow I may come through there and give that same response or do it from one ridge over. Well, from 50 yards shy and it may provoke that response. I had the ability to work that gobbler tomorrow because I didn't go in there and blow him out the day before.

When did you learn to hold back?
OWENS: It's something that's happened with me in the last probably half-dozen years or maybe even less—the ability or the desire to go into a place and instead of going, "I'm gonna go in here and I'm just gonna blow through it." Now, if

making time with that hen. I've yelped a little bit. Now I want him to think that there's a gobbler over there with that hen and bring in that jealousy part of it, cuz that's a huge part. In the turkey world, there's a definite pecking order. There's the number one gobbler. There's a number two. They all know their place. They're all trying to fight every day and re-establish, climb the ladder, but they all know who's who. Same with the hens. All the hens know their pecking order. So you can evoke different, emotional responses from a turkey, whether that be a gobbler you can evoke the desire to breed, the jealousy, the desire to fight,

> I get the satisfaction, whether I killed a turkey or not, that I slipped in there, I got inside his world, and I did so in a way to where I don't think I interfered with his daily activities. Being able to step into the turkey's world without forcing anything, I think that's the biggest thing.

there's a turkey in there and I find it, fine. If not, I wanna be able to sneak into a place and know that that place is just as well hunted tomorrow as it would have been today, because I didn't disrupt anything.

Doc, what, from your point of view, what are the sounds in nature you're trying to emulate?
WEDDLE: Well, like he says, we're trying to be a hen on the periphery. The tom only gets to do this breeding thing once a year, so he's always trying to gather more hens with him; he's never satisfied. If he hears a hen off here to the side, he's wondering: *Why isn't she over here with me? She's supposed to be coming over here and running up to me, because I'm so pretty. Why is she over there?* So I want to pick at his curiosity and get him to come look for me—always *him* looking for *me*. That's crucial to the ruse.

What are your tricks?
WEDDLE: I spit and drum along with yelping, because I want him to think there's another gobbler

etc., etc., etc. Basically, it's trying to add realism to the situation and make the birds want to investigate your presence.
OWENS: I think what we're trying to say, which is something that's very difficult, is that there's a fine line there between trying to walk into nature without disrupting nature and be real, but also provoke a response. So there's a fine line there where you wanna be that hen that'll provoke a response, but you don't wanna be obnoxious and do something that's unrealistic.
WEDDLE: Again, we all sorta project our own personalities into each hunting situation. There's no right or wrong. What works for me might not be how others think it should be done. What works for Joe over on that ridge is fine but that's not how I wanna work over here on my ridge.

Among the infinite number of birds that you've encountered over the years, do you remember one that strikes you as the most difficult?
WEDDLE: I can't single out one without bringing

up a thousand. They're all tough. They've all whipped my ass. Some days it feels like every one of them has kicked my butt all over the woods. I mean, I could bring up 20 right off the top of my head. But I had one gobbler that took me 12½ hours to kill. It was in Minnesota—he was tough. That was a chess match. Countermove, move, countermove. All day long. I finally got the best of him.

How?
WEDDLE: Scratching in the leaves—the cadence of feeding turkeys. Wild turkeys are tough! That's what keeps us going back. It's the hard ones that keep you going back. Those are the memorable ones, even the ones you don't kill. Especially them.

How about you, Dave? Is there a particular bird that stands out as the most difficult? Just flat out difficult?
OWENS: Killed?

Let's take it both ways.
OWENS: Okay.

The most difficult bird you killed and then we'll turn it around and ask about the most difficult one that got away.
OWENS: Like Doc says, they're all difficult. And a lot of times, they're all difficult in their own specific ways, and there's a ton of them. If you do it, see, like for more than a minute, you're gonna bump in to that. They're all difficult; they're all there to survive. We're stepping into their world. But the most difficult one I killed? Let me think. I would guess one that comes to the top of my mind: there's the bird in Oregon that I wrestled for several days and ended up killing. One of those perfect situations to where I found him, kinda mid-morning, late morning and. . . .

Eastern Oregon?
OWENS: This was in northeastern Oregon, so I think they're Rios there and they're "easy" birds—right, Doc?
WEDDLE: Right.

OWENS: "Easy" Rios, "easy" Merriam's—they just gobble and run at you and commit suicide. This bird gobbled like crazy. Every time I touched my call, it gobbled. I quickly figured out he was gonna be like many birds I fooled before. He wasn't gonna close the ground like I wanted him to. He gobbled so I can keep up with his direction. Well, eventually he just walked right out of my life, still gobbling. Because the terrain was open, I couldn't move on him without bumping him. Next day I found him. Took me about to mid-morning again to find him because he was a little ways away, but I found him again.

Did he behave any differently?
OWENS: Same story. He's just gobbling his head off and I can't put myself in the right position. Here again, it's all about position. Called a hen up. All right. And I'm thinking, *This bird is really weird.* He's gobbling like he's alone. But he's really weird. He's not moving. This hen comes by me and she's just cranking it, just *pow, pow, pow, pow,* just cranking it out and really doing what a hen, what should provoke him to come. I watched her, was able to see bits and pieces of her walking right down past him. I never did lay eyes on him. He's on this hill. She walked right down through there and I know he had to see her. And he just stayed up there gobbling at her just like he was gobbling at me without ever meeting up. I was, like, *okay so it's not just me.*

You weren't the only one snubbed!
OWENS: The very next day, I was able to get close enough to him roosted. When he started gobbling, I was able to basically just, inch by inch, crawl my way in extremely, extremely close to him. Keep some cover between himself and myself and get extremely, extremely close to him. And he's gobbling like a fool, like he had been the last two days, and just put myself into a spot to where as soon as his feet touched the ground, he flew down and was right over a little rise. He came right up my hill and, here again, the only time he heard the call was to get his head up high enough over that hill

for a good kill, for a clean shot. And I was able to kill him. That was one of those times I was dealing with all the snow. So that was frustrating. I was hunting in the snow every day. Every day I was expecting it to be pretty weather: *I'm gonna catch a break*. And every day it wasn't but I remember shooting him, and once I figured out that I had him, and it's snowing like crazy again, I just remember laying back going, "Finally!" I'd heard him gobble hundreds of times over the past couple of days, and now I've got my hands around him.

WEDDLE: I think a lot of times we make the birds more difficult than they really are by doing something stupid.

OWENS: Yeah, for sure.

WEDDLE: This is a sport that you can never perfect. It's like golf. You simply cannot go out and shoot 18 birdies. You'll never perfect golf and you'll never perfect turkey hunting. We're screwing up all the time, every day. I screw up every single day I turkey hunt. You will never be able to kill every tom you set up on. There are too many factors, too many variables. Throw in the human element and that really throws a monkey wrench into the works.

OWENS: Another one of those same type birds that was just a very difficult bird, a challenging bird was a bird I killed in Louisiana. It was less to do about the bird. Well, he had plenty of quirks and tendencies that made him difficult to deal but it was also the place that he called home. Which is a lot of times the situation. It's the terrain.

WEDDLE: Or the number of hens he's got with him—that's the most difficult aspect right there.

OWENS: Yeah. First time I struck out in Louisiana, the year prior. The next year I chose a different area. I'd walked 16-some-odd miles, about half of it through water the day before without finding any turkey sign. Really feeling like I was just as lost as I was before I even got there. Went into this next area. It looked pretty. Found some pretty stuff. Then I thought, *At least I'm in pretty ground.* I was fortunate to find some scratchings. Well, I was deadbeat tired. I ended up leaning against a tree, making some blind calls and

I kinda kicked back and dozed off. Next thing I know I hear feet in the leaves, and I open my eyes and here stands a gobbler, probably 15 feet away. The hen's to my right about 10 yards. He makes out probably my eyelids moving that close and he starts kind of booking out of there, not very scared, but somewhat alerted. She never even knew what happened. But he ran back into this little area. She went off about her way. Well, I just busted them up. This is my second year going to Louisiana trying to kill a turkey and I just missed my chance.

Should you have killed him?

OWENS: I had him at 15 feet. There's no reason I shouldn't have killed that turkey. So I give him about an hour and I decide I'm going to make a loop and set up about 100 yards down—maybe 150 yards down. The only thing is it's palmettos, just a palmetto-choked place. And I'm thinking to myself, *that turkey didn't gobble when he came in last time.* And just when I was fixing to set up, he let one out. And I thought, *we're working with money here!* I yelped to that turkey and he gobbles, just hammers it. It's "go time." I yelped again and he hammers it again. We're ready to go so I climb up on him and then I don't say anything else. I know this turkey, he is a sneaky turkey.

What do you mean?

OWENS: He's one of them that when he decides he is gonna come, he is not gonna say another word. And it's really hard in that terrain with those thick palmettos to see him before he sees you. I heard him fly across, I guess across a little wet spot, cuz he spooked a squirrel when he did it. And it was one of those little things that I heard I knew what it was—sure enough, I made eyes on him as he's coming up through there. It didn't do any good. He saw me and before I was able to get what I felt was a good shot, I had to let him drift off. I gave him another hour. I'd looped around, doing little half-moon loops and got to where I thought I'd be in earshot of him again, yelped to him, and bam! He gobbles again. So I tried to be

Dave Owens and Tom "Doc" Weddle **56**

The Connecticut River Valley along Vermont's border with New Hampshire holds a good population of turkeys—where Weddle found this one strutting in 2016. Dave Owens first met Doc on this trip at Doc's campsite behind the barn.

wise in this situation: I'm gonna stand up. I'm gonna get behind a tree and try to stand up. The only problem was, he wasn't rushing in. It may take him 15 or 20 minutes. So you're sitting there trying to hold your gun up against a tree or whatever and you know he's going to see you. Here again, about that time there was a little bit of an opening there. I called from the middle of that opening, hoping I could get him in it. Here he comes again. I called that turkey up three or four times that day without killing him. Very next day, I walk in there and I'm able to get him off of that palmetto flat into what is like a river swamp, wide open: beautiful, *beautiful.*

Are you sure it was the same bird?

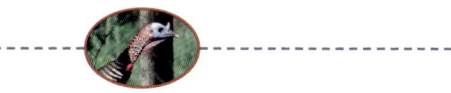

OWENS: I don't know if it was the same turkey, because there was two turkeys at this time, but same situation. They started gobbling a little bit later in the morning. I called to them and then I shut up. His only mistake this time was he was in open terrain. So I clammed up. They were gobbling their heads off and they shut up. Fifteen minutes later, after shutting up, I see them. I see them coming down through there, and they were coming straight to the call, and they just shut up 20 minutes prior to their arrival. At the time I was able to see him before he saw me. I was able to work it out and I killed the turkey. But that was another one of those never-going-to-happen situations. When it happened.

some styrofoam and made a stuffer. This was back before B Mobile and Pretty Boy or whatever they are became big and we killed some turkeys over that thing. But I just felt like I was selling myself short. It took a lot of that chess match out of it. It provokes a response from turkeys, but I just don't like killing them that way.

How about you, Doc?
WEDDLE: Yeah, from early on in my career, decoys were a no-no. That's not how we wanted to kill our turkeys. I can count on one hand the number of times I've had a turkey decoy out when I'm hunting. When I'm guiding it's a different thing altogether. My first priority then is to get results. Decoys work especially well in the cattle pas-

> I called to them and then I shut up. His only mistake this time was he was in open terrain. So I clammed up. They were gobbling their heads off and they shut up. Fifteen minutes later, after shutting up, I see them. I see them coming down through there, and they were coming straight to the call. . . .

Do you ever use decoys?
OWENS: Used to, I think that we all go through a progression, or at least I did. Coming up as a turkey hunter without a mentor, I didn't know. In fact, I quickly figured it out. I did it for a couple years but it just wasn't the way I liked to hunt.
I know this past year, I didn't stick a decoy in the ground one time. The only decoy I own now is a little Dave Smith hen decoy and a lot of times, if I'm using it, I'm videoing. I'm not hunting. I'm doing it to basically capture better footage, something to keep his attention off me so I can get some good footage for video purposes. But as far as hunting myself, I very rarely if at all use decoys. Now, there was a time when I used them—I even made a stuffer once upon a time. I had killed a turkey down in south Florida and I took him home and filleted him out and put him around

ture and sod farm country of Florida, where I do most of my guiding. Down there I even do something that I've never seen done before, and that's put out a whole flock of Dave Smith dekes. They're the only ones that I will use because of just how lifelike and real they look. I've had as many as 14 out at a time in a spread, including a pair of strutters and a couple of jakes.

And that works?
WEDDLE: I've had turkeys start running from half a mile away. They absolutely come to them. And there's going to be a brawl or there's going to be some X-rated scenes going on. Something's going to happen. And it usually ends in a dead gobbler. I mean, it's unbelievable.

Is there a special way or pattern you display them?

WEDDLE: Not really. In using a flock you're simply appealing to the jealousy factor and their natural-born flocking instinct. But they gotta look real. One time I had three guys to guide at the same time: a grandfather, a son and a grandson. And I thought, *I want to see how this works out.* So I went in at about 3 o'clock in the morning, I had already built a big—what I call a log cabin—blind, draped with Spanish moss. Big enough for four of us to sit in.

There's a latte machine going. . . .
WEDDLE: Everything but! So I go out at three in the morning and I set up the flock: I had 10 and a buddy loaned me his four. I've got a couple of

as much as I have. I know that he could have jumped up and done jumping jacks and that gobbler would have still ignored him. But he was afraid to move. Finally—it took five minutes—he finally got his gun in position and he killed that gobbler. So we got two dead gobblers in the decoys. I crank up the calling a little, and the other two gobblers are still out there in the fog, but they've moved off a little bit. They've now just heard two gunshots. It's really foggy. But the sun's warming up, the fog is starting to lift, and when it does I can see there's two gobblers out there and a bunch of hens. And now they're about 700 or 800 yards from us and I crank it up on the call and they gobble. And I can see every head in the flock

> So we go deep into the property and, sure enough, there they are, standing around in a pasture that had recently been sprayed with manure—human manure from the local sewage lagoon. Common practice there. Really makes the hay grow.

strutters and then the hens spread around like a normal flock would be. And at daylight, we had two gobblers gobbling over here and two gobblers gobbling over here. It was a real foggy morning. But both of them, both set to respond. And the first two from the right, they come in right at daylight and of course, this is how it happens. When you've got a strutter out, the gobblers run up to the gobbler and there's gonna be a fight. So I always set that decoy where I want the shot to be. Two gobblers rush up—the grandson kills one right off the bat. Now it's the son's turn to kill one. Well, the gobbler ran out a little bit and then he ran right back and wanted to flog that gobbler. His buddy is laying there flopping on the ground but he's still wanting to whip that strutter's ass! He's jockeying around and moving and his head's bobbing back and forth. And the guy that's shooting now, he's kind of in an awkward position. He can't, and of course, he hasn't been around turkeys

comes up and they're looking and you can, I just know what's gonna happen. Here they come and here comes a whole flock of hens and here these gobblers come: three toms, six jakes, and 22 hens—all into my flock of 14! And those decoys are so realistic, and everything's going on at under 30 yards and unless. . . .

How'd he get a shot?
WEDDLE: Well, the gobblers of course run up. Now there's two dead gobblers in my spread and now here's three more. And unless a turkey was moving you couldn't tell whether it was alive or not. Those dekes looked like turkeys and so finally the grandfather gets a shot on the gobbler. He kills that. All three birds were big: cool limb-hangers. We went to the nearest oak tree with a horizontal branch and we hung them all on those limbs.

So decoys do work.

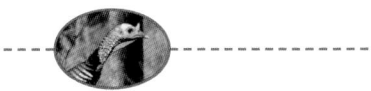

WEDDLE: That's the kind of results you can get with a flock of decoys. But it's not something you obviously can carry out into the field in a sack.

It's not like goose hunting. You can't drive your trailer out to most places you hunt.
WEDDLE: Not most places. I can drive my van out there on the pasture in Florida but it's kinda a unique situation down there.

What's the strangest place you remember killing a gobbler?
WEDDLE: This one's memorable. [laughing] Same place, across the road, same landowner. All my clients had already killed their birds. I was having a hard time killing one on the state ground that year. My landowner said, "Why don't you just come over and kill one of these birds?"

Generous of him.
WEDDLE: He still had some leftovers. Well, I don't normally like to do that. I like to kill my birds on public ground. But, like I say, I was having a hard time. My girlfriend Jen from back home [in Indiana] was with me that year. And as we were coming back from town in the afternoon, I stopped to look for a trio of toms the landowner had been seeing. You can hunt on private land in the afternoons, so I'd been intending to make a try for those toms. So we go deep into the property and, sure enough, there they are, standing around in a pasture that had recently been sprayed with manure—human manure from the local sewage lagoon. Common practice there. Really makes the hay grow.

Lovely.
WEDDLE: And very aromatic! The bouquet was really, really sweet. Well, it stunk so bad that I didn't even slow down, just kept right on driving out the gate and 12 miles back to camp, where I dropped off Jen. There was *no way* she would have hunted with me or even stayed in the van. I told her I'd be back.

You weren't leaving those turkeys behind!
WEDDLE: [laughing] They had been on one side of a big cypress head. On the other side was a pasture—I'd park there. The manure there had been spread a couple days earlier. At least it *looked* dry. Well, as soon as I pulled off the two-track road, I was stuck. I'm spinning my tires. Shit is flying everywhere. Human shit—everywhere! It's all over my van. I'm spinning my tires trying to get out, which only made matters worse. A horrible mess. I texted the landowner: "Have you ever heard the expression, you've got yourself into this mess, so you can get yourself out? That might be true some days, but today, PLEASE HELP ME!!!"

Did he save you from your very own proverbial shit storm?
WEDDLE: He texted me back and said he was tied up in town. It would be at least a half-hour before he could come get me. I told him that I would be the one hooking up the chains.

Yikes. . . .
WEDDLE: There was nothing left to do but grab my gun and a diaphragm call and tip-toe across the field of human manure. I got to the other side of the cypress head, set up, called a couple times, and within 15 minutes I had the three toms standing 12 yards in front of my gun barrel. As I'm walking back to the van, here comes the landowner.

To the rescue!
WEDDLE: He towed me out of that mess and I headed into town and spent $40 worth of quarters at the car wash hosing off every inch—the tires, the wheel wells, everywhere. What a god-awful mess.

Was it worth it?
WEDDLE: Hell, yes!

Classic. [Turning to Dave] Well, young man, and what's the strangest place you remember killing a bird?
OWENS: Mine pales in comparison to Doc's story! [laughing]

Doc took this difficult, gorgeous Georgia gobbler in 2014 from a heavily hunted wildlife management area.

Naturally. We knew that going in. We just knew he was gonna win that contest.

OWENS: Yeah. [laughing] I'm guessing the strangest encounter—like strangest place I've ever was lucky enough to kill a turkey—was in Hawaii this past spring. I started in Hawaii. The very first turkey I killed for the 2016 season was on a very, very well-maintained, beautiful, busy golf course. This guy did a lot of trapping for them and had permission to hunt it after the golf course was closed. Which was after 6 p.m. so there was a couple of hours of daylight there. The place was covered up in turkeys but I was able to kill my first turkey of 2016 and my first turkey in Hawaii right in the middle fairway, right down from the tee

boxes, and straight across the fairway from the sand trap. A whole flock of gobblers right down the middle of a beautiful fairway in the rain was the only nasty thing about it. But, buddy, they were out there in those fairways. And I killed a turkey right out of the middle of a very, very nice golf course.

Did you ever purposefully pass up a bird that you could have easily killed?

OWENS: There's a lot of guys, these old timers and people that turkey hunters have always talked about calling them up. And you don't become a turkey hunter until you can call one up and not kill it. I can't say that I've ever just straight up done that!

Never?

OWENS: Well, only in one situation have I ever called a gobbler up and not killed him when I had the opportunity. There's has been times when I called him up and had a shot opportunity because I didn't want to kill two, or I didn't want to kill hens. Only one time did I call a gobbler up and not kill him and that was solely because my brother had a girlfriend that he wanted to help kill a gobbler. This was on a piece of private ground that we had, and I actually had no intentions of hunting it. I ended up getting up late one morning before work. Didn't have time to get to where I wanted to be on the state grounds, so I just went over there, more or less called him up in expert fashion. But knowing that my brother wanted her to kill a turkey—and this was a perfect situation,

How about you, Doc? Have you ever purposefully passed up a bird you could easily have killed?

WEDDLE: Yeah, a number of times. The first one was in 1988, in New York. I remember it like it was yesterday because it was a watershed moment for me. Before that I always took the first good opportunity to kill a bird. You make it count. But on this drizzly morning in New York, a bird waltzed in "fuzzin-'n'-buzzin," and I consciously made the decision that it just didn't feel right. I can't even explain why to this day. I whispered "BANG" over the gun barrel. I counted coup on him and just let him wander off.

What were you thinking?

WEDDLE: Like I'd raised the bar in some way. It felt like I'd taken a step up on the ladder to becom-

> At least it *looked* dry. Well, as soon as I pulled off the two-track road, I was stuck. I'm spinning my tires. Shit is flying everywhere. Human shit—everywhere! It's all over my van. I'm spinning my tires trying to get out, which only made matters worse. A horrible mess.

this was actually the place that we had said that she should be able to get her turkey—I called him up and didn't shoot him. That's the only one that I can say I've actually called up.

You pass up birds going to roost, don't you?

OWENS: I don't like shooting turkeys on their way to roost. I don't like setting up where turkeys roost and shooting them on their way to roost. I have been close to roosting turkeys, or watched turkeys in late evening and had them walk by within spitting distance, and not shot them when it would have been perfectly legal and okay to shoot them. I was just in the right spot. That's happened numerous times but I just don't have any desire to shoot a turkey on the way to roost. But calling a turkey up and not shoot it? I'm not that good yet, I don't think.

ing a better turkey hunter. From that point on, I think there's been less panic when it's time to pull the trigger, even though I still manage to freak out enough at the moment of truth to booger-up more than my share of opportunities.

By then, did you perhaps feel a bit more mastery of the hunt, such that you could afford to pass up a sure thing?

WEDDLE: I did, yeah, yeah. It was definitely an enlightening experience. And I've done it a number of times since. But most of the time I'm ready to kill him when I see him.

OWENS: Yes, we're out there to kill turkeys! I've had that moment where I've sat there and go, why haven't I already killed this turkey? But I was able to talk enough sense to myself. [laughing]

Dave, counting on one hand, what are your favorite turkey states?
OWENS: It is virtually impossible to say. It's probably gonna be taking a combination of things into consideration.

The assumption is that this is within your experience.
OWENS: Yeah, yeah, and one of the things that Doc and I were talking earlier is with an itinerary. There are some really awesome places that I really wish I could have spent some time. There were some places that I regretted having to leave, but that you're only allowed one turkey. And what are you supposed to do after you killed that one

terrain. The public lands a lot of time not nearly as manicured as cattle pastures and such. Those birds are just more finicky, and so is the challenging aspect of hunting that terrain.

How about outside the Southeast?
OWENS: Once you leave Georgia and Florida, there's always one place that jumps out at me as my favorite. If I had to list some others, let's say Black Hills, whether it be the Wyoming or the South Dakota side. The Black Hills is just wildlife rich. There's so much wildlife to see and experience there in the Black Hills. I think it will always be one of my favorites, not because it's overrun

> But on this drizzly morning in New York, a bird waltzed in "fuzzin-'n'-buzzin," and I consciously made the decision that it just didn't feel right. I can't even explain why to this day. I whispered "BANG" over the gun barrel. I counted coup on him and just let him wander off.

turkey? I felt like I sold myself short because I didn't get to experience it well enough.

Still, name a few—and tell us about the reasons they're your favorites.
OWENS: Georgia. It's my home state. I'm more familiar with it. There's something about the hardwood ridges of Georgia that I just love. It's where I learned to do what I do, where everything started. So Georgia is probably at the top of my list. Florida is a very close second—first place I'd ever hunted out of state. There's just a very strange draw to Florida. And a lot of turkey hunters, I found, for some reason, they can't really explain it. Maybe because it's so unique. There's things when you're hunting Florida that don't make sense, where I am hunting and you're working a gobbling turkey. It's like turkeys shouldn't exist here. So the terrain there and the fact you are hunting all Osceolas—their nature to me is just more wary, especially if you're hunting the thicker

with turkeys. A lot of people talk about all the turkeys. I've actually found there's been some difficulty in finding them. Once you find them, yeah, but it's not just overrun with turkeys like other areas. Let's see . . . if I had a couple more. I only spent one day here but right up here in Indiana. Just because I love hunting eastern turkeys and I love hunting turkeys in the hardwoods. And these rival some of the prettiest hardwoods, which is the type of terrain that I really like to hunt. Really look forward to getting back to Indiana and hunting again. Wish you could kill more than one turkey. That's the only reason I didn't get to experience it more. [laughing]

Doc, you've certainly been just about everywhere chasing wild turkeys, many times over.
WEDDLE: Yeah, that's one of the first questions that people ask me all the time.

You've put lots of miles on those trucks over the years.

WEDDLE: Yeah, and yet I would be hard-pressed to give you a top 30 list. There's a lot of things that go into a turkey hunt. There's the aesthetics, there's the quality of the turkey hunting, the people you meet, the weather. It's the total package. That's really what defines how good or bad the hunt ends up being. But if I had to name my top five, I might say Florida's there, Indiana, Hawaii—those are my definite top three—and then Pennsylvania's awful good because they've got so much public ground. Virginia cuz I love the history of the area and the beauty of the state. But I could just as easily pick five different states for each one of those picks and I wouldn't have any qualms about it. I've had great times in every single state. Virginia was the first place I killed a bird outside Indiana, and then I didn't come back for about 20 years. I've been there the last two years in a row. Once I hunted there again, I thought, *Man, why did it take me so long?* I'm kind of a Civil War buff—like you, Tom—and those battlefields all around the areas I hunt intrigue me. Virginia's got mountains, oceans, foothills. And besides that, I could sit and listen to that particular southern dialect all day long. Like a babbling brook to my ears.

OWENS: Now that you say stuff, I'm like, man—*Virginia was my favorite!* I told my girlfriend that this is one of the first places I'm gonna go back to.

WEDDLE: There's a guy—you know who Shelby Foote is?

Of course. I've read his books. I have his wonderful three-volume narrative on the Civil War. He made Ken Burns's series come alive.

WEDDLE: I could sit and listen to Shelby Foote talk forever. I love that old Virginia dialect. It's so melodic. It's like rippling water to my ears. Comforting.

In your travels you must get some interesting reactions to your Georgia accent.

OWENS: All the time. It depends where you're at. When I'm up in the North, when I was up in Rhode Island, I heard: "My gosh, you've got such a southern accent." "Well, you retarded *bastard*, in

your own way you sound just as silly as I do! That's what my buddy up there says, all the time: 'You're a retard.'"

Ah, "Little Rhody." I have cousins there. You gotta love the Portuguese stuffed quahogs, with a splash of hot sauce. Delicious.

OWENS: As soon as Doc said "Virginia," I thought, *Man, I sold myself short.* I can't believe I didn't say "Virginia!" because the turkey hunting there is top-notch, and the terrain is just kind of like somewhat behind us [looking up at green beech woods in Indiana]. Where I hunted was hardwoods, rolling hardwoods.

WEDDLE: It's got a variety of all that stuff.

OWENS: And you said Hawaii. I've heard more turkeys gobble in Hawaii than anywhere in my life.

WEDDLE: Yeah, I obviously don't have any Polynesian blood in these white legs, but I felt more at home and welcome and at ease in Hawaii than any place I've ever been. It was kind of magical.

Speaking of Rhode Island, and having been brought up 15 minutes from the border, it is not Rhode Island [enunciated], it is Rah-DYE-lan. . . .

OWENS: All right, all right. [laughing]

As the locals say: "Wicked good, wicked good." Doc, I am turning to page 165 in your book and the state-by-state rundown. I can't tell you how utterly honest—even hilarious—I found it. I have to tell you, the first time I read it I actually laughed out loud. I thought, No "respectable" turkey-hunting magazine or any other patronizing publisher would ever have run this.

WEDDLE: I might have gotten a little carried away with that one!

It's classic. It's so colorful and candid and I just can't resist. Occasionally, an author deserves to have his words thrown right back at him—particularly from a fellow reader who perversely appreciates them:

WEDDLE: Delaware is hard for me to categorize, because the state is a place of contradictions . . . it

has some good aspects, and some extremely bad ones. When I compare it with other places, I somewhat tongue-in-cheek refer to Rhode Island as the very armpit of the nation in terms of its turkey hunting, and Delaware as the butt crack.

You are insane! [laughing]
WEDDLE: I can't dispute it—I said it.

You can't top that.
OWENS: No, absolutely not.

Indiana Jones has beaten you again.
OWENS: Yeah, absolutely.
WEDDLE: I wanna put a caveat in here, though. I've had some really awesome turkey hunts there.

that chicken shit and they spread it over the whole state. So everywhere you go it just smells like chicken manure. Nevada's tough, also. I would list that with my least favorites—and, again, I really like Nevada. It's got some fascinating scenery but it just doesn't have many roosting trees and it's got damn little water which limits turkey abundance. A lot of times our least favorite turkey states have little to do with the state—it has a lot more to do with the difficulty in getting there to legally hunt. And I'm a public land hunter, so I'm gonna make my judgments based on accessibility, on how good the turkey hunting is that I can find on public ground. Some of these states have phenomenal turkey hunting on private ground. That doesn't apply to me.

> There's a lot of things that go into a turkey hunt.
> There's the aesthetics, there's the quality of the turkey hunting,
> the people you meet, the weather. It's the total package.
> That's really what defines how good or bad the hunt ends up being.

I've met some absolutely fantastic people. I've found wonderful diners. I camp in a great little campground that's. . . .

Delaware, Maryland, New Jersey: they all specialize in diners. Did you ever see the movie, *Diner?*
WEDDLE: I did not.

Set in Baltimore. Barry Levinson, 1982. Remember it: *Diner*. Watch it.
WEDDLE: I like hunting in Delaware. What I don't like about Delaware are the glaring negatives. Which are: it's the trashiest place I've ever been in my life. It looks like you're walking around in a landfill. Everywhere you go.
OWENS: There's couches and a lot of stuff along the road.
WEDDLE: Everywhere you go. Speed traps everywhere and chicken farms everywhere. And they take all

What's the secret, in your experience, from day one, in effectively scouting a new place, a place you never been before?
OWENS: First off, once you have the place, I guess there is no secret that this is where Doc and I disagree. Maybe not disagree—we just have different methods about going to do it. I'm a little bit, obviously being younger, I'm a little bit "new age."
WEDDLE: Exactly.
OWENS: I'm a little more, I won't say myself as being a computer guru at all, but the ability to use all the imagery and the stuff you have available, get that new piece of ground.

Plus you don't have as many ex-girlfriends as Doc.
OWENS: [laughing] You can get the satellite imagery and the topo maps and get them in your hands. Here again, it's gonna take that experience in knowing what to look for. Where is that turkey

Doc Weddle loves hunting Florida's deep, dark swamps among the cypress trees. When restoration efforts began in 1949, the statewide population had been decimated—only one-tenth the birds breeding in the wild remained from an estimated historical population of 250,000.

gonna have access to have everything that it needs? I'm a mobile turkey hunter. I like making sure I'm not tying myself down. I like making sure I have option A, B, C, D—on down the list. And I also like making sure each option gives me the ability to cover quite a bit of ground. I like being able to put my ears on a lot, so I like finding hardwood ridges. I'm going to go revert back to that, since that's my favorite terrain to hunt turkeys. I like finding hardwood ridges that a lot of times have roadbeds or something on them. But even if they

don't, you can walk the spine or the top of that main ridge—it gives you access to all these finger ridges. All these little finger hardwood ridges that will jet off of it and these little hollows and ravines that will a lot of times have turkeys. You can put your ears on. You can put a call down and see if you can provoke a response. So it gives you the ability, as long as you plan it, and you start in the right spot. You can steer the course. Then you can stay on that ridge top and cover a huge amount of ground within the first couple hours of daylight.

So therefore you put yourself in a good position to hear one of those turkeys by calling into what you deem is already good turkey ground. Just from looking at the online imagery and basically put yourself in the mix, right off the bat—that's what I kind of look for.

What about where there isn't much high ground?
OWENS: Gets more difficult when you're hunting places that are flat. Obviously, you don't have the ability to look for spine ridges because topo lines are virtually non-existent. Places like Florida, places like Mississippi, Louisiana—then you got to go more toward the satellite imagery and being able to determine trees types. Look at when the

don't have a fear of snakes, which is a lot of people's reasoning for wearing tall boots and stuff. So I wear Crocs. It's comfortable. Within minutes of me getting out of the water, receiving a little air, the type of pants I wear are dry, and my feet are dry.

Doc, what about you? Over the years, have you developed any particular secret or key to effectively scouting a new area?
WEDDLE: I do a lot of research before I ever get there—so I know what areas have got turkeys. And then the actually scouting, I don't do much Internet scouting. I depend on scouting with a gun in my hands. Hit an area, if you've got high ground, get up high. Listen. Listen at daylight and then, if,

> But there's always that desire to turn a new leaf.
> I love new ground, you know. I love to see places
> I've never seen. I like to walk over to that ridge over there,
> cuz I've never been there.

picture was taken. What does that mean? If you see cypress, then a lot of times that means it's wet. That means that you can expect there to be water there. So, if you're looking to get from point A to point B, there's a lot of that between there. You might need to either have an alternate route to get around it, to get to where you want to be. Or plan on walking through a lot of water, which is part of hunting Florida and Louisiana!

Do you ever hunt in hip boots there?
OWENS: Never hunted in hip boots. In south Florida I hunt in Crocs [sandals]. Cuz I know I'm gonna get wet. So let's just get wet right off the bat, wear something that's comfortable and that dries really quick. It's kind of refreshing. A lot of times it's hot in Florida at the beginning of the day. That first little bit of daylight may be a little cool on your feet. And I have gotten flat out cold down there before by jumping in the water. But, no, I

whether you do or don't hear turkeys. Then, you're scouting for tracks, droppings, feathers, dust bowls, strut marks, if you can find them. The first thing with scouting is to know whether or not you're even in an area with turkeys. Once you've established that you've got turkeys in there, then you're looking at terrain features and fence lines, creeks, ridges, contours. Trying to discern what the land features are gonna allow you to do or get away with or where the turkeys wanna be or not be. And then spend a lot of time on the ground.

Boots on the ground.
WEDDLE: I still do go back to a lot of places that I love, back to familiar places. But there's always that desire to turn a new leaf. I love new ground, you know. I love to see places I've never seen. I like to walk over to that ridge over there, cuz I've never been there.
OWENS: Yeah.

WEDDLE: Even back here behind my house. I'd never been on that ridge at all. And this year I got back in there, and it's the most beautiful ridge you've ever seen in your life. I think that's something that's pretty consistent with most turkey hunters. We wanna see around the next ridge.

But not all do?

WEDDLE: I don't know. There's a lot of people who are scared, I think, to see new ground to get lost or whatever. They wanna keep going back to the same spot to set up their tent, put their decoys out, and that's where they're gonna hunt. Now, the wanderlusting types, the traveling hunters like us, we wanna see something new.

OWENS: I wanna jump into this piece—*man, that looks like a good hilltop from the road right here.*

WEDDLE: But there's turkeys over there, man. I gotta check it out.

OWENS: I'm gonna run up there real quick. It's gonna take me 20 minutes. I'm gonna get up there, just see and check it out. Next thing I know, three hours later, I'm trying to finally make my way back to the truck, because you see this one! That one looks just as good, let me see, you know, next thing you know you've picked your way around everything, and making notes along the way.

What do you guys shoot?

WEDDLE: I recently changed two years ago. I spent 30 states worth carrying a Remington 870 Express Super Magnum. Something I bought, lord, I guess it was in high school I bought that gun, or maybe college. Something that I was comfortable with, and I shot some Hevi-Shot in it, and whatever. I recently just changed over to loading my own shells, shooting what they call TSS shot, Tungsten Super Shot. Started reloading my own shells.

What size shot?

OWENS: Nines, where legal. Nines. Yeah, a lot of states you get into, you got to watch it. Some of them it's 7s and larger. Some states say 6s. I reload that TSS shot to give me the ability and the confidence to carry a smaller gun. Now I hunt with a 20-gauge after the last two years. It's a Franchi Affinity Compact, so it's basically the youth model. It's got a really short stock. I think it weighs a little less than five and a half pounds—or right at five and a half pounds. I can put that on my back. With that gun, I put up patterns that will rival any 12-gauge out there.

WEDDLE: It's an interesting choice.

OWENS: I'm not a numbers guy. I'm more focused on consistent pattern. And being fanatical about everything turkey related, I do spend time on a patterning board, making sure my gun is equipped to take care of what I need to do. And that gun puts up, you know, you're talking about a 20-gauge shell that's got over 500 pellets in it. So, I'm putting 270ish in a 10-inch circle at 40 and another, you know, 230ish about is about my average in a 20-inch circle. You're talking about 500 pellets in a 20-inch circle. Forty yards is what I feel like is comfortable turkey range. Fifty yards—I know that gun will kill it 10 times out of 10. So if I make a mistake it's lethal out to that distance. But on the other side I can throw that thing across my back. It weighs less than six pounds and I can walk for miles and never even know it's there.

How about you, Doc? I imagine you've gone through many guns over the years.

WEDDLE: Yeah, I have. I killed turkeys with eight different 12-gauge shotguns and a bow.

Is that your preferred gauge?

WEDDLE: Yeah, I never shot anything besides the 12-gauge. This new 20-gauge and TSS stuff is interesting but it's also expensive to load those shells.

The shot itself is expensive.

WEDDLE: Yeah. For years my favorite gun was a Ruger Red Label over and under. I hand painted it camo. I sanded it down and sanded the stock down and took a beautiful gun and camoed it. And my purist bird hunting buddies just [laughing] shake their head and wonder at me sometimes. I put sling swivels on it, rifle sights. It was an awesome gun. I killed a bunch of turkeys with it. Then

I picked up a Benelli. An old one, a used one. And I really liked it. Killed a number of turkeys with that. And then Benelli came out with a new model, the M2, and I bought it. It's much lighter than my over and under. It shoots the point-of-aim. It's got a 20-inch barrel and a pistol grip stock and it shoots devastating patterns, and so I've been carrying it for a number of years and I love it. It's an awesome gun.

Do you use any kind of a sight?
WEDDLE: I've got a three-beaded Tru-Glo sight, which is just two green beads in back and a red bead in front.
OWENS: Like a rifle sight.

But this new red dot sight is phenomenal. I don't see myself changing anytime soon. I don't see myself changing. I've got that little Franchi Affinity compact. It's got a 24-inch barrel. I had it dipped in bottom-land camo. So it's got a good matte camouflage finish and I put that red dot on there. It was kind of my off-season project a couple of seasons ago and started the TSS reloading and been hauling it ever since. I hold that gun tighter than I do my girlfriend. I love my little gun. Sick bastard. [laughs]

Of the 49 states in which you killed your turkey, do you remember how may birds you took in the morning and then how many later in the day?

> The first hour after official sunrise
> is by far the biggest percentage; it goes down after that.
> A lot of people say that they kill a lot of birds at 10 or 11 o'clock.
> But my percentage figures show otherwise.

WEDDLE: Yeah, yeah—not a rifle sight but beads.
OWENS: Same thing I had on my 870.
WEDDLE: So they glow in the dark. Or not in the dark, but low light.

What about you, Dave?
OWENS: For sights? I put one of the Burris Fast-Fire sights on there, kind of one of the holographic sights. Gives you the ability to—I mean, as long as that dot's on, it's gonna hit whatever you're aiming at. You can literally hold the gun out like a pistol and shoot it if need be. Cause I've missed turkeys over the years by not getting your head down on the gun or trying to look up over the barrel of the gun too quick. I was really hesitant. I had a bad experience before by using a scope. I said I'd never use any optic like that again.

OWENS: I don't. If I went back and looked through my turkey log I probably could. Very, very few in the evening. First off, because evening hunting is not allowed in a lot of states. It's only legal until lunch or 1 o'clock, or 4 o'clock in some. I wouldn't be scared to say over 90 percent of them were morning or lunch and a.m. kills.

How about you, Doc?
WEDDLE: I keep a lot of data and do some figuring up between seasons, and so I do keep specific data on time of kill and how it relates to sunrise or sunset. The first hour after official sunrise is by far the biggest percentage; it goes down after that. A lot of people say that they kill a lot of birds at 10 or 11 o'clock. But my percentage figures show otherwise.

FACING PAGE: Doc's palmetto "limb-hanger" during March 2008 in Florida had one-and-a-half-inch spurs. He was well on his way to his second U. S. Super Slam, which he completed in 2011.

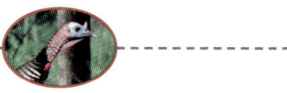

Well, people's perception is what they think they know.

WEDDLE: Yeah, yeah. Here, again, it's always mentioned on hunting videos and how-tos: those late morning birds are better. That's where they get that perception. But then there is a peak in the late afternoon. Now, a lot of times, okay, so you've gone out in the morning and you've killed a gobbler first thing—well, you're not out there at 8 or 9 o'clock or noon or whatever. You've already killed your bird.

So that's gonna skew the results.

WEDDLE: Skew the results. But then, of course, some states, most of the states don't allow you to hunt in the afternoon. But there is a spike in kills

acting like a turkey is supposed to. Beautiful hunts, both of them. An hour and a half apart, 400 yards apart in the same woods.

OWENS: Yeah, and I've had that with Merriam's and I've had it with easterns. It's just like so, much less, if I can say it, I've had it more with Rios and Merriam's, given my limited experience with them compared to easterns. I mean, I just have found that they're more receptive.

How do you guys deal with the rain and wind?

WEDDLE: Hate it is all you can do.

Start drinking?

WEDDLE: [laughing] Heavily. Wind is the biggest deal.

> When it's drizzling rain it's cooler than it's been.
> In my experience, when it cools off a little bit . . . gobbling
> kind of peaks. In a downpour? That's hard hunting.
> I think I'll sit in the van for a little while!

three to four hours before sunset. And then it goes down too because that last hour or two of daylight, you might hear turkeys gobble.

OWENS: They don't respond as good as they do three or four hours before sunset.

WEDDLE: Not nearly as well. I had a lot of fairly good a number of afternoon hunts but by far and away the best percentage is first thing right off the roost.

OWENS: I've had some really memorable and good afternoon hunts—very much fewer for easterns.

WEDDLE: We've had some awesome easterns. We had two in Virginia this year.

OWENS: Really?

WEDDLE: Yeah. Gobbling hard. The first day, half the season in Virginia you can hunt til noon, then the second half, well, the very first day we could hunt in the afternoon, we killed two birds. One at 3 o'clock and one at 4:30. Screaming, strutting,

OWENS: Wind.

WEDDLE: Wind will always be the biggest deal.

OWENS: I hate wind.

WEDDLE: You turkey hunt with your ears a lot. And you use the turkey's ears for success a lot. So the wind just flat out puts muffs on your ears and not much you can do about that. You can hunt with the wind, find open areas in the wind, try to target places that are out of the wind.

OWENS: Yeah, east side of hills.

WEDDLE: Ravines, valleys.

OWENS: Yeah. Rain—obviously, I would rather it not be raining, but if it's gonna be raining, as long as it's not a torrential downpour, I'm gonna hunt, regardless. Torrential downpour or not. I just hate getting all my stuff wet. And having to dry it out is just annoying but, I mean, I've had some phenomenal hunts in the rain.

WEDDLE: Rain, a lot of times, pushes birds out

a miserable day to hunt. They're not gonna gobble. Time and again that's been proven. I keep track. I observe that stuff. And they are *not gonna gobble.*

WEDDLE: Yep, it's like they're already preparing for it a lot of times.

OWENS: Yeah, I think it's the pressure.

WEDDLE: The pressure, yeah, but a lot of times with that drizzling rain I think that's got something to do with the temperature. When it's drizzling rain it's cooler than it's been. In my experience, when it cools off a little bit, granted, it doesn't drop down to some sub-zero freezing temperatures. But when it cools off a little, gobbling kind of peaks. In a downpour? That's hard hunting. I think I'll sit in the van for a little while!

How about thunder and lightning—how do the birds react?

OWENS: You can't hear.

WEDDLE: They gobble good at the thunder, but the aspect of getting lit up and electrified doesn't really do much for me either.

Who is or was the best turkey hunter you've ever known?

WEDDLE: I'm gonna read my answer on this one cuz I prepared it. [laughing]

All right, you're allowed. As long as they're your words.

WEDDLE: First, I'm gonna say the *best* turkey hunter I know is sitting right here beside us: Dave Owens. This young whippersnapper is death on birds everywhere he hunts. I'd put him up against anybody to get it done, both in the woods and on the calling stage. I swear the kid's got turkey feathers instead of body hair beneath that shirt! As good as Dave is, though, I'm going to declare David Caudill as my *favorite* turkey hunter. David has spent his whole life of 87 years in the wilds of Florida. He's still hunting turkeys. His parents, I think, they settled on the island that is now Cape Canaveral. So they came to Florida back when Old Florida was really wild. David has spent his whole life hunting. He worked as a heavy equipment operator

Weddle drove all night to reach Kansas in 2012 to hunt a Walk-In Private Access area: private farm land leased by the state for public hunting. Within 10 minutes of fly-down he had this tom pounding dirt.

in the open, which I think is what a lot of us capitalize on. A light drizzle, at daylight, won't make any difference.

OWENS: No. Whether they're going to gobble or not—and I've heard a lot of gobbling when it's lightly drizzling. If it's raining hard, yes or no? Probably no. If it's not raining at daylight, but it's gonna rain within an hour or two of noon, that's

for the Florida Wildlife Commission, and then became the lead turkey trapper and guide for [game biologists] David Austin and Lovett Williams at Fisheating Creek, back in its heyday as the premier turkey-hunting spot in all of Florida. This was the place where the two renowned biologists did their groundbreaking research on the wild turkey. David Caudill has quite literally held thousands of turkeys (alive and dead) in his hands throughout his many years. His brain holds a vast amount of knowledge and wisdom about wild turkeys and turkey hunting. He is such an astute observer and a consummate storyteller. He's our joy in camp. We sit and listen to David. He'll just talk for hours and hours, regaling us with stories. Part of that is that he's so deaf he can't hear what anybody else is saying, so he keeps talking, but that's part of his charm. If David and I were out scouting, and he was to tell me that the visible sign around us indicated that a turkey with a nine-and-a-quarter-inch beard and matching spurs of one and an eighth inches came down Sandy Road at 3:10 pm on last Saturday afternoon—and scratched up a June bug from beneath a dead pod with his left foot and ate it—I *know* all of this happened just as he said it did. [laughing]

Are you planning to see your friend next spring?
WEDDLE: Lord willing. [Doc did spend time with David one last time, listening to his stories. Caudill died the following summer at age 88.]

Your best man—the best turkey hunter you ever met?
OWENS: That's a very difficult one for me because I don't know a lot of other turkey hunters. I am not acquainted with many other pure turkey hunters. I know a lot of hunters, but mostly gentlemen that I have met on this journey that I don't want hunting my turkeys. Be glad to help them anywhere else but home. There's some good, good turkey hunters. As far as naming the very best turkey hunter that I know, or else known through any type of avenue, it would be Doc, sitting right here beside me. How can you dispute 26, 28 years worth of experience? When people say, "Yeah, I

turkey hunt," they mean they turkey hunted this spring, which may be 15 days, 20 days they went out. Doc has hunted from the beginning of every spring to the end of every spring for 28 years! You really can't deny that.
WEDDLE: That doesn't mean I'm good—it just means I do it a lot.
OWENS: That just means [laughing] that he's got the experience to know when there's a turkey in here that needs to die.
WEDDLE: There's been a lot of screwing up in those 34 years, brother. [laughing] Every blind hog finds an acorn now and again.
OWENS: There is no substitute for experience. In my opinion, the best turkey hunter I've ever met has got to be somebody with that type of experience, not only with just turkey hunting. There's some old timers that I'm sure are very successful turkey hunters, but say they just hunted in Georgia for 50 years or something. They've turkey hunted since there was a season. But the thing is that, they've only hunted in Georgia. We have a really long season but our season isn't in when it starts down in south Florida and climbs up to the Northeast where it ends the last day of May.

Doc, what are favorite books and favorite writers about turkey hunting?
WEDDLE: *The Old Pro Turkey Hunter* by Gene Nunnery [1980], that was kind of like our Bible when we were first starting turkey hunting. That was our inspiration, me and my buddy. We used to read that one every year. Everybody ought to read that. Every turkey hunter ought to read that book. Besides Nunnery, some of the old timers like Dave Harbor, who wrote some early stuff. He kind of established the world-record system used for turkeys. But he was also a very colorful writer and wrote stories that really captured the essence of turkey hunting, for me. So that was kind of inspirational. Dwayne Bland, Charlie Elliot, Kenny Morgan are all really good, for their inspiration and their knowledge. All these guys are dead, by the way. Lovett Williams for his technical and biological stuff.

So there is hope for you yet!

WEDDLE: Yeah. [laughing]. A couple of living writers I admire are Jim Spencer and John Mc-Daniel. They've both written several books and countless magazine articles. I like their take on the hunt. There are a bunch of turkey books out there in lots of different styles and content. I collect turkey books. I've got just about every one that was ever written. Searching for books in the off season, for me, is almost as big a challenge as turkey hunting during the spring. There's a lot of turkey wisdom in those books.

About all most people read nowadays is their phone.

And just by him just sitting over there mentioning all the titles, I'm like, *I couldn't name you that many turkey books!* It's embarrassing what little bit of turkey literature that I'm familiar with and a lot of it is very fresh, like I just read it or something. But someone that has the ability like Gene Nunnery in *The Old Pro Turkey Hunter*, I couldn't get to the next page quick enough. I would read it and I would want to flip back and read right back through it because, I was like, it made me shake my head sometimes and just lean back and just remember. It provoked that response that I thought only a real encounter could provoke. Whereas, just a turkey hunting story, while I do enjoy them, it's just a turkey story: "Hey, I went here. I heard him

> And for somebody to have the ability to bring that to life through words and to paint that picture to where it makes your heart flutter a little bit and catches you in the throat, that keeps me flipping the pages.

WEDDLE: Unbelievable as it is to me, I read a statistic that 75 percent of people will never read another book after they graduate from high school. That amazes me.

Dave, what style of writing about wild turkeys, either in magazines or books, do you find most interesting?

OWENS: I like a writer that keeps me turning the pages—something that I can relate with, something that really stirs an emotion that I feel like you can only get through writing. You can't get it from a video. It's something that really puts you there. Taking a turkey is an experience, it kinda stirs your soul, so to speak. And for somebody to have the ability to bring that to life through words and to paint that picture to where it makes your heart flutter a little bit and catches you in the throat, that keeps me flipping the pages. What I've read pales in comparison to what Doc has read.

here, I went there, called him up here, shot him here." I can read it. I love reading anything about turkeys but it doesn't get me as fired up.

And, finally, you both represent two quite separate generations of turkey hunters. We've talked about many of the changes in the sport over the years. Dave, having come to turkey hunting relatively recently, where do you and your peers see the sport going?

OWENS: The sport as a whole, I feel there's people like myself that appreciate it for how at least I feel like it should be taken. Really a slow-down approach—a "really-appreciate-what's-there" approach. I always feel in debt for some reason, like I owe somebody or something, just for that experience. And there will never be any way for me to repay that debt but there's a certain amount of us out there that'll always be there. There's a certain amount of turkey hunters that love turkeys and

will always be there. There is this new crowd that's come in and I'm treading lightly here because this is one of those debates that will set you in a fire, so to speak.

Go ahead and speak your piece. This is your opportunity to do it.
OWENS: The attitude that if it's legal in your state to do, then, by all means, you have all the rights to do it. But there is a group that's out there, I feel like, just for the head smashing, bloody pictures, kill, kill, kill everything. And that is completely opposite of what I feel like turkey hunting is and means to me. But I don't feel like that group of people will ever go anywhere; they will always be there.

think they'll always be there and I don't wanna—the word is so terrible—but the purist, and I'm gonna say that in a positive light right now. When I say purist, I don't mean that they're overly critical of what anybody else does. They're just very comfortable with the way they're doing it and the way they're doing it is in the woods or in one on one, them and the turkey-type settings.

Instead of "purist," I think I may have a better word for you—how about traditionalist?
OWENS: Yeah, let's do that. Okay. Over what's there now which is the blinds, and the decoys, and that whole deal that is so much different than the turkey hunting that I do know. I'm not going to

> I think the biggest threat probably to turkey hunting is just the general disconnect that the general population has from hunting, wildlife, our place in it all.

Are they a threat to the sport, though? These bad boys, or the bad attitude, whatever you want to call it?
OWENS: I don't think so. The only thing that I feel like they're being a negative influence on is the new and up-and-coming turkey hunters. I don't know if there will ever be measures taken. Turkey populations are, in a lot of spots in the Southeast, they are falling off for some reason. Nobody really has an explanation. I think hunting has very little to do about that. I think it's habitat and predators.

Well, some of that, along with natural cycles, may be out of our control, but we can control hunting ethics and attitudes.
OWENS: Who's to say that changes aren't going to be made? I don't know those changes but as far as getting back to your original question, the sport of turkey hunting I feel like it's gonna be there regardless of where the population goes. Maybe they will limit the seasons, knock down on the limits. I

look down on anybody for doing it. I won't say I never done it before, but I won't do it again.

Well, you've said it before, but in the end it really amounts to a matter of respect for the. . . .
WEDDLE: Respect for the quarry.
OWENS: Yeah, I really love that predator–prey relationship to where, I don't know, the minute you say it's you against him . . . well, *you're using a shotgun,* you're not using a slingshot! But I think there's a line in the sand for everybody. A certain amount of people feel like this is acceptable and a certain amount of people feel like it's not acceptable.
WEDDLE: But in the end if it's legal then nobody can stop you and dispute.
OWENS: You hate to criticize anything.
WEDDLE: Yeah, you don't want to criticize anything that's legal.
OWENS: What's right for me isn't right for you, and vice versa.

Illinois always seems to produce big, beautiful toms for Doc Weddle. This this one fell during the 2014 season. It was the highest-scoring bird he has ever killed.

And Doc, in the big picture, where do you see the sport of turkey hunting heading? You've been doing this for a long time. You've seen a lot of people come and go.

WEDDLE: I think we have a good foundation that will be around for a long time. I think the biggest threat probably to turkey hunting is just the general disconnect that the general population has from hunting, wildlife, our place in it all. I mean, our numbers are going down as a percentage wise, as hunters. And I think that's gonna be a factor in years to come, probably not in my lifetime. Maybe in Dave's. I look at how as a population we have such a disregard for the natural world. And so many people just live in their own little world and

they don't think about the whole big picture. We continue to poison our oceans and our waters and our land and ourselves, and we don't learn from our mistakes. I think the world is going down the tubes but it's gonna take a while to get there. I think turkey hunting's pretty strong in this country. The people that do it, and that love to do it, are gonna do it and if they said it was illegal tomorrow, next spring there'd be a lot of outlaws, in my opinion. We're over-populating the world, so we're losing ground every year, and that's number one. You gotta have the ground. And resources—you got to maintain it. If we don't have places to turkey hunt, we're not gonna be turkey hunting.

2

James F. Hascup Jr.

HOME:
Ringwood, New Jersey

OCCUPATION:
Retired C.E.O. of building contractor supply company

FIRST WILD TURKEY:
1984, New Jersey

COMPLETED U.S. SUPER SLAM:
1997, West Virginia

**IN JIM HASCUP'S BASEMENT** at his home an hour's drive from Newark International Airport, among the turkey tails and prize calls and a map pinpointing every bird he's killed, are two elegant walking sticks carved of ironwood with turkey heads for grips. At the base of each cane are turkey feet— actual scaly turkey feet.

In the early years after wild turkeys were reintroduced to New Jersey, birds were scarce. But enthusiastic hunters weren't. Hascup and a friend had the canes made up to plant turkey tracks down around waterholes to guide other hunters in concentrating their efforts, which happened to be far from where *they* planned to hunt.

When Hascup started pursuing the Super Slam in earnest, he bought a wall map of North America. When he came back from a successful hunt he placed a red dot on the location. Then he took the shotgun shell that killed the bird, wrote the date and the state on the plastic shell, and hung the spurs and beard above it.

"What are these round stones?" I asked.

"They're from a dinosaur's gizzard," Jim said.

My eye stopped on what looked like a mummified hand. *Anything is possible,* I thought. *The guy hunts Africa.*

On a spring day in 1995, Jim Hascup was descending a steep mountainside in Tennessee's Cherokee National Forest. He took a nasty tumble. When he got home his left hand was red and throbbing. His wife, Cathie, told him he needed to see a doctor. The doc told him he had broken a bone below his pinky finger.

"I'm going to put you in a cast," he said.

"You can't do that," Hascup said. "This is only my first week of turkey hunting—I still have 11 more states to go."

"Well, you gotta have a cast on it." the doctor said. "Otherwise it will never be right your whole life."

"Okay," Jim said. "Wait a minute. Stay right here."

He had his Browning in the car. He took the walnut forearm off the shotgun, put his hand up and laid the forearm in there: "Can you make me a cast so that I can hold the gun like this?"

"Yes, I can," the doc said.

Jim put some paper around the stock to protect it while the cast was molded partially

around it. Once home, Jim pulled on a glove and taped it on. On the road again! Nevada: *boom*—19½-pound tom with a 10½-inch beard and one-inch spurs. Oklahoma: *boom*. Kentucky: *boom*. Missouri: *boom*. New Hampshire: *boom*. Rhode Island: *boom*. Wisconsin: *boom*. . . .

James F. Hascup Jr. was born in Paterson, New Jersey, in 1942. The family had a country house and went "up to the lake" every summer. Jimmy spent his days near the water with no shoes on. He loved swimming. He did a lot of walking in the woods. Later, all of his teenage friends were the same: they fished, trapped and hunted.

He went to work for his father, in 1960, right out of high school. Back then, there were lots of manufacturing plants in New Jersey. Their company, A. W. Meyer, sold drills and taps and all types of supplies to the machine shops and the woodworking shops. Young Jim was an outside salesman. He loved calling on all the plants and manufacturing job sites. And during the next 50 years, as manufacturing disappeared, Hascup steered the family company to becoming the premier contractor supply company in the state of New Jersey and most of New York City. They imported drywall screws, and sold all the big drywall companies in New York that did the high rises. Hascup worked on the World Trade Center when it was built. And he was there the day it came down.

Cathie and he were driving into work that morning, on the highway that parallels the Hudson River. They looked over at the Manhattan skyline and saw smoke coming from the first tower. As they were watching they saw the second plane hit the second tower.

"You could see it clearly," Jim told me. "We were right across the river."

Hascup could do only one thing: he acted. He got one of his manufacturers to donate a whole container of generators. He and seven of his guys somehow made it through the Lincoln Tunnel. They unloaded the generators, preparing them with gas and oil, and gave them to the firefighters. They spent the night there, as the firefighters searched for bodies. They delivered to the site every day. The State Department gave Jim a special pass to get there.

"I was on this site when it was built," Hascup recalled, "but when I looked around I couldn't recognize a single thing. Buildings were on top of one another and the streets we used every day were gone, replaced by rubble."

One of his drivers had been scheduled to make a morning delivery, but he got held up in Brooklyn and didn't make it. He was going there when he heard the news. He asked Jim if he could keep the delivery invoice: it read September 11.

You were the first modern hunter to get a Gould's turkey in Arizona.
JAMES F. HASCUP JR.: I was.

When was that?
HASCUP: Two thousand two.

The native birds had been wiped out.
HASCUP: The federal government actually brought Gould's turkeys back from Mexico, cuz they originally were in New Mexico and Arizona. Those were the two states where they were. And so our government went to the Mexican government, and requested they give them some Gould's turkeys. That's how they were brought back into the U. S. They didn't put them in New Mexico. They are in there now, but they weren't back then. They had to find a safe place to put them, cuz they wanted to reintroduce them. So, close to the Mexican border is an army fort called Fort Huachuca. The government put the turkeys on the fort. That way, they would be taken care of until they acclimated. There wouldn't be anybody in there shooting them, and they could be protected. So, they put them in there for three or four years out of the fort. They're everywhere in those mountains around the fort. You can't hunt the fort anymore. That was after 9/11/2001—everything closed. The fort secured itself and doesn't allow hunting. I was there in 2002. The National Wild Turkey Federation got a tag. One tag. They only had one tag that year. They gave it to the organization to raise some money to put back into the project. The birds were starting to move out of there, and they wanted to get land and get farmers, so they could put them, and not allow people on. So, they had a drawing for one tag, and then one tag was gonna be auctioned off. I bought the tag at the auction in Nashville, and I had my buddy [wife Cathie] over here sitting behind me, helping me. Otherwise, I probably would have stopped bidding, but she didn't let me stop and I bought the tag. There was a guy at the auction, his name was Ralph Anderson. He was from Tucson and worked for the N.W.T.F. in Arizona and New Mexico, so he knew the area really well. He told me now that I bought the tag he would come with me to the fort and be my guide. I flew to Tucson and we drove to the fort. I got to meet the company commander and he gave us the run of the fort. The birds had never heard a call before—we took a bird in the first half hour. When I got the Gould's tag, it also came with a tag for a Merriam's turkey, so after the Gould's hunt Ralph and I drove four hours north to Williams, where I took a nice Merriam's that afternoon.

Nice.
HASCUP: Yes, it was. It was an historic moment, that the first Gould's turkeys were back in the United States, and I took the first one.

FACING PAGE: Hunting his second state of 1995, Jim Hascup fell on a mountainside in Tennessee and broke a bone in his left hand. He asked the doctor to mold a cast so he could still hold his Browning shotgun—and went on to hunt 11 more states. Jim cheerfully recorded the dates and places of all his turkey kills that season on the plaster.

James F. Hascup Jr. **82**

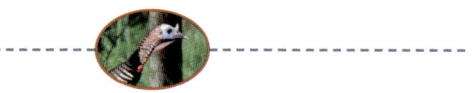

A number of years earlier you experienced an extraordinary day when you took three birds in three states.

HASCUP: I wanted to hunt Nebraska and South Dakota. I contacted a man that I had hunted mule deer with in Colorado. He lives in Minnesota. I mentioned that I wanted to hunt those two states for turkey. This man wasn't a turkey hunter but he told me he knew a man named Chris Yeoman who works for the railroad and he guides in both states. I called Chris and talked at length with him. We worked out a deal to hunt both those states and Montana, also. I figured three days in each state so I was going to go for 10 days. Chris said he had to work so he would be with me for the weekend and then I would be on my own. That was fine with me. All I needed was access to where the birds were and he definitely knew that. I flew to Rapid City, South Dakota, and met Chris. It was April 14, 1994. We drove all the way down to Crawford, Nebraska, which was just over the Nebraska line. We go there late, about 11 p.m., but Chris knew the motel owner who left the key under the mat. The next morning, we were up at 5 a.m. No more than a 15-minute drive and we were at the ranch. Chris thought he knew where the birds usually roosted and he was correct. They were there. The birds flew down by 6 and by 6:30 we were on our way to breakfast with a beautiful 20-pound gobbler. After breakfast, we headed north to a spot Chris knew near the Black Hills. About one and a half hours later we were driving on an old country road and there right ahead of us was a gobbler strutting in the middle of the road. And he had a bunch of hens with him and he was showing off his stuff. We passed him and ran into the farmer about a half mile down the road where he was working on his fences. We stopped and I asked if I could hunt that gobbler. He said, "Sure, I'll watch from here." Chris stayed with the farmer and I got in the ditch on the side of the road and crawled down towards the bird who now was on the other side of the road. It was slow and wet in the ditch. Every time I called he would come up on the road but he was too far for a shot. I think he knew I was there somewhere. I crawled closer and closer but this time I tried a different tactic: I called behind me in the opposite direction. Suddenly he came up on the road and this time I was close enough and took him. When I got back to Chris and the farmer they said: "Jim, you put on quite a show. You had turkeys coming from everywhere. There were three toms behind you, and the big gobbler was on the other side of the road and there were two more toms with him." They added that behind where they were standing, two more toms came running up the hill, but when they saw them they left. I thanked the farmer and he said, "Don't thank me—I enjoyed the show." Now it was 10 a.m., and we were on our way to Ekalaka, Montana, which is a 550-mile ride. With no speed limit, you can make some time, which we did. We stopped at Chris's house in Rapid City to put the birds on ice, had some lunch, and we were off again. We pulled into Custer National Forest just outside of Ekalaka at 7:30 p.m. We pulled in a spot that looked great. The plan was to sleep next to the truck. I said, "Let's take a little walk down in that patch of woods and call." Chris suggested that we do it in the morning. But I had a feeling, and said, "We have time—let's try now," and off we went. We only walked about a quarter-mile and I called and heard a reply. I said: "Chris, did you hear that? It's a gobbler." He told me to try again. I did and again he answered. This time he was getting closer. We didn't even have face masks or gloves so we hid behind some rocks. Lo and behold, here comes that big gobbler looking for us. I shot him at 7:45 p.m. I couldn't believe that I took three beautiful gobblers in three states all in one day. I was ecstatic! I never have done that before. I took two birds in two states the same day twice, but never three.

A perfect day. Sometimes it all works out.

HASCUP: Well, now I had completed those three states in one day. After saying good-bye to Chris, I went back to the hotel. I had figured this hunt would take 10 days, and here I was with nine more days before my flight home. I remember when I hunted the San Carlos Apache Reservation in Arizona,

On one extraordinary day in 1994, Hascup killed three wild turkeys in three states: Nebraska, South Dakota and, finally, in the Custer National Forest near Ekalaka, Montana.

I met a fellow turkey hunter who was in the same motel. His name was Fred, and of course we got talking about turkeys. He was from Michigan. I asked if he had ever hunted an Indian reservation before. He said yes, he had hunted the Standing Rock Lakota Sioux Reservation in South Dakota and North Dakota. I couldn't believe what I was hearing. The State of North Dakota doesn't allow non-residents to hunt their turkeys. I had actually contemplated buying a piece of land in North Dakota just so I could hunt. I asked Fred, "Did you hunt turkeys?" He said, "No, I hunted sharp-tail grouse." I asked if he hunted North or South Dakota. He said both. I asked if he saw any turkeys, he said, "Not in North Dakota, but I did

see them in South Dakota." I was hooked. I called the reservation and asked if they had any turkey licenses. They said sure: the cost is $50. The next morning, I checked out and was on my way to the reservation—about a six-hour drive. When I arrived, I went into the office and bought a license. I asked one of the officers where the turkeys were. He took me to a map and pointed to South Dakota. I told him no, I want to hunt in North Dakota. I know in the western states, water is the key, so on the map at the top of the reservation, I saw a river. "What about up there?" "That's the Cannonball River," he said, "and it's all private ranches." I said, "Okay, I'll ask people." One of the other officers told me where he saw turkeys but

that the landowner probably wouldn't let me hunt. I figured I would try. I'd been a salesman all my life and I know how to gently get my point across. I drove up to this ranch and went to the trailer and asked this nice young lady. She said, "No you can't hunt, they are like pets." I explained the cycle of turkeys and how the males are here all winter and now they're all out breeding with the females. I explained that you only need one tom for 15 to 20 hens. She listened and finally I could see she was coming around, then she said, "Okay, go ahead." I walked along the river and found a spot that was covered with signs of turkeys. I think I sat down and called for about an hour and here they came, all of them: four toms, five jakes and a dozen hens. What a picture. I took my time enjoying the view and finally I took one of the big toms. I went back to the trailer and thanked her for letting me hunt. I had killed the first non-resident turkey in North Dakota and I didn't have to buy the land. Now it was time for the long drive back to Rapid City and the flight, so off I went. I was driving excessively fast but it was 3 in the morning. When I got close to Rapid City I was stopped for speeding. The officer was a nice guy when he saw my camo clothes and asked if I was hunting. I told him where I had been and told him about what I was trying to accomplish. He was very interested. He said he collected police arm badges and could I get him one from New Jersey? I said sure, because I know several officers in New Jersey, and I was sure I could get him one. He didn't give me a ticket, but told me to slow down. I shook his hand and was getting into the car when I remembered the bird in the trunk. I called to him and asked if he would like the bird. He said, "Wow— I'd love it!" I gave it to him, he turned on his siren and lights and took the bird home: another satisfied customer. When I got back to New Jersey, I sent that nice young lady a two-pound box of chocolates for letting me hunt.

And that was approximately halfway through your quest for 49 states?
HASCUP: Yeah, that was in 1994, and I finished

in '97, started in '89. So, yeah, a little over halfway through.

Tell me about your first turkey hunt in the South.
HASCUP: I was hunting in Georgia and went to South Carolina first. When we met the guy from South Carolina, my friend Ronnie was with me. And when we got in this guy's pickup truck, he's got a full glass. It wasn't soda. [laughing] Full glass, and a .357 Magnum sitting on the seat right there next to him. I sat next to him. Ronnie sat in the back. So he took us around and showed us where we could hunt the next day when we came back. We had talked to him, wow, it must have been an hour and a half, two hours. And we're leaving and he said, "Okay, you guys have a good time tomorrow." He says: "You know what? You're all right for a Yankee." We were the first Yankees he ever met. [laughing]. Anyway, that was a bust. It was terrible. We never heard a bird, never saw a bird. Very little sign where we were. We only hunted two days and then we went to Georgia. Georgia was great. I killed a bird the first morning right off the roost. And then the afternoon they sit you on these plots, which is a bean that they plant, and the turkeys like to come to that and dig them up, and eat the beans. They're like peas. So, I sat on this field. And son of a gun, in the afternoon here comes the big gobbler. I shoot him too. So now I got two birds the same day. You're allowed two birds. My buddy is there and he is gonna stay for another two days. I got nothing to do, so I've been talking to this young guy, Major Talent, that was there. And he had dropped me off out in the field there, and we had talked about he was originally from South Carolina, because we were talking about how I didn't have such a good time in South Carolina. So, I said: "Listen, you're from South Carolina. Can you find me a place to hunt a couple days? Can you find me a place?" He says, "Well, I might be able to." I said, "Okay, let's go make a phone call." This is pre-cellphones. We went to the phone booth and I had to beg change from everybody. [laughing] So I got a couple of dollars' worth of change, and we went over and he calls. He gets off

the phone and he says: "Okay, we're set. We're going to my uncle's place." He hadn't been in there in years. He says, "My mom and him are brother and sister, but they haven't talked in years."

Great—the Hatfields and the McCoys!
HASCUP: He said they had a big fight and the family doesn't talk. "But I told him that you were my future father-in-law. And that you came down and you wanted to turkey hunt. So, I'm gonna bring you up there to the turkey hunt if that is okay with you"

Are you kidding?
HASCUP: And he says: "Yes, that's fine with me, you come ahead. But I don't want you to kill the

this piece of woods. So, we go back there and we worked on these birds four hours and we couldn't get them to come close. We were right next to each other and he's a good caller. And I thought I was a good caller, too. We both were calling. We'd take turns. Nothing. We couldn't get them. We could hear them. We could hear them in the leaves. We knew they were close. Probably, if I would have stood up, I could have killed one. But I didn't. And finally, I turned around and I looked at him, and I went like this [motioning to throat] to cut the sound and we both stopped cold. And we sat there it felt like hours, but it wasn't. It was probably only 10 or 15 minutes. All of a sudden, I look up and I see this blue and red head coming. Here he comes. When he went behind the tree I picked the gun

> He gets off the phone and he says: "Okay, we're set.
> We're going to my uncle's place." He hadn't been in there in years.
> He says, "My mom and him are brother and sister,
> but they haven't talked in years."

bird that's behind the house because he gobbles every morning and Mother likes to hear that bird." So, we go there the next morning. We're right outside the place and we're looking at his house. Beautiful old southern mansion. Beautiful. And sure enough, as soon as it gets light, that bird gobbles behind his house. I said: "We're going to have to figure out how we're going to get to that bird. Maybe we can call him across the road." I look down and I said, "Major, look down." He said, "What, Jim?" There were old drag marks. You know, how they spread their feathers out? I said, "There's drag marks everywhere—look." And we're walking around in this little field line and I said, "There is more than one turkey making these drags." He said, "My gosh, it's getting lighter now." All of a sudden, a bird gobbles behind us. Well, that one's legal. As we're on our way back, there are four more. There's five different gobblers in

up. He walked out the other side, I shot. Then I jumped up to run over there and there were two birds dead. Two big gobblers. They were with each other and I never saw that. Both had one-and-a-half-inch spurs and 11-inch beards. Anyway, we go down to meet his uncle, because he says I want you to meet him, meet my uncle. Okay. So, I go down there, and he's a fine southern gentleman. He had a bathrobe on and he had his cup of coffee. And he came right out and sat on the porch with us because no way he's letting us inside. We're covered with dirt. [laughing] But came out there and sat with us and talked with us and he says, "Well, I'm real proud to meet you and I'm glad you could come down here and help me." And he looked over at my guy, Major, and he said: "Major, you tell your mother to call me cuz it's about time we ended this." So, I got to put two families back together besides killing two big gobblers. Actually,

four in two different states. I had a great time.

Little did you realize you had a potential career as a family feud counselor. [laughing]
HASCUP: I still see Major when I go to Tennessee. Now he hunts with my friends in Tennessee. And he's in their old apartment. He greets me and says, "How you doing, Dad?" "I'm all good, good." [laughing] "How's my daughter?"

Jim, You seem to have hunted everything that walked Noah's plank. [laughing] In a general sense—not specific to turkeys—why do you hunt?
HASCUP: I've loved the woods since I was six or

thought, *man, that's the ultimate.* **And yet you keep coming back to the ordinary and—by some aesthetic measure—homely American turkey.**
HASCUP: The best thing about turkey hunting is that they answer you. You talk to them and they talk back! Some other animals like moose and elk talk, but not like turkeys. When we first started hunting turkeys, and that's probably part of the answer, it was something to do in the spring. Because here in this state, you hunted grouse and ducks, and then the ducks all flew south. The grouse were still here but the season ended in November. We could hunt ducks down in the shore areas until February, and then it was done. You were done, until the

> I remember an old fellow from Tennessee,
> Jim Arthur. He taught me a lot about the woods and life itself.
> He would say to me, "Listen, Jim, she's coming alive,"
> in the morning when the birds would start

seven years old. Why do I hunt? I hunt to be in the woods, to be away from people, to be away from all the political things that are going on. It's who I am. Out there nothing changes—it is all the same. And I like the idea being there to see the sunrise; I like to be there when the sun goes down. And I like to listen to the birds. I remember an old fellow from Tennessee, Jim Arthur. He taught me a lot about the woods and life itself. He would say to me, "Listen, Jim, she's coming alive," in the morning when the birds would start. And then they all would stop, the birds would stop, and I'll tell you, it's a feeling that I get all the time when I'm in the woods. And I remember Jim, or, as we all called him, "The Old Man."

And what is it specifically about hunting wild turkeys that you most love? That has over the many years kept you coming back? You've successfully pursued African big-game animals. One would imagine many hunters would have

following fall. When turkey hunting came in, it was, *my gosh, here's something to do in the spring.* And once you've started, it's a whole different thing, because, the buds are just coming out. I mean, it's a whole different thing that I've never seen before. The trees are blossoming, the trees are budding—especially when you're in the South, the redbuds. It definitely got under your skin to be out there in the spring. It's warm. That's another thing. The air smells so fresh in the spring, compared to the fall when everything is dying, the leaves are dying they're falling off the trees. It's a different smell.

When did you kill your first turkey?
HASCUP: Nineteen eighty-four.

How old were you?
HASCUP: Forty-two.

Do you remember the hunt?
HASCUP: Absolutely. I'll tell you exactly. They put

Jim at his office surrounded by memories of his many hunts in Africa, where he visits several times a year.

birds into New Jersey in 1976. We got them from Vermont. Yeah, Vermont. We traded them for grouse. And they opened the season in 1980. So, I started hunting turkeys in 1980, and it took me four years to kill one. It's not like it is now. There was nobody to tell you how to hunt. We could read some books, but they didn't really tell you. And I read articles. Nobody told you: this is what you do. I scared off more birds than you could ever guess because I didn't know what I was doing. I didn't know how to call. I didn't know when to call, when not to call. All these things I learned over the length of time. The bird that I killed, I had heard him there the week before. And, again, I could only hunt on the weekends, cuz I worked. And there was no taking off from work. So the following Saturday I went back there. And the bird answered me again. And he was down a little draw.

I was on top of the draw. I called, and he answered. I got all set up next to a tree. My friend was with me and he sat behind the tree. And I wait a little while, I called again. He gobbled again and now he's closer. I said, *boy, this is great, he's finally coming.* I got the gun up, and a couple seconds later here comes a red head up over the side of the bank. *Bang!* I shot. And I got up, I'm jumping up and down I'm so happy. I run over there—it's a jake. And as I looked down the hill, I watched the big bird. He actually looked back at me as he was walking away. He wasn't even running; he was walking away. I'm not sure, but I think I heard that turkey laugh! I went back there every year after that. I don't think I ever killed him. But I've heard other birds, I did kill other birds there. But never in that spot. So that was my lesson. I killed my first bird and it was a jake.

At any point in your evolution as a turkey hunter, did you ever have a mentor? You said you sort of learned it all early on. But at any point during that progression, did you ever link up with somebody who really knew the game?

HASCUP: When I started, there were no local mentors. No one in the North hunted turkeys because there were none. There were no old turkey hunters like in the South. We had to learn all by ourselves, and by our mistakes. I ran off a lot of birds before I figured out what I was doing. But after a while, absolutely. I mean, a couple of them who really taught me because they hunted turkeys all their lives. One is "Peck" Martin from McMechen, West Virginia. And the other one is Russ Arthur from Cleveland, Tennessee. Those two guys are probably my biggest mentors, without a doubt.

Tell me a little bit about of each of those guys and the characteristics that make them so good.

HASCUP: Well, Peck is just about the same age as me; I think he's about a year younger. And he's been turkey hunting his whole life. He calls himself a West Virginia redneck. And he taught me a lot of things about when not to call. When to switch calls. See, these are things that you'd never know until someone with experience tells you. But I didn't meet him until I was well into this hunting deal. He is a great turkey-call maker and a great friend. I was killing birds my way, and having a hard time, too. I'm very aggressive. He is not very aggressive. He is very slow. He's laid back. He did things different than me but he taught me his way. And I used his way a lot. And, of course, he is a call manufacturer so I learned a lot with the box call and mouth call: all were from him. I also got slate calls and glass calls from him. And they came with lessons on how to use them! He taught me how to use a lot of calls, which I'd never used before. Still can't use the wing bone, but I try. [laughing]

How about Russ?

HASCUP: Russ is younger than me. Russ is in his early 60s. And he actually just retired. But he is without a doubt the best turkey hunter in the country. If you heard him you would not believe it. I mean, the man doesn't even need a call. He uses calls, but he doesn't need to, cuz with his mouth he can make all the calls. His owl calls are unbelievable. We'll be in the woods and when he gets to calling, two or three owls come in screeching at us with birds gobbling everywhere. He can do jake calls. I remember we were in Connecticut once and we had this tom hung up at 60 yards. I had him hung up. I went back and got Russ. We came back there and the bird was in the same position. And he proceeded to have a jake fight. He beat the ground, beat the bushes, had two jakes screaming back at each other. I'd be damned if that big bird didn't walk in and I killed him. But that's Russ. He's very aggressive when he calls, and he gets them one way or another. And talk about walking! My gosh. My one leg was short on one side from side hilling, up and down, because that part of Tennessee is straight up and down. Anywhere you went, there were beautiful Tennessee mountains.

Where in Tennessee?

HASCUP: Cherokee National Forest, north of Chattanooga, near the Georgia border. It's about two hours from Atlanta and two hours from Memphis.

In the early years, before you met and hunted with these gentlemen, do you remember any particularly memorable mistakes that you made? Where I'm going with this is: what would you advise a beginner to carefully avoid?

HASCUP: Okay, the main problem that I had, and it happened to me several times: you hear a bird gobble on the roost, or gobble on the ground. You don't know, but he's facing away from you. So now he gobbles. Well, he sounds like he's 300 or 400 yards from you. He's not, but you don't know that. So now, you take off to get close to him because you need to close the gap. That's too far to call. I have called them that far, but it's too far. So you try to close the gap. You call him again. All of a sudden, my god, he's right there. Here he comes right at you. He sees you. It's over.

What do you do?

HASCUP: This is the time to change things. I call again; he answers you. All right. The next call is not with a turkey call. I don't want a turkey call. I don't want him to come. I want him to stay right where he is. So, I'll use an owl hooter or a crow call. But I use several different calls: a coyote call, something that'll pierce the silence, and he'll answer. At least he's not coming at you, because you're not using the turkey call. And so I would say that what people should do is try to learn that distance, and be careful. Getting closer and switch to a crow call to locate that bird, rather than run into them. That happened to me so many times.

one. And then we went to kill a Rio Grande bird. We had hunted an eastern, and then we had to kill a western bird. So we went to Colorado and killed a western bird. So now we had all four of them. We wanted to do the World Slam, but besides that my friend said, "Why don't we hunt a little bit here in New Jersey?" He hooked us up to go to California, to Redding, which is in the north. And then he hooked us up with Medford, Oregon, so we could hunt in two states. We went out there, and I killed a bird in Redding the first morning. My friend did not. I hunted two more days with him. I just went with him. Didn't carry a gun, and we just couldn't get birds to work. Then we drove up to Oregon,

> He calls himself a West Virginia redneck.
> And he taught me a lot of things about when not to call.
> When to switch calls. See, these are things that you'd never know
> until someone with experience tells you.

Did you ever consider how many birds you've killed over the years?

HASCUP: I lost track at 100. I'll be honest with you. I kept track up to 100, cuz that was another goal. And when I got to 100, I stopped. And now, I don't care if I ever kill another one. I just wanna kill one with my grandson.

Do you remember the time when you made the conscious decision to get a wild turkey in all 49 states?

HASCUP: Yeah, it was with a friend of mine, Ronnie Wright.

I assume that goal was not from the beginning.

HASCUP: No, no. It was not. First of all, we were just hunting in New Jersey. Then, we decided: let's try to get the Grand Slam. So we went to Texas first cuz that is the easiest. We went to Florida, which was easy for me, but not for my friend. He went three years in a row before he finally killed

which was really, really difficult, cuz it was right at the beginning of their first turkey season.

Why was it so difficult?

HASCUP: Nobody knew how to hunt turkeys. We ran into people hunting turkey like deer. They'd put a drive on to drive the turkeys, like they did deer. They didn't know, they had no idea. And they would wear red bandannas and a red hat. Because you had to wear red to hunt deer. You didn't have to wear it to hunt turkeys, but they didn't understand that. We stopped a bunch of them and talked to them about it, about wearing camo. They thought, *man, that'll get yourself shot!* They thanked us. They were nice enough people but they had no idea what they were doing. We tried to teach them a little bit. On the first day, there was one bunch of birds there. And there had to be 20 guys trying to kill these birds. The birds went across the field and went into the woods. And I said, "Is there any way to get up on top of that

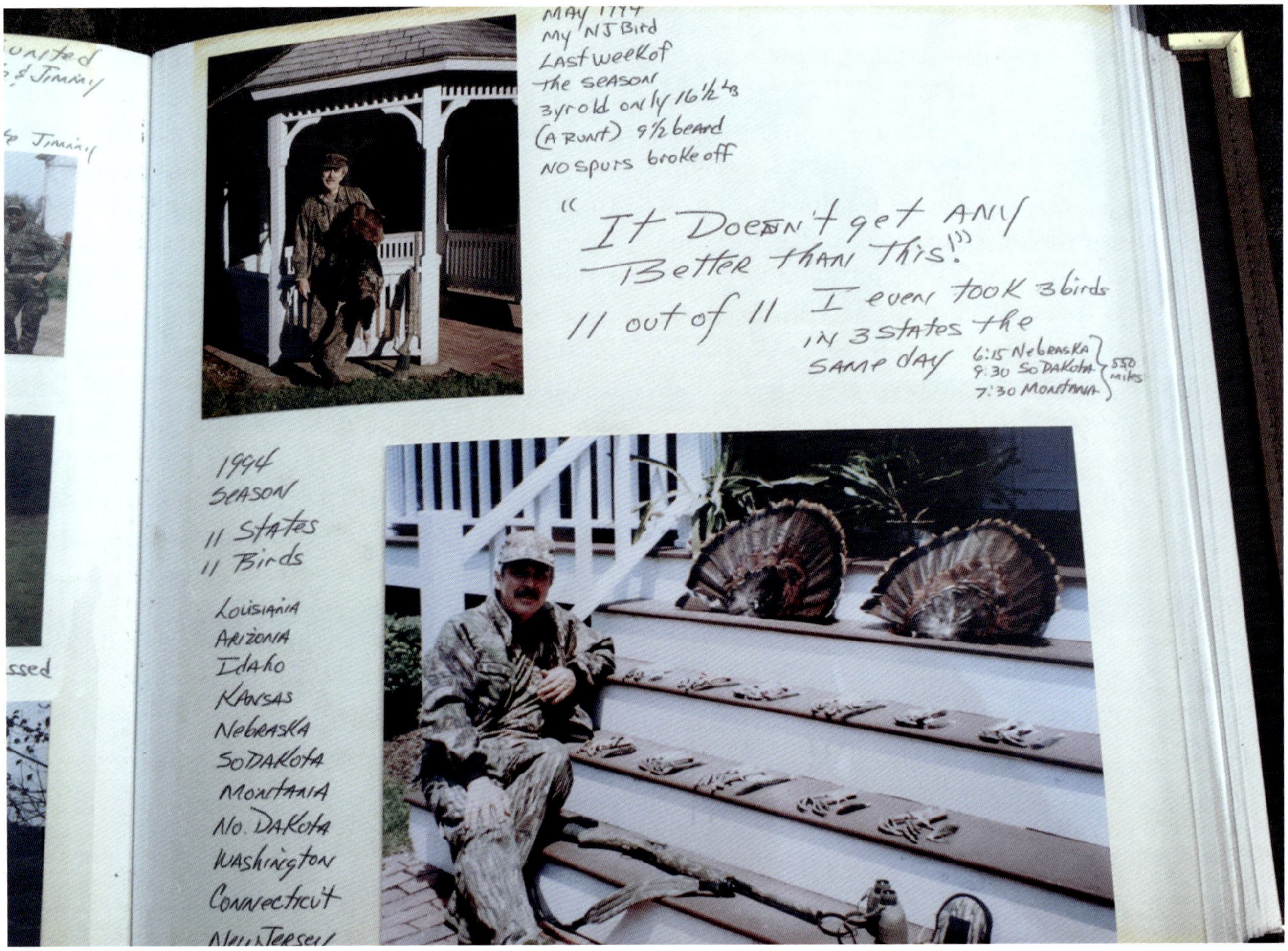

Hascup kept extensive scrapbooks and detailed records of his travels while seeking a wild turkey in all 49 states.

hill?" One guy said, "Yeah, I know a road." So, we drove up and got up above them. And we called. First day we never heard them. The second day, I didn't even bother to go down to that field. I said, "I wanna be up on the top." Finally, around 10 o'clock, I was able to pull a bird up the hill to me and I killed the bird. We stayed, but my friend, unfortunately, did not get a bird. He wanted to leave, so we did. It was a shame. It just happens. It's luck. And so he said: "I'm done. You do it yourself from now on." From then on, I started doing it myself. Then, started to hunt six states or 10 states or whatever.

So, in your quest for 49 states, after Oregon you pretty much did them all on your own?
HASCUP: Yes.

How long did it take you, from the time you decided to complete the Super Slam?
HASCUP: Well, I killed my last one in 1997. I guess it was eight years. I guess that was '89 to '97.

Obviously, your first was here in New Jersey.
HASCUP: Yes.

And you have quite a story about your last bird. It was electric! [laughing]
HASCUP: Yes, it was. I was hunting with James Martin. His nickname is "Peck." He owns Martin Brothers Wild Game Calls out of McMechen, West Virginia. And I had got out there the day before, because I had two states to do: I had Ohio and West Virginia. And Ohio opened the day before West Virginia opened. These were my last two

states. So we went out to Ohio and, boy, we walked ourselves to death. I ended up getting a bird, and that was another great story, but I'll tell you more about the last bird. The next day, we woke up and I said: "This is it, Peck, this is the last bird. I'm so happy that I'm able to do it with you." And this was, by the way, my third time that I was out there to hunt with him. The other two times, I did not get a bird. That morning, turkey conditions were terrible. There are two bad things for turkeys: there's rain and there's wind. And this day, I didn't have any rain but the wind was blowing the tops of the trees like you cannot believe. You can't hear the birds and the birds are scared to death on windy days cuz they can't hear the coyotes. They are quiet. We went to this place where we knew there was a bunch of birds—we had seen them there before. When I called, Peck goes, "I heard a bird." I said to him: "Get outta here. You didn't hear a bird. You didn't hear nothing." "No, Jim, I heard a bird." I said, "all right." So we walked over there. It had to be, 300 yards from where we heard that bird. There was a side hill and the birds were down the hill. I still don't know how he heard them. When we got to the edge of the hill, I called again. *Damn* if that bird didn't gobble. I said, *holy mackerel*, so we backed up. The only tree that was there was right on the fence line. And I didn't know it, but the top wire on that fence was electric—and it was hot.

Oh, no!

HASCUP: And we sat down next to that fence. Peck was alongside of me. He wasn't against the tree—I was. He was down low. So, I got my face mask on, got my hat on, got the gun, everything all ready, and I leaned back to be flat against that tree. The back of my head hit that wire. The hat went up in the air. I dropped the gun. "Jesus, Peck," I said, "it's hot!" And he's laughing now, and here comes the bird up the hill. I don't even have a face mask on because it was all sideways. And here comes the bird. I could see the head. I'm laying down now. And I picked my gun up, and as he popped up, I shot him. I did get the bird.

But that's not quite the end of the story. . . .

HASCUP: Yes. That's not the end of the story. About two years later, I went back out to hunt with Peck in West Virginia. I did hunt with him almost every year, but we would go to different places. We went back up and we went up to the same area. Not that part of the farm—the same farm, but on the other side. And this was great because we called this the "Train Whistle Bird." Because we didn't have to make a call. As we were coming in, the train in town blew and the bird answered. It's all good. We'll go that way. So we started walking over that way. Train whistle went again, and the bird gobbled again. My God, this is great. "I don't have to make a call, Peck." So we got over there, the bird's coming towards us. And every time that train blew his whistle, that bird would gobble again. I said, "Sit down right here." Well, Peck is trying to make a video of this, and he couldn't even get the camera up. The bird was coming that quick. That bird came right into sight, I shot, I killed that bird. I jumped the fence—a low barbed-wire fence—I got over there and I got the bird. On my way back, I had the bird in my hand. I'm holding him up for Peck to see. I lowered the bird a little bit as I was walking, and *I'll be damned* if it was that top wire again. It hit the bird and the electricity went right up the bird and right into my hand. Again, I threw the bird down. I had the gun over my shoulder and it went flying. Peck started laughing and so did I. The fence got me twice. Same fence, same farm—it got me twice. [laughing]

The bird was trying to come back from the dead.

HASCUP: That's it, that's it! [laughing]

What's the maximum number of states you hunted in one year, Jim?

HASCUP: Well. . . .

During this eight-year period?

HASCUP: I think it's 13. At least that's what I can see in the picture there. It's 13. But I came back and hunted in New Jersey, so maybe that's 14, I don't know.

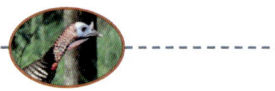

Of the 49 birds, on your quest, how many were taken during spring?

HASCUP: All of them. Yeah, I didn't hunt the fall at all, okay? I'm not really into that, because they don't gobble, and I wanna hear them gobble. So I'm really not into doing that. I know some other people like fall hunting. Did any of the other people you talked to do some of their birds in the fall?

Yes.

HASCUP: Lotta them?

Not a lot of them—a couple.

HASCUP: All toms?

Yeah.

HASCUP: No, no. I didn't have any of that. But I had people with me, because when you're trying to kill a turkey and you're only figuring three days for each state, you need somebody to tell you where the birds are. Killing a bird is not as hard as finding them. So when you go to a state that you don't know anything about, I would say to people, I would call people on the phone, and tell them what I was doing. Then I would ask if I could hunt with them. There was a magazine from the N.W.T.F. called *Turkey Call*. It would list different calling contests in different parts of the country, and who won first, second or third place in the

> I lowered the bird a little bit as I was walking, and I'll be damned if it was that top wire again. It hit the bird and the electricity went right up the bird and right into my hand. Again, I threw the bird down. I had the gun over my shoulder and it went flying.

All toms.

HASCUP: Well, I did kill a female once, just one though, in Texas. East Texas. And it had a 10-inch beard, but no spurs.

Focusing on the 49 states, during those eight years, how many birds did you kill with a guide and how many on your own?

HASCUP: When you say guide, I don't need anybody to call for me or. . . .

That's what I mean by a guide. I'm not talking about an outfitter who points you in the direction of the turkeys.

HASCUP: Okay.

I mean, if you're being guided, you're at the guy's elbow and he's. . . .

HASCUP: He's calling for you?

calling contests. I didn't care who won—I just wanted to talk to a guy from that state. And normally I would just call up information. [laughing] Our state's terrible, people are scared to death of letting you know where they live, so their phone numbers are unlisted, but in most of the rest of the world, everybody's phone number is listed. And I would call a person up. In fact, I remember that one time I called and I got an older lady, and I said, "Is John at home?" She says, "No, John doesn't live here." I said, "Would you have John's number?" "Sure. Wait a minute. Let me get it." So that's the kind of people that are out there. [laughing] And I would talk to John and I'd explain to him what I was doing. And I would say that I'd like to come down and hunt: "Now I'm willing, if you have ground that we can hunt on, I'm willing to pay you a trespass fee. If we can hunt together that would be great, but if you can just point me in the

FACING PAGE: A triumphant Jim Hascup with his prize West Virginia bird on May 1, 1997: the last wild turkey in his marathon eight-year, 49-state quest—and the first of what would later be called the U. S. Super Slam.

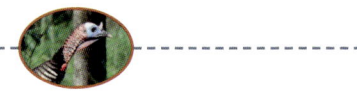

direction of some place to hunt." And I said, "I'd love to hunt with you and I'm gonna promise you something right now: I will never come back and hunt your property unless you ask me to come with you." I said, "Because I know we all have little private grounds that we don't want anybody to know about and we don't wanna take anybody there, so I wanna tell you up front that I'll never do that. And most of the people, I'm gonna say 90 percent, said: "Son, why don't you come down and hunt? I'd love to have you." And that's how it happened. And there was no transfer of money, I'd buy them dinner or something. Or when I got back, send them a little thank you. But other than

and Washington. And then, of course, I'd already been to Texas and we'd already been to Colorado, and we'd already been to Florida. So I said, "Jeez, Ron, we got a bunch of states—why don't we try to do them all?" So that was it. I went out with two maps of the United States. There was a fellow in the town that I work in that had a map store. And so I had him mount those two maps. I gave Ron one and kept this one [pointing to map on wall] to do this story and we started together. But we weren't competing with other people.

It was just a goal you set for yourself.
HASCUP: Right, set for myself.

> She's always behind me 110 percent and she just would spark me up: "Well, don't worry about it. Try this or just go and do that." And I'd get off the phone and I'd be right back up where I should be, and go back out there and try again.

that, it was just: come down and do it. But that's how you have to do it in order to find ground.

As we are looking at all your trophies and photos and all your memorabilia—really, your hunting memories—you mentioned your competitive nature. Is that what drove you to set the goal of a turkey in 49 states?
HASCUP: Okay. Well, like I said, when I started this, it wasn't competitive. I was the only one that I knew who was doing it.

You hadn't heard about anybody else pursuing it?
HASCUP: I never heard about anybody else doing it.

The Super Slam hadn't even been named yet. How did you dream it up?
HASCUP: Well, that was my friend, Ron. My friend said, "Let's go and kill one here." So, he and I did. Then he said, "Let's try two states." So we did Georgia and Alabama, and then we did California

Did you ever reflect on why you set these hunting goals?
HASCUP: Because of my personality.

Which is?
HASCUP: I'm a type-A personality. I like to do difficult things. I like to do things no one else will do, or things that are difficult to do. Like all the sheep and all the caribou and all the moose and all the elk. It was a goal I set for myself: I wasn't trying to beat someone. No, I only knew of me and I was on my way.

So it was more of a personal achievement.
HASCUP: Achievement. There you go. Okay. That's the word I was looking for. Yes, I was looking for that. All my sheep, I've never entered any of them in any record books. I did enter them with the Grand Slam Club. I'm No. 774. But not with Boone and Crockett. It's all in my head. When my wife said, "Why don't you write a book?" "No, I

got it all in my head. I don't need that. I don't need notoriety from somebody else, although if you wanna give it to me. . . . [laughing]

But there are people who would like your stories—I want your stories.
HASCUP: Well, stories are what I like. That's it. I don't want a trophy for doing what I did. I will not take that. I will not take that. But I do want people to know it. Yes, some of the stories are fun. And they should know. When I've stood up in front of people and told them some of my stories everybody enjoyed them.

Was there any point during the quest for the 49 that you were discouraged?
HASCUP: Never enough to give up.

Never?
HASCUP: Not with the type of personality that I have. Never. I just can't. I would never give up. I'd be down, absolutely.

What did you do to dig out, to pull yourself up?
HASCUP: Call my wife. Call my wife. Without a doubt she builds me up whole. That's her. She's always behind me 110 percent and she just would spark me up: "Well, don't worry about it. Try this or just go and do that." And I'd get off the phone and I'd be right back up where I should be, and go back out there and try again. But I've been down a lot of times. Getting off turkey? Not for a second.

Is hunting other game different?
HASCUP: I went polar bear hunting, okay? Which is something that's closed now, and nobody can do it. I went up there. It's a 10-day hunt. Fourteen days later and I never even saw a track, nothing. I was out with the Eskimos on a dog sled, and I came back into town and the guy felt so bad, he said: "I'd like to take you back out again in a different area after we get provisions. We have another area; they have seen a bunch of bears there. I'd like to take you. So the hunt was only 10 days.

I've already done 14. He said, "Would you come?" So I called my wife up and she said: "Of course you should go. Stay there. You're there. You might as well go with him." His name was John. I spent 14 more days. So I was 28 days on the ice and 50° below. And I killed a bear on the 26th day. It took us two days to get back to town. So a total of 28 days. But I did get a bear, and that was all my wife, 100 percent. Without a doubt, I wouldn't have gotten one. Cuz at that point, not that I wanted to quit, it was just that I thought the hunt was over. But the guide said: "No, the hunt's not over. It's not fair what happened."

So he made it fair. [laughing]
HASCUP: You hang in there. I will, absolutely, right to the end. Always. Always.

When did your turkey quest become competitive?
HASCUP: I thought I was doing it all alone until I ran into a hunter three times. That's when it became competitive. Very competitive. It didn't become a solo thing to do anymore. Now it became competitive.

Where did you run into this guy?
HASCUP: First time in Texas. The second time in New Hampshire, and the third time in—I'm trying to think—Utah. No, Nevada. I'm sorry.

Put these encounters in perspective. Where were you toward your 49th state at that point?
HASCUP: Texas, it was probably my 15th, and Massachusetts was in the 20s. And then, Nevada was right in there in the high 30s.

And you just ran into this same hunter out of the blue?
HASCUP: Same guy, same individual.

Did he tell you he was trying to get to 49?
HASCUP: The first time he mentioned it, so I knew he was doing it. The second time, he was leaving when I got there. And the third time, I saw him. I think he saw me, I don't know. But I knew

Jim Hascup (left) holding his 49th-state turkey with his friend J. D. "Peck" Martin (far right) at Martin Brothers Wild Game Calls in McMechen, West Virginia, 1997. Between them, from left: Peck's son, James "Jaybird" Martin, Jr.; Larry Sprouse; Peck's nephew, Larry Sperling. Peck Martin is a champion turkey caller and expert call maker. He was in the woods with Hascup when Jim tagged his long-sought bird.

it from the first time. Then it became competitive, after about the 15th turkey.

Did you keep track of this other guy's progress?
HASCUP: No. Not till the end, for sure. I did know where he was. The last year, when I had five birds to go, he had one. So I thought I lost. I didn't because, luckily, some of mine were in the South, where the season opened earlier, so I could get to North Carolina and Virginia and Maryland, and then move on out to Ohio and West Virginia. All of these hunts happened in March and April.

Did your quest put any sort of strain on your personal family relationships?
HASCUP: No. I have a great wife. If she was here, she might say something else. [laughing] But back then, she didn't say a thing, except, "Go for it."

When you were planning your various trips, how did you decide where to go?
HASCUP: Okay, during this time, I was thinking about nothing but turkeys. I didn't even want to deer hunt anymore. I had a hard time doing duck hunting because I was so focused on turkey. I would look at several states that I needed to go to, looking for places to hunt, and call people. But some states were a draw or a tag, like Wisconsin. It took me four years of entering to draw a tag for Wisconsin. Same with Delaware—that took me three times. I'm sure other people have told you about it. You first have to go to Delaware before you can even apply and you have to take their equivalent of a hunting exam. You have to spend two days.

Yeah, I've heard about that ordeal.

HASCUP: Eight hours a day. Listening to them lecture about safety. It was so similar to the test I took when I was 13, to get a hunting license in New Jersey. Only then you were qualified to get a Delaware hunting license. Their certificate. And then you were able to apply for a tag, which I didn't draw the first few years. I would go to the different states that had drawings, I would put into all of those. And that would change where I was going to go. But in the Northwest, I would figure all those states because there was no drawing, and just add in as many as I could. I would look at the date they opened and where I was going before there. I started in the South, mainly, because a lot of those states opened in February. I would start for there, and I hunted pretty much February, March, April and into May, depending on some of the states in the North. That's how I would come up with my plan. And then I'd draw one of those states and it would change everything. I'd have to change everything. You don't always get the bird. In some of the states I hunted twice. And two states I hunted three times. And you don't always get them. It's not a guarantee. Even when you know where the birds are, still not a guarantee. Once you got to one of these places, wherever you had a limited amount of time, you gave it your all, right to the last minute of the day.

How did you go about locating the birds?
HASCUP: Like I said, I had somebody that would tell me, or show me an area. The people or person that I had contacted would tell me pretty much where the birds were. Sometimes they took me right there and we heard the birds, and sometimes it would just be an area. Sometimes they'd just come with me, and, again, they're not calling, but they like to hunt. Most of these guys, that's who they were: hunters. And they loved it. Some of them, like I told you, I got through the *Turkey Call* magazine. Some of them I just got through friends, like the fellow that I hunted with in Wisconsin. He worked in a mill. He cut white oak barrel staves, he said, 22 and five-eighths. "I could tell if it was 22 and three-quarter," which he couldn't

use. He said, "22 and five-eighths is what I cut, and I cut that all day long." He made round barrels, that's all he did. Told me about them. I called him and asked him about turkeys. He said, "I don't turkey hunt." I said, "Do you know where the turkeys are?" "Sure, I see them all the time," he told me, cuz he gopher hunted for farmers. He put gopher traps out. And then, he'd cut off the front feet, and for every pair of feet they gave him a dollar. The farmers did it because the gophers would dig holes and the cows broke their legs in the holes. He knew all these farmers. He got me on this farm and he took me there. The night before I went trapping with him on a four-wheeler. And then he showed me where I should go. The next day I went to that spot and I killed a bird first thing in the morning. It was great. There were lots of birds where he took me. Nobody—only me—no one else. Now I came back and I had a whole day to kill. So I went and I found a spot that had catfish jerky. And I bought some catfish jerky and a six-pack, I went and sat on a rock and put my feet in the Mississippi River, and enjoyed myself until he got off work at 4 o'clock. I went and got him and he was so happy that I got a bird. I gave him the bird and then we went trapping again. And the next morning I left, so I only took two days in that place to get my bird.

In all your experiences, do you consider any particular state the easiest?
HASCUP: Not really easy, but *easier*. Let me tell you about New Hampshire. And I know other people had a hard time with New Hampshire. I did not. I met a guy who was a turkey hunter; he knew where turkeys were. But he was working. He took me to this place and he said, "You can hunt from here." Showed me where a road was. "You can walk this. It's a woods road. It goes for about three miles. I've heard birds in there." I said, "All right." Then he said, "Let me take you to this other place." He drove me up to this other place. It was up on top of a hill. It was getting to be evening now. It was spring so it was like maybe 5:30. It was getting dusky. The birds, some of them were in the

tree already. Well, I made a call. And the bird answered me in the tree. So he starts walking towards it. I said: "No, no. Come on. Let's get out of here now." So we left right away. He said, "What's the matter? I said: "I don't want to go near that bird—leave him alone. I know exactly where he is." I shook his hand and he said, "Okay, good luck tomorrow." So I went back, had dinner, went back to the hotel. Tried to sleep. There was no sleep. All I was doing was thinking about that bird. *My gosh.* I couldn't wait. It was 4 in the morning. I couldn't take it any longer. I got up, I went down and I bought a huge cup of coffee and a roll from an all-night store. And I went back up and I sat in the woods, in the dark. About, maybe, 80 yards from

Which was your most difficult state?

HASCUP: My most difficult state was Delaware. And, again, I'm sure that other people hunted that state and they hunted on private land, which would probably make it easier. But when I went, which was early in this quest, I drew a tag for state land. I could only hunt on state land—I couldn't hunt on private land. There were no birds in this area, even though they told me there were. I talked to the people from the state, and they told me there were birds. They wouldn't tell me where. The piece of property was long and there were little pieces and then you would go across a road, and then it picked up on the other side. I figured three days, but I had more time, cuz I was driving. In

> Now it gets light enough and I make a call. He gobbled three times.
> The third time, he was on the ground. He shouldn't have been
> on the ground for another half hour. He's on the ground
> coming fast. He was running so fast he ran right by me!

that bird. I sat there and never made a sound and I drank my coffee, ate my roll and watched the sun come up. Then, all of a sudden, a rooster crowed, and the bird gobbled. He was right where I thought he'd be. Right in the same tree that he was in last night. This is great, *this is great.* So I waited. Never made a call. And the rooster called again; he gobbled again. I said, *My gosh, I hope somebody doesn't hear him and come in here, after I've been sitting here since 4 o'clock in the morning.* Now it's 6:30. Okay. Now it gets light enough and I make a call. He gobbled three times. The third time, he was on the ground. He shouldn't have been on the ground for another half hour. He's on the ground coming fast. He was running so fast he ran right by me! I don't know where he was going. I called and he stopped. He turned around and I shot him. I was at the check station two hours before it was open. Mine was the first bird that day, for sure.

three days I never heard anything. I figured, okay. I'm going to give it another two more days. I went and I saw tracks; I saw scratches. I said, *Well there's birds here somewhere.* Or maybe they were hens and they weren't coming to me. And they weren't calling. So finally, on the fifth day I found another spot which showed a fair amount of tracks. And I called. Early, early on the roost, never heard anything. Covered this piece and it wasn't that big. And I was on the edge of it, on a farmer's field. I wasn't allowed to go into that field. And a bird answers. I can't believe it: five days and I finally heard a gobbler. I move back off the field and I called. It took him an hour but he came across the field. It was my hardest state ever. I never want to go back there. [laughing]

What was your most challenging bird?

HASCUP: Not *challenging*, because once you found them, it was a slam dunk. But I had to find

them. It took five days. I've had many birds, but right here in my own state, I worked this one bird on and off for four years. And I still haven't killed him! I talk to him every year and every year he does something different: he'll sneak up behind me; he'll come in a different direction. He is a very smart bird, at least a four-year-old, maybe a five-year-old by now, and I have not killed him yet. This year, I hunted him early in the season and there was a pack of dogs that came in. Screwed the whole thing up. Then I hunted him on the next-to-the-last day. And when I went in there—there's a campground right near there where he roosts—I figured, I'll get in there early. Nobody's in that campground. Well, they had an outing that weekend—there had to be 30 people there. He never made a sound. He is one tough a bird. Next year. . . .

Where is the strangest place you've killed a gobbler?
HASCUP: Okay, the strangest place was in Florida. Because the ground is so different and I'd never seen a turkey stick his head under water and feed off the bottom. And I saw this in Florida. I hunted in a place called Fisheating Creek; it's on the south-western shore of Lake Okeechobee. It's a series of swamps. I remember, when I was there, I hunted with a guy called Lovett Williams; he was a very famous biologist. He was instrumental in restoring all the birds throughout the state of Florida. He moved them around. And this area, Fisheating Creek, is where he took most of the birds from. So when the state decided to stop the program, he was able to get that area as his hunting lodge. And the first day I said, "Where am I going to find these birds?" He says, they like to go on the ridges. So, I go out the next morning; it's all swamp. I came back that night and I said, "Lovett, what are you talking about—where are the ridges?" He said, "You know, the high spots." "What are you talking about?" "In the swamp, there's a high spot. It's only got maybe a half-inch of water in it, and they like those ridges."

Not a ridge where you come from!
HASCUP: I ended up killing two very nice birds

there. Two birds. Both had one-and-a-half-inch inch spurs. Really nice birds. I was very happy.

Were they the birds you saw duck under?
HASCUP: Yeah. They were feeding, coming towards me, strutting in the water. They have longer legs than the other types of turkeys. At least that's what they tell me.

Osceolas.
Yeah. But they would walk in the water, only about an inch or so deep. And stuck his head right in the water, and feed off the bottom, like they pick in a field. He's picking off the bottom. I couldn't believe this. I saw a hen, I mean, her whole head disappeared under water. This was in another spot.

And when you pulled the trigger, what was it doing?
HASCUP: I would call him, and then he would puff up, he would gobble, and he would start to walk towards me. When he got close enough, I shot him and he fell over. He was soaking wet when I got to him.

Have you ever purposefully passed up a bird that you know you could have killed?
HASCUP: Most times, it was because they were jakes. I passed up plenty of them. I would not shoot a jake now, that's for sure. But I got to say, there was one bird that I worked all day, and I did let him go. But I'm not sure whether I could have killed him or not, the more I think about it. He was in view at the time. I could have shot. But the circumstances of this bird, he worked so hard and so long. He left me and then he came back. And then, he'd leave again. I wouldn't hear him. I'd sit there. All of a sudden, here he was back again. I said, *I can't believe this bird keeps coming back.* But he just stayed that little bit out of range. Now, could I have shot him? *Should* I have shot him? I don't know whether I should have or could have, but I didn't. And I'm glad I didn't because he lived to go on. I never killed him. I never heard him again.

These Osceolas had inch-and-a-half spurs.

Which turkeys tend to, by their behavior or whatever, give you the most satisfaction?

HASCUP: Well, the birds that are in the South are much harder to hunt, especially back then. They don't gobble much at all. Sometimes I would sit for an hour or so blind calling. And not a sound—and then, all of a sudden, there he was. The birds in the West are the easiest. The Merriam's are very vocal and call a lot. This makes them easier to locate. The eastern birds are the hardest. I'm talking about the easterns in the South: Tennessee, Mississippi, Alabama, Arkansas, Georgia, South Carolina. They are hard to locate and hard to kill. These are the toughest birds.

Confederate turkeys.

HASCUP: There you are. I'll tell you, talk about that place in Tennessee where I hunted. They tell me that I'm the only Yankee they allowed there. [laughing] There's 15 turkey hunters there. I'm what they call their pet Yankee. I know, when I hunted with some of the people down there, they said the less calls you make, the better. Calling very softly, you can get louder. You can't get softer when they're close. So, you call very softly. You'll hear them on the roost. They'll hit the ground, never say a word. So now, you're playing with ghosts. You're calling and sometimes they come in, sometimes they don't. Sometimes the next call they make is a quarter of a mile away, going the other way, and you'll never catch up with them.

You talked about most difficult birds—what about crazy experiences?

HASCUP: While hunting for my Connecticut bird, I met a man named Lee Helmers. Lee and I hit it off right away. And when I told him what I was trying to do, he said: "Let me help. Maybe I'll do it also, and you can help me." When I asked him which states he could help me with, he said Rhode Island. I said, "That's great; I need to go there." He took me to his spot which wasn't far, and showed me where he had hunted. The following year I hunted with him and we both took a bird. I asked him about Maine. It had only opened a few years before, and they only shoot 25 to 30 birds a year. "That is going to be a tough one." But he said: "Okay, I'll go up there and try to find us a spot. The license is a draw, so let's do that next year." The following year, we both got a license and Lee went up to Maine, and did a lot of scouting. I didn't hear from him for a while, which was okay because I had lots of other states to hunt in the Southeast. One day, Lee calls me and says, "I've found some spots." "Great," I said, "I'll meet you in the L. L. Bean parking lot the day before opening day." Now, I was really excited about this hunt and the time dragged on till I could meet Lee. I flew to Boston, then drove to Maine. He was there waiting. After discussing a few thoughts, we took off to look at the spots. Well, the first spot had seven trucks parked there—all turkey hunters.

Jim was a member of the first group at Fisheating Creek Hunting Camp in Florida in 1986, the year it opened by the famous Lovett Williams and David Austin, who had been state wildlife biologists leading the Sunshine State's wild turkey restoration project. Jim recalls that each afternoon Williams gave fascinating lectures on turkey biology and behavior.

Some of them were camping and I knew tomorrow would be a real mess. I said, "What about your other spot, Lee?" "Okay, I have two more spots," he answered. So off we went. We pulled up to a dairy farm and there is a turkey hunter standing behind the barn cranking on a box call in the middle of the day. Lee said, "That's a good way to educate the turkeys." We talked to the farmer in the milking barn, and I asked how big the farm was. He answered 60 acres, and my next question was how many hunters will be there tomorrow. He said, "Six, including you guys." I asked Lee how many birds were there: one group with one tom. Well, that wasn't going to work, either. I said, "Lee, let's try the last place." He said "Okay, but it's about

an hour drive." I said, "Then I'll follow you." We started off and it was getting dark and I was driving and daydreaming about some of the other places I was going to go this year. All of a sudden, I noticed that Lee wasn't in front of me, so I sped up. I still couldn't see him and I have no idea where I am or where I was going. This was way before cell phones. Now I'm really flying down the road and I see a car coming at me. Well, when he passes me, I see it's a cop and he puts his lights on. Now I even go faster as I see him turning around in my rearview mirror. I finally catch up to Lee. I'm blinking the lights and blowing the horn and he's not stopping and the officer is right behind me blowing the siren louder. Finally, Lee pulls over

to the side of this desolated country road and I pull over behind him. The officer gets out of his patrol car, asking: "Where the heck are you going in such a hurry? Give me your license and registration." I started apologizing to him and explaining what I was doing because I was lost and needed to catch Lee. Finally he says, "Okay, you win, I won't give you a ticket." I thanked the officer and said: "Now, I'd like to ask you a question. I know you drive around town all the time. Please tell me, have you seen any turkeys? He smiled and said, "You're kidding, right?" I said, "No, I really want to know." "You're standing on the spot where 50, 60 turkeys walk right across this road and go up the hill onto Fred Schultz's farm. The lady across the street feeds them all winter." He said: "I see the light's on in the barn—Fred's probably milking. Go on up the street and tell him I sent

HASCUP: No, I never did. I never added it up. But it was plane tickets, hotels, food, licenses and car rentals in all the other states. And some of the licenses were inexpensive: 40 bucks, 50 bucks. Some of them were 250. I don't exactly remember. You want me to add it up?

No, no! [laughing]
HASCUP: I guess we could try to figure it. But, it's gotta be a fair amount of money. Especially over eight years.

When I asked Clyde Neely in Texas the question [in *Turkey Men* Volume 1], he wouldn't answer it. And then, he kind of thought and looked around. "See this house?" he said. "I could buy another one."
HASCUP: Yeah, it was expensive!

> It's not so much killing a bird, because everybody knows how to call, everybody knows how to shoot. I would presume that if you're going to do this, you must be woods smart, that you know the woods and you know how to look for sign, how to know where they are.

you." I thanked the officer and off we went. Fred was in the barn and was a great guy, and we helped him move hay for the cows. I told him I was trying to take a turkey in every state, and I asked if we could hunt there tomorrow. He said sure, and I asked, "How many acres do you have?" When he said 500, I said, "Well, that's great—and how many hunters will be here tomorrow morning?" "Only you two." I couldn't believe what I was hearing. By 8 the next morning both Lee and I killed our birds. That spot in the road was the place that was meant to be for Lee and me to stop. And blind faith took over.

Have you ever thought about how much these 49 states cost you?

From your experience, Jim, if you were to advise somebody who is maybe thinking about or is on his way to doing the U. S. Super Slam, what are some of the most important considerations in setting out?
HASCUP: Finding the birds—I told you that from the beginning. It's not so much killing a bird, because everybody knows how to call, everybody knows how to shoot. I would presume that if you're going to do this, you must be woods smart, that you know the woods and you know how to look for sign, how to know where they are. But finding property that you can hunt on, it's difficult. Getting a farm you can hunt on because, you know, people tie them up so you can't hunt on them. So getting access is your main objective. A

"The season of the cast," 1995, when Jim hunted 13 states and took 11 birds. As his exuberant entry declares, he had now tagged a turkey in 37 states with only 12 to go.

lot of the states like in the West are all open. They're public land, so you'll have no problem getting on. But, again, where do you hunt there? Like Nevada. Only 13 percent of the state is owned by private citizens. The rest of the state is federal property. You can hunt anywhere you want, but looking for water and finding a bird is difficult. You have to spend some time finding places to hunt. I always figured three days for each state but you need to make sure that somebody knows where the birds are before you go there. You know, I went to Idaho, I had a friend of mine that moved out there and so I wanted to hunt with him. He's not a turkey hunter and he didn't even hunt when I was there—he just came with me. But he talked

to the game wardens and he talked to the police. He found the general area where some birds were. I was there for three days. It took us two days to find them, and the third morning, we killed one. But it took us two days to find those birds in an area where we knew they were. *But where were they?* Tucked away in a canyon. Took a while. So that's what I would say: Water is the key. Water's the key in the West. Water's a key anywhere. They need fresh water. They have to have water. In the South, there's a lot of swamps. There's water everywhere, so there's not a problem. But, in the West and in the North, that's a very big thing.

Let's talk about your easiest states in this quest.

HASCUP: My top state is Tennessee. That's without a doubt. I have got to say New Jersey's gotta be up there close, cuz I still love this place, and I'm very familiar with the woods here. They're the same grounds, same trees, same everything. Vermont terrain is the same, so is Connecticut—they're all the same. They're exactly the same. There's very little difference. But I have the most fun and do enjoy the mountains in Tennessee. There's just a lot to enjoy there, there really is. I enjoyed Michigan a lot. Different woods, different trees, but still hardwoods, lots of hardwoods. And I enjoyed Georgia a lot, too. And, of course, I en-

HASCUP: In the other states that I like to go and I like to hunt, my friends there go out and do some. But here in New Jersey I only do it probably two or three weeks before the season starts. Because if you go too early, they're still bunched up together and the hens haven't split off. That's why the toms leave—they leave because the hens leave. There's probably 75 to 100 birds that stay here, around my house. We feed them all winter. And they don't break up until around the end of March, the first of April. You go early in March you are not gonna find them. You can only do it two to three weeks before the season.

> I've killed many birds just sitting. Sometimes it took a long, long time. That one bird in Michigan, I sat there the one day, and I got four inches of snow on me, and I laughed. It was snowing and I just sat there. And when it got to be four inches I got up, and packed it in.

joyed Texas. I've probably killed 20 birds in Texas. I used to go back often because I have friends there, and I used to bring groups of guys there.

Do you most enjoy hunting familiar territory?
HASCUP: I truly—thank God—like hunting a familiar piece of land. After I did this quest I kind of cut myself down to doing one or two states a year, all with familiar guys, usually two states a year, and I pick ones that I really like and people I really liked. I like to go out and hunt with these particular people.

When you were chasing the Super Slam, how many days a year did you devote to turkey hunting?
HASCUP: I would do at least three months. At least half of February, all of March, all of April, and all of May. So, three to three-and-a-half months. And that's all I did was turkey hunt. I worked a little.

Pre-season scouting?

Any particular secret or strategy to effectively scouting a new area?
HASCUP: A new area in New Jersey?

Anywhere.
HASCUP: These birds in our area, they're so domesticated anymore. They're in people's backyards. All of them, lots of them. It's a tough thing, because you can't hunt them there, and you got to call them away from there. Like this year, my grandson and I, we found probably 10 different birds. But a lot of them were right in backyards. And we tried to call them out of there. [laughing]

I remember reading a news piece a year or two ago about some mailman being chased by wild turkeys.
HASCUP: That was here, in New Jersey.

Was it really?
HASCUP: Yeah, it was stupid. It was a stupid story. I don't think he was being chased. I think he was

just afraid and ran. Ran cuz he saw the birds. It was in an area where you can't hunt them. That county, Bergen County, which is just below us, you can't hunt in that county. There's very little open ground. There's parks, which is where the birds live. There's golf courses. That's where they live.

Away from the putting green, do you prefer to sit and wait or run and gun?
HASCUP: Mostly run and gun. But it depends on the bird. If you hear them, and then as you get close, he shuts up, then you got to sit and wait, you got to spend a lot of time. Sometimes it's two hours. You just sit there and make a little call. It depends. That bird there, you might not get them at all that day, but you remember that. You come back another day and do the same thing with him. Try to get close to him, try to sit there and call him. I've killed many birds just sitting. Sometimes it took a long, long time. That one bird in Michigan, I sat there the one day, and I got four inches of snow on me, and I laughed. It was snowing and I just sat there. And when it got to be four inches I got up, and packed it in. Next day most of it was gone. And on the fourth day, I went there in the morning, never heard them. I went there at 11 o'clock and I'd be damned if there they were: two gobblers together. The hens went to sit and lay their eggs. Here they came in, both of them together. And here I'd been playing with them for four days— and the fourth day I figured them out.

When you're planning a hunt, what are the key elements that you check off in preparing for the trip?
HASCUP: For a trip you have to come up with where you're gonna hunt and what seasons are open. Sometimes one season is almost closing, so you might only have a couple of days to hunt. And then, you're moving on to the next state, and whether you have more time there or not, it all has to do with the correct timing. It also has to do with weather—that's a big thing. Rain is the worst thing, but you can kill them in the rain. It's very hard to kill them in the wind, but in the rain you

can kill them, because they like open fields in the rain, where they can see. When they're in the woods, they're bothered by the noise of the rain. They can't tell where the coyotes are, so they go into the fields. Right away, I have to plan and I ask people, if it looks like it's gonna rain when I'm gonna be there: Do you have some fields? And some of them would say, "Yeah, I see the turkeys in the field." Yeah you do, because it's raining.

Do you have a favorite shotgun for turkeys?
HASCUP: My favorite gun was a humpback Browning, A5 Browning automatic, which has a hump on the back. I actually have three of them and used that for most of the birds. I did switch off about maybe a third of the way through. I bought a 10-gauge Ithaca semi-automatic, which shoots three-inch shells. Now, they shoot three-and-a-half. But back then, three-inch was tough because I started with two-and-three-quarter.

How about calls—you have quite a collection.
HASCUP: Dick Kirby—familiar with that name? Okay. He was kind of an icon in the turkey-hunting industry. He was a barber in upstate New York. And he loved turkey hunting. He came up with different calls that he manufactured himself. He was one of the first. With so many on the market now, he was one of the first guys that made such beautiful calls. And he is the one that bought out Neil Cost's rights to make calls. He bought the rights to the Boat Tail calls, so Neil could no longer make that call because Dick Kirby gave him a bunch of money—I don't know how much—in order to buy it out. I was influenced by Dick; he did some things I'd never heard of. And I remember talking to him one time and I asked, "What do you do sometimes, Dick, when I call a bird and he answers but he won't come?" He said, "Jim, run at him." [laughing] I said: *What?* What are you talking about?" "Sometimes you run at them. They don't know what you're doing. They've never had anybody run at them, so they'll stand there confused and bump into one another, deciding which way to run or fly. And you've got a couple

When Jim's daughter was away at college, he borrowed her Suzuki Samurai. "I got to places I never could before," he said. What's a little mud that a good detailing won't erase?

minutes before they fly off to kill them." I tried it, and it works! I've killed a couple of birds running at them. So that was Dick Kirby. That's what he was all about. [laughing] He's passed away now, but I will never forget him.

The Browning you shot for so many years, what gauge?
HASCUP: It was a 12-gauge. And there was another, I had a regular standard barrel, which is like 26-

inch. You can't have a barrel any shorter than 20—in our state that's the law. Otherwise they call it a sawed-off shotgun. I was able to buy a 20-inch short barrel. The problem was I carried my gun on my shoulder. A lot of guys don't; they carry it in their hand. But I like to walk. I'm a walker. Miles. And when you go down under trees that long barrel would whack on the branches. Sometimes the birds could hear it, especially if you were trying to be quiet. But with that short barrel it was

the same height as my shoulder, so I have that Browning with that short barrel, and I used that for most of the birds. And I tell you, I bought it not from Browning, but a re-manufacturer—not a gun manufacturer, a barrel manufacturer. And I put that on and, boy, that thing was great, great. Killed tons of birds with it.

Did you use a sighting device?
HASCUP: Back then, no. I'm getting older now. Back then, though, what I used to do was paint the front sight white so I could see it, cuz in low-light situations, early in the morning, sometimes it's hard to find that bead. But now, I use one of those red dots.

Well there's the bird! It comes up and now you're sneaking out there to put it in the ground and the bird sees you. I have my grandson, we hunted and we used decoys, especially in the beginning because I didn't want to catch his movement. He started when he was 12. And they do work, they definitely work. But they weren't for me.

How about blinds, do you ever use blinds?
HASCUP: I didn't during that whole time, but now I use pop-up blinds, not often, but I do have them. Especially around here, if I have a place where I like I put a blind up and then go there, call from there, especially with my grandson. We've used them several times.

> I don't use them anymore.
> You'd hear a bird and you'd have to sneak out there and get your decoy ready. Well there's the bird!
> It comes up and now you're sneaking out there to put it in the ground and the bird sees you.

Over the years, with the tremendous advancements in loads, I'm sure your choice of shell has changed.
HASCUP: In the beginning, it was No. 6s.

Two-and-three-quarter shell?
HASCUP: Two-and-three-quarter, right: two-and-three-quarter No. 6. Now I use three-inch No. 5. They didn't even make No. 5s back when I first started, so it was either 4, 6 or 7½. And 7½ was like a pheasant load or a quail load, so I wanted something a little stronger than that. A lot of guys shot 4s but that's a much less dense pattern.

Do you ever use decoys?
HASCUP: Well, I tried them, of course. I have them. I've gotten caught putting them out so many times that I gave up with the decoys. I don't use them anymore. You'd hear a bird and you'd have to sneak out there and get your decoy ready.

And since you like to move around a lot, how do you carry your things, your calls, etc.?
HASCUP: Well, back then I used a turkey vest, which has about 1,000 pockets in it. And you're carrying too much, way too much: a holder, a scale to weigh them. You had four or five box calls, you had slate calls, and glass calls, and I don't know how many mouth calls. Little screw-off things you can put mouthwash in and you can store your mouth calls from year to year, one you really like, so it didn't dry out. And you'd have so much in there, it just doesn't pay, so now I don't. Now I have a little pack that I bring and I take a box call, and a couple of mouth calls and the slate call. That's all I bring. I can tell you a little story about that, this is a little story about a turkey vest. I was hunting in Connecticut with these friends of mine from Tennessee. They wanted to go on and extend their season, cuz in Tennessee it ended so early, and up here it went all of May. So I hooked them

Brooks (the Turkey Hollow man) & me with my tom

My 3year
old tom
17 lb 6½lbbr
7/8 spurs
1st thing
2nd DAY
52yd shot
he wasn't
oming any
loser

The Lodge

up with my friend from Connecticut, Lee Helmers, and we took them up to Connecticut. Well, we're out the day before, just roosting a bird—the season opens the next day. We hear this bird and he says to Terry MacDonald and me, "Okay, I'm gonna let you guys off down here." It was at the top of this huge field. Well, the bird was almost in the middle. So I said, "I'm gonna get that bird, I'm gonna outrun Terry, I'm gonna run down the bird." [laughing] So I go out in the morning and I got that turkey vest on and I get down, I hear him gobble, and I'm now close to him, and I start to walk in on him. The bird is roosting in the tree. I gotta cross this area and I'm afraid he's gonna see me. So I get down on my

call when they get close, cuz you can't crank on that while you're trying to hold your gun up. Now they got holders to hold your gun up; we didn't have them back then, we rested it on our knee, but [laughing] it's changed a bit. But I have probably four different calls: a box call, a mouth call, a slate call, a glass call. And then some locating calls, like I said, a crow call, a coyote call or a woodpecker call.

Is there one particular call that you tended to use in all 49 states when you were on your quest?
HASCUP: The one call I used all the time was the mouth call. I started using commercial calls until I met Peck, and then I used his mouth calls exclusively. And I also hunted with his box calls the

> Now I'm crawling. Another rock falls out. I reached in my pockets.
> My friend MacDonald, was hunting below me.
> He filled my pockets with rocks to slow me down. [laughing]
> I'm telling you, I must have been carrying 25 extra pounds of rocks.
> Jeez. But I did kill the bird—he didn't, I did.

knees. When I get down on my knees a rock fell out of my pocket. *What the hell?* What the hell is that doing in my pocket? I threw the thing over there, took a couple of more steps on my knees. Now I'm crawling. Another rock falls out. I reached in my pockets. My friend MacDonald, was hunting below me. He filled my pockets with rocks to slow me down. [laughing] I'm telling you, I must have been carrying 25 extra pounds of rocks. Jeez. But I did kill the bird—he didn't, I did.

Now that you prefer traveling light, what calls are your essentials?
HASCUP: Well I like a box call, I like a box call a lot: my buddy Peck Martin has made me some beauties. I use a box call and a crow call for locating, but I also like a mouth call. You can't use a box

whole time, too. I was a walking testament for Martin Brothers game calls!

What sound or voice do you think has brought more birds to your gun?
HASCUP: It has to be the mouth call.

What are you doing with it: clucking, yelping?
HASCUP: Okay. The yelp is the call that everybody makes. That's what the hen makes. But as they get closer the purring and the picking—*pick, pick*—that's the kind of calls that they wanna hear. The kind of calls where the turkey is now, it's eating, it's feeding, it's just hanging out, it's making a little sound to another hen that's with it, that's the call that brings them in, all the way in. I have my own sounds I make that are tried and proven. It's

FACING PAGE: Hascup in 1990 in Selma, Alabama, with Brooks Holloman, the legendary "Turkey Hollow Man," and one of the founders of the National Wild Turkey Federation.

a combination of calls that work. If you start yelping when they're that close you're gonna scare them. So I would say the purr is the one that will bring it in the most.

What about time of day, do you have a preference?
HASCUP: I like early morning, I like off the roost. But 11 a.m. is a super time. The hens are sitting and the gobbler is by himself and ready for action if it comes his way. But I've killed a lot of birds later on. Hunting is over in our state at noon. Some states it's 1 o'clock. Michigan is 4—I can't believe that one! The hens stay with the toms in the roost, they fly down, they get bred by the tom, and then they hang around. And then around 11 o'clock, 12 o'clock, or something like that, they leave and go lay their eggs. They lay one egg a day. And all birds, doesn't matter turkeys or whatever, have a number. And when they get to number— some are up to 16—when they get to the number, then they sit down and incubate them. They don't incubate until the last egg is laid. So they close the season at noon, so that you're not scaring that hen off the nest when you're walking around. So that's what the idea of that is. Why Michigan would close at 4 in the afternoon, that blows everything out of the water.

After fly-down or, say, by mid-morning, do you change your strategy for the rest of the day?
HASCUP: Absolutely. You read the barometer, because on low days they don't gobble. You have to know what's smart—what to do and where to go that day. You have to know what the birds do at certain times of the day. What they're doing early in the morning. Some of them have a mission. They're going someplace. You'll never kill that bird. You gotta go to where he wants to be. So you remember and then you go in that direction. By 11 o'clock you'll get an answer. You will if you find them, *if* you can find them. So, less in the day in

Among the voodoo turkey spirits in 1994: Jim Hascup deep in the appropriately named Devil's Swamp in Baton Rouge Parish, Louisiana.

the morning early, you move around, call, try to hear one, and then try to get close. And then, try to call them to you. But when it's all died down, 9 or 10 o'clock, there's no gobbling anymore. It's real quiet. Then you gotta know the ground, look for turkey signs, get to a place where they are. You can sit, call slow, call quiet. It's all different. Do they work? Yes, they all work, but they don't work all the time. So you keep trying.

What about henned-up gobblers? What's your approach?

HASCUP: Difficult. If they're henned-up, like I say, you come back to that one, because there's one

henned-up or not, and you call, they're gonna come. They're gonna stick their head up. They're gonna wanna know what the heck is going on—what's she doing over there? You will kill them.

What's your heaviest gobbler?

HASCUP: My heaviest gobbler was in Arizona, on the San Carlos Apache Reservation and it was 25½ pounds. I'm sure people have killed bigger ones.

The longest beard?

HASCUP: The longest beard wasn't in the United States. It was in Mexico. It was 12½.

> But there might be another buddy that's not real close to him, that he's kicked out of the bunch. Well, he's around too. That's the guy you're going to kill. He's a two-year-old and you're going to kill him.

gobbler that has all the hens. Usually, he has a couple of buddies with him. Okay. But there might be another buddy that's not real close to him, that he's kicked out of the bunch. Well, he's around too. That's the guy you're going to kill. He's a two-year-old and you're going to kill him. You may not kill that four-year-old or the three-year-old that's with him, or the two or three four-year-olds. Get them together there, those are henned-up. Those you're not going to kill until that hen goes to sit on her nest. When she goes to sit on her nest, then they're all vulnerable. But early in the morning, when they're henned-up and you can't get them to come, forget about it. Go someplace else. I do. Other people have different strategies, okay? Sometimes, you crawl to try to get close to them. Some of them, they'll strut around, they'll gobble, they'll move off. Then they come back cuz that's their strutting area. You try to close that distance. When they've moved off, then you just be very quiet. When you're real close to them, whether they're

How about spurs?

HASCUP: Well, I killed one that was one-and-five-eighths inches at the Kennedy Ranch in Corpus Christi, Texas.

What changes have you seen in turkey hunting over the years?

HASCUP: Less people, especially in this area. We have a drawing for weekdays and Saturdays and different zones. And the first two weeks and Saturdays were impossible to draw. Now, no problem to get any zone, any day of the week you want.

Fewer hunters now.

HASCUP: Fewer hunters. Right. Much more when I hunted in 1997, much, much more.

That seems counterintuitive.

HASCUP: It is. See, we used to have a drawing, which we still do. But it doesn't matter. You don't need to draw. And they would have only so many

tags. They had four weeks of the season, but each week is separate in itself. They have zones, they have so many zones in the state. So you get to pick a week and a zone. There were all—especially the early weeks, the first week, the Saturdays—they were always sold out. You'd be lucky if you ever drew a Saturday. And to draw opening week was difficult. There was never a problem to draw the last week. In fact, after that initial drawing, then all the rest of them were over the counter. And I was always able to buy the last week. I always do that because I know there's nobody else out there but me. Now I can go buy all of those over the counter. So you could probably buy 10 tags if you

some of them, I won't even get a chance to get out. I was working at the time, and you get busy and you can't go.

What's your next challenge?
HASCUP: To get my grandson a Grand Slam.

What can you share from the kitchen of Cathie and Jim?
HASCUP: Our white bean turkey chili.
   2 cups chicken stock
   1 cup sour cream
   1 pound wild turkey breast meat
   1 medium onion, chopped

> There's less hunters. Less turkey hunters. Less hunters, period.
> Less turkey hunters, for sure. I'm trying to think, this year I think
> we saw one other hunter. We might not have seen a hunter at all.
> Yes. We saw a car from another hunter. We never saw the guy.

want and kill 10 birds because of so few hunters.

Why do you suppose that is?
HASCUP: There's less hunters. Less turkey hunters. Less hunters, period. Less turkey hunters, for sure. I'm trying to think, this year I think we saw one other hunter. We might not have seen a hunter at all. Yes. We saw a car from another hunter. We never saw the guy. But we saw the car, so there was another hunter out there. That's it. We went every Saturday and we saw one guy. And that's Saturdays, not even during the week.

You think that's an indication of a broad decline in interest in the sport?
HASCUP: I think in all hunting. I think it's on a decline from back in the day, back in the 1990s. Also, halfway through turkey season, trout season opens. Goodbye. Half of them are turkey hunters, sometimes, but they'd rather fish with friends. I've done that many times. I'll buy all four seasons and

   2 cans great northern beans or navy beans, rinsed and drained
   2 cans (4 ounces) chopped green chilies
   3/4 teaspoon bouillon
   1½ tablespoon garlic powder
   1 teaspoon salt
   1 teaspoon ground cumin
   1 teaspoon dried oregano
   ½ teaspoon black pepper
   ¼ teaspoon cayenne pepper

Cut turkey into strips or chunks. Melt three tablespoons butter in pan. Add turkey and cook until tender. Put chicken stock in medium sauce pan and bring to a boil. Stir in sour cream. Add turkey, chopped onions, beans, chillies and seasonings. Bring to a boil. Reduce heat and simmer uncovered for 30 to 40 minutes or until unions are tender. Garnish with fresh cilantro, diced tomatoes, crushed tortilla chips or shredded cheese. Hope you enjoy!

3

Jon D. Pries

HOME:

Trout Run, Pennsylvania

OCCUPATION:

Retired commercial airline pilot

FIRST WILD TURKEY:

1960, Pennsylvania

COMPLETED U.S. SUPER SLAM:

2008, Virginia

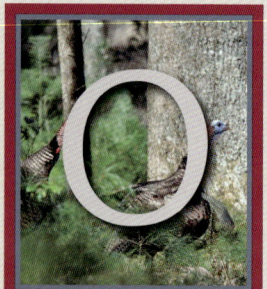

ON A SOFT SUMMER EVENING, I drove up a country road and off the cracked blacktop, turning right at a mailbox with a small weathered sign: GOBBLER'S KNOB. I climbed uphill along a long gravel driveway, through a patch of hardwoods and through green fields. At the crest stood a stone house.

I got out and surveyed the scene: 93 rolling acres, ringed by an old logging road. I heard a doe's soft grunt at the edge of the woods and the sharp call of a nighthawk above. The golden light was a picture of serenity. I imaged that this is what the man I was here to meet had seen and felt, 16 years earlier, when he first gazed on these beautiful Pennsylvania hills, and walked around what would become his new home.

Jon D. Pries had driven the two and a half hours from Carlisle to Trout Run, to scatter his father's ashes under the beeches on the grounds of an old, rambling 14-bedroom hunting and fishing club to which Jon's grandfather had belonged for years. Jon loved the times he spent here as a youngster, splashing in the stream and catching crayfish, poking around to see what was around the bend.

Jon heard a bulldozer working up in the mountain above the clubhouse. *That must be Tommy Patterson up there*, he thought. *I wanna go say hello.* They talked for a spell. And Tommy said, "Jonny, I have a place you ought to take a look at." Fresh off a divorce, the commercial airline pilot wasn't looking for a new place to live. But the elderly owners from Philadelphia couldn't make it up here as often as they used to; their son in California didn't care. The property wasn't even listed yet.

"I had a mortgage on a home down in the Carlisle area," Pries told me. "And I thought, *I've got to get to the bank and find out how to do this.* "I didn't want this to get away from me."

When Pries was in college, an older Navy veteran was earning his degree on the G.I. bill. The man had his pilot's license. He checked around the fraternity to ask if anyone wanted to go up for a plane ride. Jon had never been up; it sounded like fun.

"And I just loved it," Jon recalled. They flew out of the Williamsport airport down to Wilkes-Barre, had a cup of coffee, hopped in, came up over Eagles Mere, a resort area, circled there a couple times and then back to Williamsport and landed. "I just thought that was the neatest thing. So, my next couple of summers, I worked as a line boy refueling airplanes at the Harrisburg airport and washing planes down." And he worked on getting his own license."

From 1969 to '71, Jon Pries was part of the Vietnam War, but not in heavy combat. He was based out of Korat Royal Thai Air Force Base in Thailand, flying classified electronic reconnaissance of Cambodia and Laos in an old Super Constellation, four-engine prop with three tails in the back. It wasn't all that dangerous. He signed up for a second tour. He took his 30-day leave in New Zealand, stalking huge rainbow and brown trout—

FACING PAGE: "The Sultan" on display at the 2009 National Wild Turkey Federation Convention. From Mecklenburg County, Virginia, he was the 49th and final longbeard in Jon Pries's quest for the U. S. Super Slam. Ten months earlier, in 2008, Ron Fretts, member of the Federation's Board of Directors, and Jon spotted him late on the morning of their first day hunting. Three mature gobblers were in full strut across an open grassy field. From 200 yards away he was noticeably larger. "There he is," Pries said, "the Sultan—that's the bird I want." He closed the deal the very next morning. As the Pennsylvanian kneeled next to this magnificent gobbler, "my body shook and tears streamed down both cheeks!" After six long and wonderful springs, the quest was complete.

the spookiest he had ever seen—in crystal-clear streams.

While cavorting on the South Island of New Zealand, Pries had the good fortune to hook up with a man named Mike Bennett, a government hunter. Occasionally, Mike took a guest hunting. Jon flew on a small plane from Christchurch, into the river bed in the forest land where Bennett hunted.

"We landed on a real short sand bar, got out, and there was Mike," Jon recalled. "He had shorts on—a stocky little guy. We hit it off. And we stayed in a hut that he built. I don't know, it was 12 feet square, maybe, and very crude."

In three days Pries shot five red deer stag, which were flown out and down river to a meat-processing place to dress the meat and send it to Europe, for serving in restaurants there. And then Mike Bennett did something that he said he rarely had done.

"In fact," Jon said, "I don't think he'd done it before. He took me up on the mountains to go after chamois, and we got caught up there in some ice and snow. But I was able to shoot two."

To this day Jon remembers that week with Mike Bennett as one of the richest experiences of his life. Years later, he was at the Harrisburg Outdoor Show, and ran into an outfitter from New Zealand. He stopped and said, "Boy, I love New Zealand—what a beautiful place!"

"You've been?"

"When I was in the service; I was down there hunting."

"Who'd you hunt with, mate?"

"A fella named Mike Bennett."

"*Mike Bennett?*"

"Yeah, do you know of him?"

"He's only the most famous deer hunter in all of New Zealand!"

Jon learned that Bennett was still alive and living in Berry Town.

Jon wrote an old-fashioned letter to Mike and sealed the envelope. One day, a couple of weeks later, Pries was going through his email. There was one from Mr. Bonehead NZ.

"He told me that he had been going through an old leather trunk and came upon a picture of me," Pries said. "He wondered whatever happened to the American lieutenant that he had taken hunting 35 years ago." The next day the old Kiwi received Jon's handwritten letter.

Several years ago, Jon's son, Tim, who worked at an advertising agency in California, was was named employee of the year out of 600 to 800 employees. Tim's reward was a two-week vacation, anywhere in the world he wanted to go. The company would pay for the transportation to and from, and they gave him $2,000 to spend. He had to agree to video the adventure and present it at the next Christmas party. Tim decided to go to New Zealand. He would take his brother, Todd, who lives in Florida. They invited Dad to come along.

"New Zealand is such a wonderful place, boys," their father responded. "I'd love to. But I'm really busy here at the house. I just have so much stuff going on. You two have a great time."

On the first day the brothers went sky diving. On the second day they went sea kayaking. On the third day they hiked up to a glacier. On the fourth day they planned to go trout fishing.

When Todd and Tim pulled up in their rented Volkswagen caravan the next morning, their fishing guide was waiting—Dad.

The three stayed with Mike Bennett, in a hut right behind Mike's house, the spitting image of the one Jon and he had stayed in those many years ago along the river bank.

What drives you to kill turkeys?

JON D. PRIES: I'm glad you used the word *kill*— I don't like the word harvest.

We're predators.

PRIES: I take things, but I don't harvest them. And I find that one of the toughest questions. Because I don't want to give some corny, canned answer. I want to discuss my hunting in such a way that it does not offend people. Although I'm not worried about political correctness. Well, I guess so. And I jotted down some things. I wrote: to cleanse my soul. And that's really, I guess it's an evolvement from when I was a child and spent time along the stream and in the woods, just exploring and poking around and taking apart a tree stump to find the grubs that were in it. You know, looking at nature in so many ways. And then as I got older and was able to have a BB gun and a .22 and so forth, hunting became a natural extension. Now it's really just something I've done all my life. The more time that anybody spends in the out of doors, the more you're gonna see and experience. And be witness to some great amazing things. Whether it's wild flowers or whatever. So, I hunt to spend time in the woods. I don't mind killing things. And I do it in such a way that it's a good and, I hope, easy, clean-standing shot. I'm not interested in throwing lead and hoping I get something. I'm respectful of the animals and the birds and the fish. It's where I like to spend time. And on the few occasions that I've had some real difficult times in my life—divorce, a close family member passing away—spending time in the woods was where I got my head on straight. Part of that is the gathering part,

whatever it is I'm after, be it an elk or a turkey or squirrels. It's a matter of gathering some really good, high-quality protein, nutritious meats that are good for you. And again, I throw out that it doesn't have government-approved chemicals. I like to eat meat, so it's something that I enjoy, being able to provide for myself. Which is something that may be going by the wayside: people providing for themselves and doing their own butchering and canning and everything else. But it's all part of the process that I enjoy.

What is it, specifically, about wild turkeys that you most love and that's kept you coming back all these years?

PRIES: Well, there was my "Ultimate Gobbler Quest" for a while. That's done and I've hunted now in New Zealand and Mexico for turkeys—about every place that I know of that any turkeys exist. I still enjoy it every time I go out, although I would never brag to say I'm a great turkey hunter. I've been lucky. I had to go back to Alabama three times before I finally got a bird. It was an interesting, special story in the way it unfolded. But the fun thing about turkey hunting is, for me, every time I go out, it seems like everything I think I've learned and know about turkeys doesn't seem to apply. You think they're gonna come this way. All of a sudden, you hear them behind you; they've circled. You never know what they're gonna do next. There are a lot of people on television that say, "Yep, I bet he's gonna come up that roadway—get ready." And he'll come up the roadway, all right, but that's all filmed and canned. I just think that more than most other species—even elk, and

The nicest of three longbeards that were strutting in the morning sun on a remote hillside field at the farm of Jeff and Jenny Welliver in Lycoming County, Pennsylvania. They put on a show for almost an hour until they finally moved far enough apart for Pries to take the fatal shot.

deer, and bear, and so forth—they're the least predictable at times, and that's what makes it fun. You think you know that bird is roosted up on that side hill. You think you know where would be a good place to set up for it. And he comes off the roost, gobbling and gobbling and goes the other way. What the heck? And for a while, you'll think: *Boy, my turkey calling must be falling off. I'm not doing very well here.* And then, when the gobbler is ready, he will come. You know, if he's ready to come into your call, he'll come in. And you'll be lucky.

Do you remember your first turkey?
PRIES: Oh my, yes. I sure do. I was 16 years of age and we lived out in the country, on a 45-acre farm. There was a farmer who put some corn in. But 45 acres surrounded by other bigger farms and a

mountainside nearby. I got off the school bus and ran across the field to get to the house as quick as I could. I had my school clothes and my loafers on, grabbed my grandfather's double side-by-side 16-gauge Lefever and took it for a walk. I didn't know whether I was going to see a rabbit or a pheasant. Turkeys weren't even a consideration that day. I walked down the dirt road, cut up a logging road, and entered the woods. As I started to enter the woods on this logging road, I stopped for a minute and there was a lot of noise up in this flat up above me on a bench. I listened for a while, but I couldn't figure out what the heck it was. I thought, *My God, that might be a bear!* What was I thinking? So, I took one of the shot shells out—I think I had No. 6s on both sides—and put a slug into one side, just in case it was a bear. I mean, it's

not bear season. Maybe he was going to attack me, I don't know. I put the slug in the left barrel and I slipped my loafers off so I'd be more quiet as I worked my way up. And it was maybe 30 yards that I had to go and I could start to see up in the bench. As I rose up, all of a sudden turkeys were running and flying all over the place. I wasn't anticipating or even thinking about a turkey.

Had you seen them before?
PRIES: Yes, but in very limited numbers. In 1960, there weren't many wild turkeys around. I'd seen a few but, like I say, I wasn't even thinking about turkeys that day. So, I raised up, and all of a sudden these birds are running left and right, flying. I pulled up and BOOM, shot at one. All these birds continued to fly and move off. And I looked and I thought I shot at a stump, so I walked up maybe 30 yards or so, and I looked down and here's this turkey lying dead. I had gotten it with a slug at the base of the neck.

Wow.
PRIES: It was a hen, probably weighing six or seven pounds. It was not a big bird, not a big target. I just was lucky. I picked that bird up and I whooped and I hollered. Honest to God, I did. And I raised it up and I ran home the whole way. I couldn't believe it. I was so excited about this bird. And it's the first one I had ever gotten and first one I ever hunted, although I really didn't hunt that much for it. But I was so excited. My mom was home and we cooked it up for dinner the next day. It was a big deal, a big deal.

Did that make you start thinking about wanting to go after more of them?
PRIES: Yeah, but I knew at the moment it was just the luck of the draw, that I happened to stumble into it. There still weren't a lot of birds around. So it wasn't like, *I'm gonna start turkey hunting.* I didn't even have a turkey call. But by the following year, that fall, I had a turkey call. And used that Lynch box call. It was my granddad's. And I called a bird in. It came off the top of the mountain, came

Schuyler County, New York, is the home of wonderful spring gobbler hunting and many beautiful backdrops for pictures. "I never heard a gobbler that fateful morning until he did the old 'spit and drum,' Jon Pries said, "*behind me*—Lady Luck was with me for sure!"

sailing in. And I mean, all of a sudden, it dropped 10 yards from me. I thought, *What the heck?* I was surprised. And that started to get my interest.

Did your grandfather teach you to call?
PRIES: Not really. I just kind of picked it up on my own, talking to some people. Granddad wasn't a big turkey hunter. He was more of the deer and bear hunter, and a fisherman.

So how long was it before you got to the point where you actually, consciously, went out to hunt turkeys? Did that come years later?
PRIES: It would be about three or four years later. End of high school, beginning of college, I started to really enjoy turkey hunting. One of my friends,

Charlie Matter, from college, was, at that point, big into spring gobbler hunting. And I had never done it before. He and I went out—he took me along. In those days, they called it "running and gunning," which is not necessarily a favorite of mine. I went out with Chuck that first time, and we were on a hillside, working several benches where Chuck would call. Then we'd wait a few minutes, and we'd get up and go. And we'd move several hundred yards and call again. Well, two times on that morning, we bumped turkeys, meaning that Chuck would call, and didn't hear anything gobble in return, so we'd get up and a turkey would fly off that was coming in silently, which they do on

looking down on, I mean, I just started to shake.

Literally shaking?

PRIES: Most people will tell you, "If I ever lose that excitement, I might as well quit hunting." I was young then, but I still get the shakes when I see them. So, the bird came up and he was right in the open. I couldn't move, and my gun was on my lap, not pointed toward him. I couldn't move cuz they've got such excellent eyesight. And he was maybe 70 yards away, but walking toward me, looking for this hen. And he got to about 20 yards from me, and I just sat there and I had tears rolling down my cheek. I was just so intense watching this

> And he got to about 20 yards from me,
> and I just sat there and I had tears rolling down my cheek.
> It was just so intense watching this bird, and I couldn't,
> I didn't wanna blink.

occasion. The next time, about a week later, I had an opportunity to go out in the morning by myself. That was a great hunt.

Do tell.

PRIES: I went in before daylight, into a logging road that entered the woods. And I thought, *Wow, I can' go any farther until I really can see where I'm moving in here.* I sat down at the base of a tree and, as it started to get light, I hear soft clucking in the tree above me. These hens were roosting right above me! And I thought, *Great, now I'm nailed down until they fly off.* Which they did after about a half an hour. And then I worked up the logging road, sat down and called. And a bird gobbled farther out on this bench. I sat there and I called. He would return the call, he'd gobble back. You could tell he was closer, and I thought, *Man, this is great.* This was the first time that I'm on my own doing this and I was using a mouth call. As that bird came up over the rim of this bench that I was

bird, and I couldn't, I didn't wanna blink. And at one point, he finally turned to walk away, and he gets behind a big rock. I thought, *great!* And I quickly snapped the gun over and began waiting and waiting and waiting—and now the gun's getting heavy. It seemed like forever. But all of a sudden, without seeing him step out, he was five feet away from the boulder, standing back where he had been. *How the hell did he get there without me seeing it?* Anyhow, he's there. I just had to wait again until he looked back down over the hill. He finally glanced back to see below the bench: BOOM! I was so excited, I ran up to the bird, put my foot on its neck so it wouldn't flop in case I didn't hit it well.

Had you?

PRIES: It was dead. But, for safety's sake, I unloaded the Remington 870 pump, thought a moment and loaded the gun back up cuz no one was gonna get that turkey from me! That was a nice

bird and the first one that I'd killed on my own.

We all begin somewhere. From your experience during those early years, do you have one piece of advice for a beginner?

PRIES: Yeah, I mean I've thought about that, and I think probably the most important thing is to have a mentor, someone who will teach you. Who will take time to spend time in the woods with you, too, because in all hunting, but in particular turkey hunting, a lot of people believe that calling is the biggest, most important thing. And I'm not sure that I agree with that. I think woodsmanship is one of the most important things in turkey hunting. So find someone who will take the time and walk through the woods with you and teach you to identify a beech tree that produces beech nuts that the turkeys like. Have them teach you the difference between a white oak and a red oak, and the fact that a white oak produces oak acorns every two years, a red oak is every year, and the preferred acorn is the white oak. Those sort of things. And the fact that in the springtime, finding a seep along a stream can be key, because the turkeys will come there to get a drink. Woodsmanship is critical. I think there are people who are still protective of their honey holes, and their private little spots, but are willing to share their knowledge about the sport. I think that's the important thing.

At what point in your hunting career did you actually start seriously thinking about getting a turkey in all 49 states?

PRIES: It really occurred—let's see, a couple things happened at the same time: two years after September 11, 2001, I was laid off. And just prior to that, a few years prior to that, I was divorced after 24 years 10 months and 11 days. Please put that in the book. [laughing] But the combination of that and my dad passing away in that same time period, a lot happened. And suddenly I was on my own. Part of it was that I likened my life up until the divorce as a wonderful, big, thick book. And we really hadn't argued, fought, and had a nasty

relationship. We all know people that are that way. In any event, it was a good book of stories. But it was whipped out of my hands, put up on a shelf and I can't do anything with it except learn from it. The good news was that I was given a big, thick book of blank pages. And I get to write the rest of my story in any way that I want.

Are you happy now writing it?

PRIES: I thought: *You know what? I'm single, I've got all the time in the world, I've only got to answer to me. I have two wonderful sons, but they're out on their own, working. So what would I like to do?* I thought it'd be fun to try and get a bird in every state. At this point, I had heard about that having occurred or at least it was in progress with people like Rob Keck and maybe a few other people. I would fly from the East Coast to the West Coast. And I would look down there all the time and day-dream about where was that family slaughtered in their wagon going West, and just the whole history of the country. But also in wonderment of all the different habitat and geography and things that you could get down there and explore. After years of doing that and wanting to be on the ground where I could look at some of these things, I finally thought, *You know what? I'm gonna go to all the different states, turkey hunt, try and get a long-beard in every state. And I'll have a chance to really poke around and see some things.* I was living up here then [at Gobbler's Knob] and I called the owner/editor of the local newspaper about an idea. We talked a little bit and he said, "What are you doing now?" I said: "Well, I just retired from the airlines." And he said, "What are you gonna do now?" I said, "Well, as a matter of fact, I was thinking I'd travel around and try and get a wild turkey in every state." He said, "You ought to write about that." I'd never written before. The next morning, I arrived at his office and we sat down and talked about it and that's how my writing began.

So you hadn't killed a bird in many other states when you started?

PRIES: No, no, no, no.

Jon Pries and Terry Ciechomski entered the pre-dawn woods in Harrison County, Ohio greeted by thunder, lightning and heavy rain. Every time there was a clap of thunder, several gobblers shock-gobbled. After repositioning several times on the deepest-sounding tom, Jon caught a glimpse of him at the field's edge and began making soft purring calls. The tom came in on a straight line: *BAM*. Ohio bird—check!

Had you gotten any?
PRIES: In fact, I was just thinking. No.

You are unique then.
PRIES: Yeah.

Because nearly all the Super Slam hunters I've spoken with were kind of halfway there, when it suddenly dawned on them: why not go all the way?
PRIES: No, no, no.

Very unusual. How many years did it take you to do it?
PRIES: Six springs, 2003 through the spring of 2008. And honestly, the first year I completed 11 states, the second year I completed 12 states. Third

year, I completed 13 states and British Columbia. That year one of the states I went to was Hawaii. But I drove to every other state, in a 1997 Land Rover Defender D90, with a tent on top and stickers all over the sides. You'll get pictures of it. That's an important part of me and this whole thing.

Your first state was obviously, here, Pennsylvania.
PRIES: The first state was Georgia. I mean, of course, I'd gotten a lot of Pennsylvania birds.

Yeah.
PRIES: But when I started the quest, I was geared to getting one in every state. So I figured I would be getting Pennsylvania in the midst of all the other ones.

Okay, so you made a decision to start fresh.
PRIES: Right, right, square one.

Interesting—so tell me about that experience.
PRIES: Well, I mean, the way I would lay it out is that the National Wild Turkey Federation magazine, *Turkey Country*, that came out every year around February, would publish a map of the U.S., showing all the states. And they would have a colored band where the Rio Grande turkeys are. There was a band where the eastern turkeys are and where the Merriam's are and the Osceolas. I would look at that, select and call a number of states, have them send me their book of regula-

after shooting hours began. And I was on the road and gone because the next state might take four days or whatever. But that's how I would program it out to follow the opening of the seasons back and forth across the country.

And six years later, what was your last state?
PRIES: Virginia.

Do you have a good story?
PRIES: Yeah, it really was. It was one of the great ones, if not the greatest of all the states. In this process, I met and become friends with Ron Fretts who was a National Board Member in N.W.T.F.,

> I didn't wanna get there after the birds had been harassed for a week or so. I tried to get there on opening day or so and allot three days per state. I was lucky enough in one state, Michigan, that I tagged out in 10 minutes after shooting hours began.

tions, and when the seasons and limits were gonna be, and I would just map it out. Sometimes I'd go back and forth, crisscrossing the country. One state out West, back to the East, down South, and so on. If I could, I tried to do them next to each other—I hunted Georgia and then Alabama. And so you're not wasting time running all over the country. But there were times when I had to bounce quite a distance in between states to hunt the opening days or opening week of their season. But I would lay it out, program it in such a way that I would maximize getting to a state for their first week of hunting. I didn't wanna get there after the birds had been harassed for a week or so. I tried to get there on opening day or so and allot three days per state. I was lucky enough in one state, Michigan, that I tagged out in 10 minutes

and lives here in Pennsylvania. He was following my quest, as a lot of people were, and was interested. So when I was coming up on Virginia, I had a conversation with him. He mentioned that he knew a place to go in Virginia where we should have good success. And I said, "Well, that's great, cuz I really haven't met anyone or made a contact there." He also suggested that since this was my last state we might have N.W.T.F. video it and eventually put it on television. I was excited about that aspect. The first day we hunted there, Ron, the landowner, the cameraman and I all travelled around, hearing birds, working birds. We would call to them and they'd gobble back. In mid-morning, we were walking to go to another field area when we crossed an opening and out across a big meadow. Suddenly, we spotted three gobblers

FACING PAGE: On Jon's third morning of hunting with Don Turcke of Medford, Oregon, this picture-perfect Merriam's closed the distance across a wide-open horse pasture in full strut. "I just couldn't stand it any longer," Pries said. "At 20 yards, he strutted no more."

there, all fanned out. We stopped, got behind some brush, called a little bit and they just gobbled, but wouldn't budge. I looked at them there in the sunlight, all fanned out, all mature gobblers. Even at 300 yards, you know the difference in the tail of a jake and a mature gobbler. These were all mature gobblers. But one was noticeably bigger than the other two and I said: "My God, there he is! That's 'The Sultan.' That's the one I wanna get" But because we were surely spotted by the turkeys, we knew we couldn't hunt them that day. The landowner said, "Well, I know some other spots we can go to this afternoon, where we will have a good chance." But I didn't wanna go. I almost said, "No, no, I don't wanna hunt anymore today," But he's the owner, and you gotta respect that. So I reluctantly went, hoping that we wouldn't see any other gobblers and that we could get back on this bird the next morning.

Did you?

PRIES: As luck would have it, we didn't. The next morning, we went across the field to a little island of brush that was near where these birds had fanned out and had been strutting. We arrived there before daylight, believing that's where the birds would come. We placed three decoys out in hopes they would help draw the gobblers into shooting range. But *no*, of course not. They never do what you think they're gonna do. The three gobblers and some hens entered the field where we had been standing the morning before. Had we set up there, maybe it would have worked out. We worked the birds, called to them. They would gobble back, and there were two or three other gobblers that joined them and half a dozen hens. Finally, the birds worked toward us, but never within more than 80 yards. And then they just got tired of our calling and moved away. When they were all out of sight, we quickly ran to a drainage ditch, a drop-off between us. We dropped down and came up the other side of the drainage. As I came up I could hear this one bird gobbling out in the field. I eased up and I could see him. But he was in corn stubble beyond some tall grass. It was

"The Sultan." There was no ideal cover, so I laid down at the edge of the grass and watched in awe as The Sultan would gobble and strut. I made some soft clucks. To my amazement, he came out of strut and slowly began walking my way, stopping from time to time to strut and gobble. He finally closed the distance to 30 yards. I couldn't take it any longer. I shot and he fell where he stood. I jumped up and ran to the bird and looked in sheer disbelief. Tears began to roll down my cheeks.

You really cried?

PRIES: My God, I really did have tears, I really did. Because it was a hell of a bird. He had an 11-inch beard, which is pretty long, and inch-and-a-quarter spurs, which was pretty nice. They came to a nice sharp point, all unusual, because a lot of the birds you find, those spurs would be rubbed off from the rocks and the terrain. But he was just a beautiful bird, the nicest bird that I had taken on the whole quest. And there it was. God. And my quest was over. I mean, it was an amazing moment.

You may have already told me this, but what's the maximum number of states you hunted in any one year during the six-year period?

PRIES: Thirteen.

Were all your 49 birds taken during the spring?

PRIES: Yes, yep.

All toms?

PRIES: All mature gobblers, yeah.

Did you ever use a guide?

PRIES: No. The closest I came to using a guide was in Colorado, where I had made a contact with Ash Tully, who was a guide. I told him my story of wanting to get a bird in every state. And he said, "I'll put you on some birds." He wasn't going to take me out on a guided hunt and do the calling. He was gonna just put me on some land where I could hunt. First day, we went out together and I was calling but he was kinda showing me the property. And then the next day, he let me go on

What better backdrop for this Vermont longbeard than a granite outcropping? This bird never gobbled—it came in silently. Jon never saw him until he magically appeared, standing at 25 yards with outstretched neck and looking for the "hen."

my own. And I went up to an open field in a draw between the hillsides, and was able to call in and get a bird in Colorado.

What do you think drove you to this? Are you normally an ambitious person? Cuz it's a pretty ambitious goal.
PRIES: Well, it is, but it's just that once I decided to initiate the quest, and then in the first year was able to complete 11 states. . . . I mean, it was grueling. I was excited to see it to the end.

Was it ever not fun? You used the word grueling.
PRIES: No, it was never "not fun." It was physically demanding at times—I pushed myself a lot both when I was hunting and the days I was traveling to the next state. But, with every bird, I was closer to that goal. And really, the first couple of years when I completed 11 states, the first year, then finish

12 states the second year, I was sure I would continue and complete the quest. I was trying to get a lot of it behind me so I could establish credibility, so when I talked to someone, I didn't say, "Well, I've been doing this for 12 years and I've already gotten three turkeys!"

Ha! [laughing]
PRIES: Better to say that I've been doing it for three years and I've killed 36 turkeys.

Sure.
PRIES: I would say that I would like to come to Utah (or whatever state) and get a turkey: a nice longbeard representative of the turkeys in your state. I just want to get one gobbler and then I want to move on. I'd say, "Look, I'm not trying to find a spot where I can come back and sneak into your special hunting area." And putting it that

A Rio Grande lit up by a patch of bluebonnets decorating a roadside on a 3,000-acre lease in San Saba County, Texas. Jon Pries was the guest of Sam, Hugh and Stuart McManus, and John Bradford, with all of whom he has remained friends since.

way, people bend over backwards to help. They wanted to be part of it.

Did you ever feel a sense of competition with other hunters? Either with people you knew or knew were pursuing the Super Slam?
PRIES: No, because a year or two into it I had gone to the convention and talked to Rob Keck about it and some other people. I knew the people who had completed it prior to me. And that's fine. I just thought it was a neat thing. I've got the time, I'm interested in it. Again, I'm single. I could do what I wanna do. I just thought it was a neat accomplishment to try and complete. And then I met Tom "Doc" Weddle in Delaware. Delaware is the only state where they require that you have to take a class and an exam before you can turkey hunt

there. So we met in that class, and he was almost complete with his quest. There was an instant friendship. There wasn't a feeling of competition. We ended up hunting the next year together in Hawaii. I've hunted with him down in Florida, not side by side, but we've been at a camp together. We were in Delaware at the same time, so it became just a friendship of running into a buddy that's doing the same thing. Never did I think, *I better push harder and maybe I can beat Doc.*

When you set out to get a bird hundreds of miles or even couple thousand miles away, how did you plan the attack, so to speak? How did you plan your strategy? You drove to all these places.
PRIES: Drove to every state in my 1997 Land Rover D-90 Defender—every state but Hawaii.

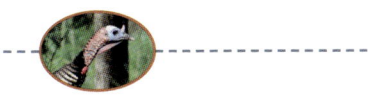

Did it occur to you that that was a bit of a paradox for a guy who has free airplane passes?

PRIES: Maybe, but I watched the way they handle bags. [laughing] I thought maybe it'd be a good idea to drive. Flying was, to me, not an option because when you get there, you're not sure that your bag's gonna get there that same day. I didn't wanna fly anywhere to turkey hunt. When I did fly to Hawaii I had a carry-on bag that I can put under the seat and a backpack. But in the carry-on bag, I put an extra set of hunting gear, camo gear, and things that I could use for hunting, in case my bag

Or I would just look at some topo maps and make several phone calls. I would call the fish and game departments, talk to one of the wardens or someone there. Again, I'd explain what I was doing. And again, everybody seemed to say, "That's great, yeah, sure, I'll tell you what, when you get here, give me a call and I'll take you out highway 23 at mile marker 105" or wherever. Or I'd stop at a local sporting goods store, or go to a cafe or diner, and just mention what I was doing. And, again, people would bend over backwards to help put me in the right spot.

> Maybe, but I watched the way they handle bags. [laughing] I thought maybe it'd be a good idea to drive. Flying was, to me, not an option because when you get there, you're not sure that your bag's gonna get there that same day. I didn't wanna fly anywhere to turkey hunt.

of hunting gear didn't get there, with the shotgun. Well, I arrived in Honolulu, and no bag. It came two days later. In the meantime, I was hunting with Doc Weddle and another couple, and they loaned me a gun. The first day I put on my nylon shirt and my nylon pants because I'm in Hawaii. We drove up the side of the volcano and get out at 8,000 feet, and it's like 35 degrees! [laughing] And I'm thinking: *My God. Boy, I really did it to myself this time.* So that's one of the reasons. But, again, something about looking down all those years and wanting to get down on the ground and move around and see things—that had a lot of it too.

Once you got to places you'd never hunted before, how did you find the birds?

PRIES: One of two ways. I would either know someone who was a hunter, and had met them either at the convention, or one way or another I'd be in contact with somebody that was a hunter, that was gonna take me to where there were birds.

What was the most difficult state for you?

PRIES: Alabama. I had to go to three times. And it wasn't the state; it was the birds. The first two years that I hunted there, I worked birds. I heard birds gobble. I would get into a position where I thought they were headed or would call and they'd be coming in, but they'd hang up. I never had an opportunity to shoot at a bird in Alabama those first two seasons. And this was interesting because, at that point, Alabama had a five-bird limit. So it's not like there weren't a lot of birds; there were. They had a five-bird limit and no tags. Now, go figure that out. So you, Mister Honest Alabama Hunter, shoot your five birds. You don't have a tag to put on them. Just put them in the freezer.

You mean there was no tag required?

PRIES: That's correct.

I thought you meant they'd run out of them.

PRIES: No. Ain't that something? That was the regulation: no tag needed to put on dead birds. So

Jon D. Pries **132**

I go down to Alabama, I hunted two years and never got a bird. But the second year I was there, I met a fellow named J. Wayne Fears. I'd heard about him, I knew who he was, that he was an outdoor writer. I went into a local sporting goods store. And the one fellow that worked there, I was asking him if there were places to hunt, and he asked did I know J. Wayne Fears. And I said, "I've heard the name, but I've never met him." He said, "Would you like to meet him?" And I said, "Yeah, sure." So we went out to J. Wayne's place, and he had about a 300-acre property, mostly wooded, but he had some food plots there. And I hunted for a couple days. Still, I didn't get a bird there. I came back the next year and J. Wayne said: "Yep, come on down, hunt here. But do me a favor. I'm gonna have some other hunters later in the week, so just one bird." At that point, I could have gotten two birds. But so with what he said, I went out to a food plot, clover plot, maybe an acre and a half. And there was a little shooting shack, hut, 20 yards off the edge of it in the woods. Well, the interesting thing was that Alabama, of all the states, it was the one state at that point, where you were not allowed to use decoys. In every other state, you're allowed. Alabama had never allowed decoys. This year, my third year to go there, you were allowed decoys. So I took three decoys with me, thinking: *They've probably never seen decoys before. This should be interesting.* On the edge of the field I put a hen decoy in a squatted position, a jake decoy behind her, and then another 10 yards off the side of the hen, kind of in the alert position looking up. I walked back into this little hut and thought I might as well relax. Took my vest off, thinking, *Let's see, which call do I wanna use?* I glanced up and here are two longbearded turkeys running from the edge of that food plot, across the field toward the decoys. Their big old bodies were swaying, their beards were flapping back and forth, and they were just running shoulder to shoulder across this field. And I thought, *My God, look at this!* It was crazy. So I put the vest down. As I'm watching them come in, I had my nice Nikon camera and everything laying there. And they just ran straight

to the decoys, gobbled at them and jumped on them, and were trouncing the heck out of these decoys until they finally had the jake and the hen smashed on the ground. And then they'd back off and they'd be looking and they'd gobble again and they'd look at them and peck at them. And after what seemed like a long time, they both kinda looked and were very happy with what they had done, and started to walk away. And as they walked away, and got out to 25 yards, I held my gun to the outside of the one bird and shot.

So the decoys worked.
PRIES: I was amazed The fact there were no decoys allowed before, and finally they were legal to use and I didn't even have to make a call.

So Alabama was your most challenging place by circumstance. Do you remember a particular bird that was your most challenging bird, an individual bird?
PRIES: Well, New Mexico was also difficult. Now, as far as a challenging bird, I'd have to say Washington State. It was around Spokane, and I had hunted two or three different areas—not near each other—for several days, not really connecting with anything. And, finally, at one point, I was working a bird on some B.L.M. land. He was going the other way. I mean, he gobbled when I would call to him. But whether or not he had hens, I wasn't sure. He was just going away. I had to move several times and climb up on a pretty good sidehill to get ahead of him. Finally, three jakes came popping up and went by me. I could tell by the heads they were jakes. And I didn't wanna shoot, and this bird gobbled again and he's below me, and I could tell by his gobble that it was the old longbeard. I'm figuring he's following jakes, which he was, and I ended up shooting him. But certainly that was the most physical move in all. I was about ready to say, "I think I'll just bag it and come back another day."

Did you ever pass up a bird that you could have easily killed?

"Having secured this gobbler on public hunting grounds in New Jersey, I felt it might be wise to wear a brightly colored shirt as I carried the bird over my shoulder back to the vehicle!" Jon said. "You just never know who might be lurking."

PRIES: Not really, in that, again, if I had a good shot, a good, clean shot, what I felt was a killing shot at a bird, I wanted to take it, and get on to the next state in case I needed more time there. The only time I would pass one up is if it were a jake.

Where's the strangest place you ever killed a turkey?

PRIES: The strangest place, I guess, would have to be Hawaii. It's so unique. So many of the states, I mean, they're beautiful, with varied terrain and habitat. But when all of a sudden, you're talking about being at 8,000 feet on the side of a volcano that's got snow on top of it in Hawaii, well, that's strange. You look out and here's the Parker Ranch, which is well known for turkey hunting and hog hunting and other hunting. You look out at this huge Parker Ranch, and right at the edge of that is the Pacific Ocean. And you're eating fresh pineapple and fresh bananas. The whole experi-

ence was neat. To anybody, even if they don't wanna do an entire quest of all the states, but they wanna hunt in a half-dozen different states, to try a different thing, you gotta go to Hawaii.

Where are the toughest turkeys?

PRIES: I think, the answer would have to be right here, Pennsylvania, because there's so much hunting pressure here. A lot of people I've hunted with would say that. We have a good number of birds, but we have an amazing large army of turkey hunters, and then the people who come from other neighboring states. The birds get educated very quickly.

What's the craziest experience you had in the course of your quest—any one stands out?

PRIES: It wasn't so much with the gobblers, but three things that occurred that were very unique and interesting. One, in Montana, I watched a bird

Jon killed this Ohio gobbler while hunting with Terry Ciechomski. Hiking back, they came across a nice patch of morel mushrooms. They celebrated the day with Terry's wife, Stacy, by preparing a meal fit for a king: pan-fried sliced wild turkey breasts and morels sautéed in butter. A dry red wine, if you please. . . .

that I saw had a beard on it, and I was calling to it. It was moving toward me. But the closer it got, the more I realized, this wasn't a gobbler, it was a bearded hen, and at one point, as she crossed a pasture area, she stopped and it was still maybe 100 yards from me. She stopped and she just stood there for the longest time, and pecked a little bit. And at one point, she took her head and tucked it under her wing, and I thought she was just preening and I watched and I watched, and I watched, and she just stood there with her head tucked under her wing. So I snuck out around in a little wash, got into about 40 yards from her, came up quietly, and she was still standing there, in the same position. I continued up out of the wash and walked straight across this open pasture, in this wide open area. I walked to within 10 feet from her. She was asleep. [laughing] I thought, *My God, girl, if a coyote saw you, you'd be dinner,* I said, "Hey, wake up!" With that her head came up and she flew off.

That surprised you?
PRIES: I never would have guessed it would have slept like that on the ground. The second experience was in Oregon, where I had been hunting in a pasture at the edge of a woodsy area, where people kept horses, but there were no horses at the time. I called and a gobbler answered and I waited. And pretty soon this bird's in full strut, all puffed up, full tail fanned out. I could see from a distance that it's got a hen with it. So, long story short, the

closer it came, now it's at 60 yards and I'm putting my binoculars on and it just doesn't look right—it was a hen!

A strutting hen?

PRIES: It was a hen, tail fanned out, all puffed out, and I guess it's the level of testosterone that some of these birds have versus others. And so I didn't shoot that bird because it ended up being a hen. But it was just bizarre to see this and to realize, my gosh, this hen was strutting as much as any gobbler had ever strutted.

You said you had three stories.

PRIES: The third was in New Hampshire. The last two days I hunted there, I had a bird gobbling. I bet it gobbled 70 or 80 times on the roost, until it finally came down. Each of those two days, it came down and then worked its way up through the woods and along the field edge, out of my sight. I thought at some point it might turn and come in—it didn't. The next year I went back and I started out at that same spot, wondering whether that bird was still around or not. I *know* it was the same bird, because it just acted and gobbled the same, and was in the same tree. I never saw it in the tree, but I was nearby enough that I knew that's where it was. That bird, the second year, gobbled again, I bet 70 or 80 times in the tree. And then I heard what I thought was a hen; turned out to be another hunter. When the bird came off, as it moved and walked up toward the field, it gobbled and gobbled, and it gobbled. And I'd call and it would gobble and then I heard boom. "Damn," I said to myself, "somebody got that gobbler." I went up to congratulate the hunter and it was a hen! It had gobbled for two years more than any other mature gobbler I had ever heard.

Do you ever think what it cost you to do all this?

PRIES: You gotta be kidding. [laughing] No, I mean, I always wanted to figure it out. I wish I had written down every mile, the miles I drove and just the cost of gas. I don't know if you wanna publish that information. If any wives got hold of

that cost, there'd be divorces, probably.

Any important considerations for somebody either part way to their U. S. Slam or contemplating attempting it?

PRIES: There are a couple of states where you have to put in for a lottery; that's not difficult. And there again, in the planning, you have to fit that in. If you want to go to Illinois, well, you may not get drawn the first year, so there's a little logistics there. What I tried to do—and was able to do through the whole process—was to reconnect with some friends, or make friends. And for instance, the fellow from Oregon, Don Turcke, I met down at the N.W.T.F. Convention. We got to talking and he said, "Come on out, we'll go turkey hunting." He's been here at my house and has turkey hunted here. One of the places I went, I stayed at some friends' home that I was in the Air Force with 15 years earlier. And so the reconnect with some family and friends to me that was all part of it, parts that I really enjoyed, since some of the folks I hadn't seen for a long time. But consider that when you think about where you're gonna go. You probably have friends either from work, maybe the military, college, whatever, that you could connect with. Maybe they're hunters, maybe they're not. But it's fun to be able to put that together too and have some nice visits along the way. Make it fun.

Have you ever thought of what your favorite hunting states are?

PRIES: Yeah, that's a tough question because there are several I really enjoyed. Hate to say that *one* was my favorite. Certainly, as I mentioned, Hawaii has to be a favorite. Texas is a favorite, partially because I ran into a group of guys outside of Brady, Texas, that had a lease on 3,000 acres. And when I first went there, I had heard of these guys—they would deer and turkey hunt there and hog hunt. I had always kind of wanted to try this hog hunting. I ended up being invited to come down and hog hunt. "Sure," they said, "kill all the hogs you want." So I went down during their turkey season to hunt

feral hogs. Over about a three- or four-year period, I went down a dozen times. That buck up there [pointing to mounted head] is the 13-pointer that I got in Texas on that lease. Texas was fun because of the people I met, and the times around the campfire that we had. I like Florida because of its uniqueness as far as the swamps and laying there at night in the tent, and hearing the hogs three feet away from the tent, rooting around. And knowing that there's some nasty snakes and alligators and all kinds of stuff down there you gotta be careful of. Utah was certainly neat because I was near

Did you do much preseason scouting?
PRIES: Well, unfortunately, I was not able to in the quest, but as far as just generally turkey hunting, I just think it's critical, it's important. And to me, it adds another layer of the enjoyment of the whole hunting experience. But you can hunt without it. It's great to go out there and know that there's some birds in the area. This place, [Gobbler's Knob] when I bought it, in the first year, I could go out and sit at the picnic table before daylight with a cup of coffee, all geared up, and as it's starting to get light, I would hear gobbling and then I

> Another thing is you can go to a farmer before the season and you can take a cherry pie. Or you can offer to split some wood. Be more than just a guy knocking on his door to hunt there. Be a friend and have a cup of coffee or a beer with him.

Cedar City with the geology, the structures, the rock formations and stuff. So many times, in any state, if you get a couple of miles off an interstate, you can see some really neat habitat.

Do you like to return to your old familiar haunts?
PRIES: Well, I guess because I'm getting older, I'm finally admitting it. It's nice to go back to familiar areas. And even then, you're always learning a little bit more about them. This year, I went with some friends up to New York State. I'd hunted there a little bit with this fellow a couple years ago, and I like to learn more each time: the lay of the land and how to maneuver around—the woodsmanship part of it.

When you were chasing the Slam, how many days each year did you devote to it?
PRIES: I'd bet 90 days. You know, Florida would start in early to mid-March. And then most of them would crank up in March and April and run to the end of May. Maine went to like June 5th. It was the latest season.

pick one and go after it. But over the years, there seemed to be fewer and fewer. I think they're coming back a little bit now, but it's that aspect of the anticipation. And knowing there are at least going to be birds there and knowing where to hunt through the scouting.

Is there a key or a secret to effectively scouting a new area?
Well, you know, a lot of people use trail cameras, and they're extremely effective. That's a great way. But, you know, you can't be everywhere. The other way is just to stop and knock on the doors and ask farmers—or ask your U.P.S. guy, FedEx guy or mailman. You know, where are they seeing turkeys. And those people are usually pretty open about doing it, except some U.P.S. guys, I know that are turkey hunters. They won't tell you! Another thing is you can go to a farmer before the season and you can take a cherry pie. Or you can offer to split some wood. Be more than just a guy knocking on his door to hunt there. Be a friend and have a cup of coffee or a beer with him.

Left to right: Stuart McManus, "Doc Sam" McManus—also known as "the Shack Bully"—and Jon Pries, all holding custom-made leather gun cases for their favorite turkey shotguns. The workmanship was performed by inmates at the Huntsville, Texas penitentiary in their shop where they hand craft beautiful boots, saddles and furniture. Jon says he designed the case for his Benelli Super Black Eagle to commemorate the U. S. Super Slam quest.

What is your preferred hunting tactic?
PRIES: In any hunting—turkey hunting or elk hunting or whatever—I think you have to find a spot where you're comfortable. When you're going through the woods, turkey hunting, we'll say, and you think, *this looks like a good spot*. You have good visibility, you have good set up and so forth. And it just seems like maybe it's an area between where a feeding area is and where they roost. But if it feels good to you, I think that's a good place to stop for a while. It's easy, especially as the season draws on, to get a little tired, you know, after getting up at 3:30 every morning. Never seem to get to bed till 10 o'clock, no matter what you do. And spending these long days, doing a lot of hiking in this fresh air, it's easy to kind of nod off a little bit. But I think when you find a spot that you like, a honey hole, you're gonna pay attention, you're gonna stay more alert. And usually, I'd fallen to sleep when those birds come [makes purring and clucking sounds].

[Laughing] Let's talk briefly about equipment. Favorite shotgun?
PRIES: I would say that the Benelli Super Black Eagle.

This Rio Grande gobbler on B.L.M. land in Stevens County, Washington, led Jon on an all-morning race through briars, oak brush and downed timber. He drove his trusty 1997 Land Rover Defender or D-90 to each and every one of the continental United States chasing turkeys—a real eye-popper when he pulled up to a sporting goods store or gas station.

Gauge?
PRIES: Twelve.

What's the length of that barrel?
PRIES: I knew you were gonna ask that—24-inch.

Sighting device?
PRIES: I showed you that, that's a Nikon Red Dot. But the brand isn't as critical as just the red dot idea. I love it. And most people who have evolved to that red dot really like it. As I mentioned, I mean, you can lay on your side, you can be hanging upside down in a tree, and the gun will shoot where the red dot is pointed. When you put that red dot on something, that's where it's going to hit. So, if you're in an awkward position. There are

times, especially in turkey hunting more than any other type of hunting, when you're gonna have to, at some point, if you do enough hunting, switch and shoot on your off-hand. But with the red dot, it's not a matter of trying to line up sights. A rear and a front sight. Again, if you center that and put that where you want it, that's where it's gonna hit. It's a great aid.

What load do you normally shoot?
PRIES: I guess I've changed over the years, but I think what I like now is probably a No. 5 or 6, or there's some blended shotshells that have 4s, 5s and 6s and so forth in it. I think that's good too. I know Winchester's Extended Range XR shells are great. And some of the others that have buffers in

them: material that holds the shot tighter as it goes through the barrel.

And these are three- or three-and-a-half-inch?
PRIES: Well, when I was in the quest, I would generally use three-and-a-half, to maximize my possibility of making sure I had a good kill.

Aside from that Alabama episode, did you use decoys much when you were doing the quest?
PRIES: I didn't use them very much. I've had mixed success with decoys. There's some good decoys out there. I've had times when birds would see them from a distance and almost come run-

make some calls with it, wait a moment, and if nothing responded, he would put that one back in. He'd go right down the row. And maybe it was the second one, maybe it was the 15th one—there might be a dozen or more calls he would try—but he'd reach one with a certain tone and pitch. All of a sudden a bird would respond and he would then hunt with that call that day at that spot. Because of the pitch and tone variance, you never know what is going to strike them.

What else is in your vest?
PRIES: Definitely locator calls—a crow call, an owl call, perhaps a coyote call or a peacock call.

> I love it. And most people who have evolved to that red dot really like it. As I mentioned, I mean, you can lay on your side, you can be hanging upside down in a tree, and the gun will shoot where the red dot is pointed. When you put that red dot on something, that's where it's going to hit.

ning into them—I told you about what happened in Alabama. And yet I've had birds that seem like they saw them from a distance and ran the other way.

If I were to paw through your turkey vest, what would I find?
PRIES: Good way to ask, paw through my vest! Well, there's gonna be a box call, and there might be a long box call, longer box than this, [holding call] because they tend to carry sound further. Two slate calls, one would be like this slate call, the other would be a glass call with Plexiglas. In rainy or damp weather, the slate call will really deaden. Out in the rain you can't work it at all. So a variety of calls and about two or three different mouth calls. I knew a fellow one time who told me he knows a guy and I've heard it from several people. This guy would go out and he had a small blanket, he would roll out and it had all these pockets with all these box calls. He'd take the first one out and

Something that really makes noise and kind of sets them off. You can set them off by slamming a car door, sometimes, or by blowing a horn or slamming a gate on a fence. You need some chalk for the box call and something to scratch up this slate call. Ziploc bags because I never know what I'll run into the woods that I sometimes can't identify, and I want to pick it up and take it with me, or when you're lucky enough to get a turkey. Whole set of nippers that whenever you set up in a place against the tree or behind some brush, you may want to create an opening. Or just where you want to sit for the good spot, there's always something sticking up there that you might need to trim away. It's not in the vest, but with you would be a foam pad of some kind. That makes the sitting for long periods of time more comfortable. I am able to sit for long periods of time with just moving my eyeballs, trying to be very still. That seat really helps. And then another thing that I won't leave

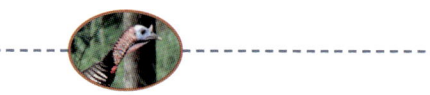

home without and that's a Thermacell. I'm telling you what, it's just God's gift to turkey hunters. I've been in a swamp one morning in Florida, and it was just starting to get light, and birds were real close. Two birds gobbling away and I heard mosquitos buzzing around my head. *My God, I forgot my Thermacell!* So you sit there, knowing these birds are close enough they can probably see you, but you got to let that mosquito just keep chewing away.

Did your use of calls change by state or region over those six years?
PRIES: No. I would tend to just start off the morning with a box call, or sometimes a slate call, to make a soft tree call. And then, if there weren't any birds within hearing distance and you were spending

from the hillside beyond. At first, we made a series of yelps, then put the call away. From there on, over about a 20-minute period, it was just scratching in the leaves: a rhythm of a hen scratching. Then wait. It might be minutes until you did it again. But the bird would gobble and be closer, and kept closing the distance, responding only to the scratching in the leaves.

Did you ever think about how many birds you killed during the morning and how many later in the day, proportionally?
PRIES: Well, certainly, the majority were in the morning. I don't recall specifically, but very few states allow all-day hunting. Pennsylvania is one that allows half-day hunting during the first half

> Where you can see the bird, the bird might see you. There's some people that like to do that. I don't like to because there's a good chance he spotted me coming in no matter what time it is. All you have to do is to spook a deer and that alerts a turkey. If he hears anything at all, he's got you spotted.

some time there, I'd do the box call periodically. For different sound, I'd mix it with different types of calls with the slate call. But it's generally the same routine.

Was there one turkey voice that tended to be your go-to, that you found yourself using again and again, or was it a mix?
PRIES: There were really two. First, I would be most comfortable and most proficient with the slate call. And then, once a bird was coming and was close enough that you were concerned about him spotting you, I'd put that away and go to the mouth call and make some soft calls. The other thing—I don't know how many people mention it—is a call that I like to use by merely scratching in the leaves. I was hunting with a fellow down in West Virginia. We brought a bird across an interstate,

of the season, and then it's all-day hunting in the second half of the season. But in most states, you hunt until noon and that's it.

Where you had a choice, did you like to hunt all day?
PRIES: Well, I'd say it's a mixed bag. Most people will tell you that off the roost or first thing in the morning it's great. Then mid-morning, after they've been with the hens for a while and the hens go off to their nest, that's a great opportunity. And then again, in the afternoon, when they're not with the hens, it's a good opportunity to strike their interest.

What is your typical approach at daylight when you're hunting a roosted bird? You know it's there.
PRIES: If you know the area where the bird is going to be roosting, and you have a good idea of

This Weston County, Wyoming Merriam's fell to the ring of Jon Pries's Benelli Super Black Eagle as it launched a load of old Winchester XX No. 5s. The photo was taken in front of a recently fallen cottonwood by his friend, Craig Ausmann, from Newcastle, whom Jon "bumped into" while hunting nearby the year before.

what tree he's gonna be in, then it's a good plan to get within 70 or 80 yards. I don't like to get closer. Where you can see the bird, the bird might see you. There's some people that like to do that. I don't like to because there's a good chance he spotted me coming in no matter what time it is. All you have to do is to spook a deer and that alerts a turkey. If he hears anything at all, he's got you

spotted. So it's a matter of getting 70 or 80 yards away from him, and get set up against a good tree and be comfortable. I tend to wait until that bird either starts fluffing around or moving or starts to talk. Certainly, if there are hens nearby and they start a little tree talk, soft calling, you want to chime in. Because you gotta let him know that there are not only hens there, but just one right

here. And you hope he likes your sound a little better and comes in your direction. But if you don't let him know you're there, he's gonna go right to those hens.

And so do you change your approach after fly-down?
PRIES: Yeah. Then it becomes when some people would run and gun. I tend to like an area where I think birds will be moving most of the day. I call a lot less than most people, I think. I think a lot of people, unfortunately, get influenced by television or videos where it's constant calling. The TV shows and videos don't include all those dead period times when they're not calling. They're waiting.

Makes sense.
PRIES: So I will call maybe every 15 or 20 minutes and it might just be short and soft, and the next time, it might be more of a louder, longer series of yelps or different sounds over that one time in the 15-minute period, or it might be a scratching in the leaves and no call at all.

What weather conditions do you find most difficult?
PRIES: Wind. To me, wind is the worst condition.

How do you deal with it?
PRIES: On the quest, you hunt, regardless. On a windy day around here, there are a few other things to do, so I get them done, because if tomorrow is not windy, you can enjoy a more successful day of hunting. But when you're out there and you've only got a certain spot, and it's windy, to me, then it's a matter of moving around. The birds are a little more alert because of all the noise and things moving with the wind. They're constantly on alert. Use your binoculars. Try to spot the bird and then get in closer to them and do some calling and try to bring them in.

How do you deal with hung-up birds?
PRIES: Go quiet, for me, go quiet. I mean, you can try and cut and really get them excited and stuff, but they'll just stand there and gobble. More often

than not, success, for me, comes from stopping calling, and let them get really curious and let them try to come to you.

How about henned-up gobblers?
PRIES: Good luck. Probably the greatest success for me is when a gobbler is with hens. Try to go back and forth with the hen by mimicking her calling. Try and get her mad at you. Do whatever they do. If they yelp a certain number of times, just give it the same thing back, maybe with a little more volume. Or if they cut, then you cut right back, and just go back and forth with her. She's gonna get mad, hopefully, and come in to check you out and drag the gobbler with her. There was this bird in California. When I heard it gobbling it was with hens. There was a little creek bed draw between us. I thought I would sneak up this creek bed to get a better calling location. When I came up, I didn't shoot because he was busy mounting the hen. I was a gentleman. I waited until he was done and then I shot him.

You gave him a helluva going away party! [laughing]
PRIES: Yeah, yeah, yeah.

Who is or was the best turkey hunter you ever knew?
PRIES: Well, there are people that I heard about by reputation. Ben Lee was a big bear of a man. My friend, Chuck Matter, who I initially was turkey hunting with in the spring, had hunted with Ben Lee. He was from Alabama, deceased now. He died at a younger age than he should have. But he was a big bear of a fellow—silent, moving through the woods, an excellent turkey caller, and he never could read a NO TRESPASSING sign. [laughing] But he was just an amazing turkey hunter.

How about hunters you've met?
PRIES: Well, if I could pick anybody I'd like to hunt with, it would be Rob Keck. Anyone who has had anything to do with N.W.T.F. knows about him. I can't believe there's anyone on the face of the Earth that had more opportunity to be turkey

hunting with extremely good turkey hunters. He has to have known and met and probably hunted with every one of them. He's been in so many scenarios, places and opportunities. He has to have learned more than anybody I have ever known.

Have you seen any notable changes in the sport of turkey hunting over the years?
PRIES: There are more turkey hunters, when there are less hunters than there used to be. So I think turkey hunting is growing in popularity more than any other aspect of hunting, more than hunting any other species.

as someone who's written multiple books is Tom Kelly. He wrote a very popular book, the *Tenth Legion*, and a whole series of books. Mostly stories, a lot of it humorous. He's fun to read. But there aren't a lot of turkey hunters that have written three or four different books. I mean, you can put down your knowledge as a hunter, I think, in one book and that's kind of it.

And finally, what's your next challenge in turkey hunting, if you have one?
PRIES: I had wanted at one point to go to Mexico and hunt turkeys in every state that was available there, but I won't do it; it's not safe to. There are

> When I heard it gobbling it was with hens. There was a little creek bed draw between us. I thought I would sneak up this creek bed to get a better calling location. When I came up, I didn't shoot because he was busy mounting the hen. I was a gentleman. I waited until he was done and then I shot him.

How about attitudes of hunters or approach to the sport—anything about the hunters themselves you think has changed in the last generation or so?
PRIES: Most of the guys that I hunt with or know tend to wanna know things. Hunters today seem to be interested in knowing about the bird, the biology and the life cycle, the habitat and the habits; and, like me, feel that's an important part or certainly very interesting part of the whole of turkey hunting.

So that's a good change.
PRIES: Yes—that hunters are becoming more knowledgeable about, more interested in the species.

Since you now know what it's like to write about turkey hunting yourself, do you have a favorite writer or writers on the sport?
PRIES: Most, most turkey writers that I know have written one book. One of the ones that stands out

some nice people and some good hunting in Mexico, but you have to be careful. I have hunted in two states in Mexico, and I enjoyed the heck out of that. My God, I loved the culture and the food and the people. And the countryside was just beautiful. I'm glad that I did it and got the coolest turkey. When I went to Campeche, I got the ocellated turkey—a peacock-looking bird. And I went to New Zealand and got 10 gobblers in three days. The rancher said, "You wanna kill turkeys? My God, get out there and kill them all!" There was a roost tree that had a canopy about the size of this living room and under it, I'm telling you, there were piles of turkey poop that were two feet deep. Amazing.

4

James
Wilhelm

HOME:

Eagle Rock, Virginia

OCCUPATION:

Retired stainless-steel machinery maker

FIRST WILD TURKEY:

1978, Virginia

COMPLETED U.S. SUPER SLAM:

2012, Arizona

Daniel Rorrer

HOME:
Pulaski, Virginia

OCCUPATION:
Retired pump and well driller

FIRST WILD TURKEY:
1997, Florida

COMPLETED U.S. SUPER SLAM:
2011, Rhode Island

I TRAVELED TO SOUTHWESTERN VIRGINIA, into the heart of the Blue Ridge Mountains, to sit down with two turkey hunters who had each killed birds in all 49 states. While they lived little more than an hour's drive apart, they had never visited each other. We met at the home of Joyce and Daniel Rorrer overlooking the New River. James Wilhelm was already there, laughing and swapping stories with Daniel. After greetings over coffee we made our way up a sloping driveway to Daniel's workshop, a spacious, modern shed where he fashions turkey calls from local woods: purple heart, walnut, butternut, chestnut, cedar, cherry, mahogany, poplar, persimmon, sassafras, maple and pecan.

ABOVE: All his life Daniel Rorrer has been skilled at making things. Here he displays a selection of fine woods he selected and cut specially for a limited edition of 100 box calls commemorating his U. S. Super Slam, begun March 27, 1997 and completed June 6, 2011.

We walked slowly, keeping pace with James, beside us, who said he would walk but had to do so leaning on a cane.

He remembers it was September. Bow season was coming. James—"Jimmy"all his life—was working on a deer stand right behind his house. He had his safety harness on while up in the tree but not going up and down the store-bought wooden ladder. He knew better. When he hit the ground he didn't pass out but came close. When he tried rolling over to get up he couldn't. At least he could move his arms and his legs and his feet.

Jimmy's wife, Judy, was in Roanoke, 35 miles away, babysitting their grandson for the weekend. A couple years back she had talked him into getting a cellphone. Never had one; didn't think he'd use it. Now, he lay there on his back, immobile, in a world of hurt. He pulled the phone out of his pocket. Some of the boys where he had worked at the machinery company in town for more than 40 years were on the rescue squad. He heard the sirens start up.

He doesn't remember much pain but he remembers them hauling him into the helicopter and his clothes being cut off. Then the world went dark. When he woke up in recovery the surgeon told Jimmy that four of his vertebrae were tied together with pins and screws under a 14-inch scar. Now, when he tries to bend over to try to pick up something off the floor, he can't. That's okay. Of four spinal operations performed in the same hospital that weekend, he's the only person who walked away.

Wilhelm had just one turkey to go to complete his Super Slam. Earlier that year he had killed No. 48. When he fell off the ladder, he had already lined up his next spring hunt on the San Carlos Apache Reservation in Arizona. He had the coveted tag. That would be state bird No. 49. It crossed his mind: *am I ever going to get it?* But he shook off the doubt. Of course he was going to Arizona—if he could walk and hold a gun he was going. First there was rehab. When he got home he was supposed to move around as much as he could stand. Four weeks out of the hospital he was deer hunting with a rifle, climbing hills with his brother-in-law.

He asked Jim Ward, a friend who makes sweet turkey calls, to accompany him West. They took a camper. They drove way back into the reservation and camped out. It was April, during the second season of the year on the reservation, on the second day of their hunt, that Wilhelm tagged his Merriam's turkey. He had No. 49.

Jimmy had come a long way from 1958, when he was 10, and Daddy took him squirrel

hunting. Jimmy's grandparents lived in the country, and he'd stay with them once in a while. Granddaddy had an old spring-loaded cocked-type .22. And they always joked about the thing shooting around corners. There was one inviolable rule: safety. From the first time Jimmy pulled the butt of the little rifle up to his shoulder, he was told what a gun could do and how to handle it. Years later, he taught his kids the same respect; he's teaching his grandkids that now.

Right about that same time, in the late 1950s, 15-year-old Daniel Rorrer was trying to convince his mother to allow him to take his father's old 16-gauge H & R single shot into the woods. Daddy was too busy with the farm; he hadn't shot it in years. Daniel's mother was afraid of the gun. She made sure the boxes of shells were kept locked in a cedar chest. Mother was a registered nurse and had seen what gunshot wounds did to human flesh. Daniel promised he would be careful. Finally, she relented, and Daniel started coming home with squirrels and rabbits for his mother to cook.

Daniel, like Jimmy, grew up on a farm. As youngsters they knew hard, dirty work. Once Daniel was old enough to be on his own, he decided that the farm life wasn't his calling. So he drove to Roanoke and got a job with Martin Well Drilling. He worked there a couple years. Then he moved on to the N & W Railroad, to keep the bills paid while he started his own drilling company. He bought a churn drill, a cable tool that was very slow and not very productive. But it's what he could swing. Still, he couldn't help feeling he was signing his life away. He worked and worked and worked—60 to 90 hours a week. He acquired an air-rotary rig. He hired people with experience, one of whom was so loyal that the man worked for Rorrer until he was 86. Daniel lost much of his hearing. He neglected his children, two girls and a boy.

Daniel's now-grown daughter Kimberly recently underwent two liver transplants. Kim's daughter, Chelsey, donated half of her liver to her mother to make the first transplant happen. Within one year that liver failed. The family was devastated. Kim went back on the liver transplant list. Her condition continued to deteriorate. She underwent endless procedures to keep her alive while waiting for a new liver. Some days were better than others. On one of her better days, Kimberly asked Dad to take her hunting. She had hardly shot a gun before, let alone hunted.

Daniel gave her a 20-gauge shotgun, and helped her get the proper choke tube and ammo. Together they patterned the gun. He put her on the shooting bench and set up

the turkey target 30 yards away.

She is right-handed but she shoots left-handed. After she took a few shot, her father said, "Kim, since you're right-handed, why don't you try shooting right-handed?" She looked down the barrel. She looked up and said, "Dad, I can't see the target." And Daniel said, "Well, you need to open the right eye to able to shoot right-handed." She had the wrong eye closed. She told him, "Dad, don't you tell this on me!"

And on opening day, last April, Daniel called in a beautiful longbeard for Kimberly. Months later, at his kitchen table, Daniel handed me a snapshot of Kim, posing proudly with the bird. "It would absolutely make her day if you could find a way to fit our hunt into your book," Rorrer said, his eyes welling up.

"She had never hunted before," I said. "Did she ever tell you why she wanted to go?"

"Yeah, she said, 'I want to do something my dad loves.'"

Miraculously, following this interview, the doctors found a match. Kim underwent a second liver transplant. It was a success. The newest family turkey hunter—a turkey woman—alive, healthy and happy.

ABOVE: A proud James Wilhelm with his 10-year-old granddaughter, Jessica, and her first wild turkey: a 20¼-pound Virginia fall bird with a 10¾-inch beard and one-and-a-quarter-inch spurs.

Why do you hunt?

DANIEL RORRER: It's something that I've enjoyed thoroughly. When I grew up it was kind of a way of life, food on the table. Nothing like getting up in the morning, too, before the sun comes up over the horizon, and going into the woods, and everything waking up, going about its day. And just all the beautiful creations that the good Lord put out there for us. It's just something money won't buy.

JAMES WILHELM: That's exactly how I feel. It's being with nature. I mean, you're actually part of it when you're out there doing this, and all the reasons he gave were exactly right. Main thing, I grew up with it, it's a food source, and you don't go to a Kroger and buy this or that or whatever. Like you say, you just get excited when the sun comes up, and the birds are singing. And at home, the turkey is great. That's what you're out there for, but you enjoy it no matter what. Whether you get anything or not.

RORRER: For sure. It's not about killing something every time you go out there.

WILHELM: That's not gonna happen.

RORRER: It ain't gonna happen. [laughing]

Probably a good thing it doesn't.

WILHELM: [laughing] You'll be home real quick.

RORRER: But just being out there and enjoying the fresh air. And it's so mind-relaxing to just get away from your everyday routine and gives you a good time to just think.

Ever since you were kids, you guys have hunted all kinds of wild game: squirrels, rabbits, ducks, deer, etc. What is it specifically about wild turkeys that keep you coming back to them?

RORRER: When that turkey starts gobbling, and he's a long distance off, and he begins closing that gap, and you know he's coming to you. And you're making the right calls and the right decisions and the right set up where he'll come within shotgun range.

WILHELM: You're fully in nature. Like I've told you before, I started out duck hunting, dove hunting, whatever; got into the turkeys, and I reckon the turkeys are more of an individual thing. You got one bird. Well, you might call in more than one bird—I've called in seven in one bunch. But it's not like duck hunting, where you've usually got partners that's sitting there with you. But the turkey is more of an individual challenge.

RORRER: It is more of a challenge.

WILHELM: Yeah. It's more just being able in full Mother Nature and like you said you don't win very often, but I mean that's part of it. A lot of turkeys won't come—they're not programmed to do that. So if you can catch them, one day you could be calling that bird, and he won't come. You can keep trying that for weeks, and nothing happens. But all of a sudden, one day, you catch that bird at a certain point, and he comes running. I don't know how you explain it, but they just changed. They're just different.

RORRER: If you persist and hunt that bird long enough, he's gonna make a mistake sooner or later.

WILHELM: Yeah, sometimes three or four years! [laughing]

RORRER: Exactly.

WILHELM: I've done that one.

Daniel Rorrer (left) was honored in 2012 by Burt Carey of the National Wild Turkey Federation with awards for harvesting a wild turkey in all 49 states—the organization's first official U.S. Super Slam with registered birds.

RORRER: The thing about it, too: a gobbler, the reason he's gobbling, he wants that hen to come to him.

WILHELM: Right.

RORRER: But he's going almost totally against his nature to come to you. But sometimes his better judgment just overrules his mind.

Daniel, when did you kill your first turkey?

RORRER: My first turkey was way back in the '60s, when I was deer hunting. In the fall, before we had spring hunting.

WILHELM: Same thing, exactly the same thing. We used to as a family. The uncles, we'd get the younger guys, and we'd go out and drive deer. In other words, it's a deer drive. That's what they call it. We set standers up, and the guys would walk through the woods and push the deer out. Well, that's where I got my first turkey, I was on a drive. And I happened to have a shotgun because we jumped grouse or whatever, and that was my first experience, like you said, was on a deer hunt. And I never did get into the spring hunting until probably I was 35 years old, before I ever started gobbler hunting.

RORRER: Yeah, back then, I carried a rifle, a 30.06, and a shotgun over and under. It was a Valmet, if you've ever heard of them. They're made in Finland.

WILHELM: I've got one.

RORRER: Sometimes coyotes and things would come in, too, and they'd be out of the range of the shotgun. And if you wanted to take one of them, you used a rifle, that same thing you deer hunted with.

Wilhelm in 1986 with a prime spring bird in his native Virginia.

When did you decide to go for spring gobblers?
RORRER: It was 1997. And I never had spring hunted before that. Like I said earlier, one of my friends got me into spring gobbler hunting. And his name was Steve Price. But he had a relation with the employer where he worked, and every morning during turkey season he was gonna be in the woods turkey hunting. He was a machinist, and then he would go in at 9 or 10:30 or so up in the morning, and work over that afternoon, and do the work that he had to do.
WILHELM: I've done that for years. I mean, I just happened to work in a place that was country-oriented, and if you come in late, that's fine, so long as you called and told them or let them know the

day before. Either worked over, or made it up some time ago, it's at the end of the week. And I tried to, a lot of it was when I first started, it was like that. Then I found out later, if you hunt all day, you do a whole lot better. But the first couple hours of the morning, if you can get a bird to work that early, that's when most of the birds are taken. But 10 to 12 o'clock, I found out now, it's a great time to hunt turkeys.
RORRER: Yeah.
WILHELM: But I never was able to cuz we had to go to work.

When you decided to hunt turkeys the right way—the way you enjoy doing it now—how

long did it take you to get one?
RORRER: It was pretty much most of the season. Yeah, on my own.

Do you remember mistakes you made?
RORRER: A lot of them. [laughing] Moving and calling too loud. You can't be slapping at mosquitos, nothing. You just gotta let them eat away, and be still as you can be.

How about you, Jimmy? How long did it take you to get your first one, once you decided to really go after him?
WILHELM: Two weeks. All right, well, here's the thing. I had a friend who worked. We both had another boy at work, his dad and stuff, we got to be real good friends. And he allowed us to hunt on his property. And then there was a paper company they had laying in behind that, which you could buy permits for, okay? So, we bought a permit and hunted, but the first time I went hunting for gobblers, of course, this one boy went this way, and I went up the ridge. I was pretty good with a box call—that's all I had back then. I just had started the diaphragm stuff, and that shook me pretty bad. So, it took me a while to get used to it, but I went up the ridge. Got up, the wind was blowing probably 40 miles an hour, just whipping. You can't hear very good and stuff and, I was standing there on the ridge, and I thought I heard a dog bark. And I kept listening. It was back the way I came in. I said, *that ain't no dog.* I started going back down there and got out on a big old flat. You could see probably 150 yards, some oaks around, but it was pretty open. And about that time, a bird gobbled just out of sight. So, what do I do? I lay down on the ground like an army commando. Got the gun up. Prone position. And I called. He gobbled, answered me. Here he comes, all right? Well, he was coming down an old logging road there. It was in the woods, it was pretty open anyway. I didn't have nothing around to get behind or up against, so I just hit the ground, and the bird came up there within about 40 yards, at least I thought it was. I had an old 1100 shotgun, and I had two-

and-three-quarter shells, that's what I started out with. And I shot that bird, and he started flopping. I jumped up and was going to shoot him again, and looked down, and the second shell had jammed in the gun. So, I worked on that, and when I looked up, he was gone. Never found that bird, never seen where he went. I looked under every log [laughing] within a half a mile there. I don't know where he went. I still, to this day, never did know. But that was the first week I was hunting, and like I said, made fatal mistakes. But the next week after that, there was a next ridge over, and I took my first bird.

You didn't jam the shell that time? [laughing]
WILHELM: No, I paid real good attention.
RORRER: I had that happen in Minnesota. I had a Benelli pistol grip shotgun, 12-gauge. And in some way of handling that gun, I must have got a hold of the bolt on that. I worked the turkey, and he came all the way down this long grass bottom, and when he got in shotgun range, I pulled the trigger, and it just clicked. Then another round had come out of the feed chamber trying to get into the barrel, and here I got two there, and I'm trying to dig the shell out. Well, lo and behold, that turkey, he got out of the distance of where I shouldn't of even shot him, and I did shoot and missed him. So, that cost me my turkey that year, and I had to go back the next year to kill my turkey.
WILHELM: That's what I say, you learn a lot.
RORRER: You gotta let that Benelli slam together.
WILHELM: Slam shut, yep.

Daniel, did you have a mentor, someone special who really taught you the game of turkey hunting?
RORRER: Yes, this Steve Price that got me into spring outdoor hunting. Steve told me, he said: "Daniel, why don't you try a spring gobbler hunt? I think you'd like it." And I told Steve, I said, "I don't know with coming out of the spring, and with having the business, and everybody wanting work done, I just don't know about it." So, on the way home, my wife and I discussed it. And she told me, she said, "Honey, you've worked hard all of

your life—why don't you take the time to do something you might enjoy?" So I called Steve and told him that I would go with him. He wanted to go to Texas. Well, I never killed a bird. It was real windy, it was raining, it was just a bad situation. Then the next year we decided we'd go to Florida and hunt. Well, we went down there, and both of us killed birds there. And then the following year, we went to Colorado and into New Mexico and hunted both states on the same trip. And after that, Steve stopped turkey hunting and traveling, but he continued hunting turkeys here in Virginia. They started having children, so he quit going, and I kept going.

much. In other words, he knew what it was. He hunted everything, like me. But for some reason, my wife says the disease got me. It become full time.

So he introduced you to the sport.
WILHELM: Right. I can't say there was any specific person that showed me or told me or whatever.

How did you learn—the turkeys taught you?
WILHELM: Yeah, I mean, but I don't know. I've always had a knack for being able to hunt things. My wife would tell that we wouldn't starve to death. But part of it's just common sense, if you think about it. Reading an animal's reactions, the

> Reading an animal's reactions, the terrain you were hunting, that kind of stuff. My thing is location. You gotta be where they wanna be. That's the main thing. If you're not where they want to be, you're not gonna call that bird. He's not coming.

You were hooked.
RORRER: He had me hooked. And I was so charged up, I just couldn't quit. In traveling all over the country, and seeing all the different parts of the states and everything, meeting new people, and friends and memories, it just don't get no better than that. And just that challenge of that turkey gobbling, and when he's coming in. And he gets 35, 40 yards, and your heart's just rushing. I mean, it feels like it's coming out your chest. It gets at 10 yards. . . . [laughing]

How about you, Jimmy, did you have a turkey mentor?
WILHELM: Yes and no. My brother-in-law, actually, married to my sister. Me and him duck hunted a lot. That's where we got to going into different things. Of course, he married into the family. He got me, took me, went out turkey hunting a couple of times. But he never was into it that

terrain you were hunting, that kind of stuff. My thing is location. You gotta be where they wanna be. That's the main thing. If you're not where they want to be, you're not gonna call that bird. He's not coming. That's just my belief.

How do you figure out where they want to be?
WILHELM: Good guess. I mean, sometimes in scouting around, you find a special strutting area where they want to strut.
RORRER: Yeah.
WILHELM: The way we did things, you go to a state.

And you'd never been there before?
WILHELM: Right. But the bird still will wanna be on the high points. I mean, not always, but a lot of times. They can hear better, they can see. They can see stuff coming. The deer's the same way. They'll go up on a side of a ridge and lay down

where they can see forever and so it's just like he said the challenge of just of being able to. . . .

RORRER: Being a good woodsman.

WILHELM: Yeah, that's it.

RORRER: But I had a gobbler on opening day about the second or third year that I was spring gobbler hunting here in Virginia, over at Draper. I had a farm that was about 400 acres that I could hunt on. I was the only one they allowed to hunt on it. And it was windy as it could be that day. And I had a jake and a hen decoy sitting out. And I decided about 10 o'clock that I just couldn't hear a turkey gobble and they couldn't hear me calling. So I decided I was gonna get the decoys up. And I went over and got one up and stuck it in my vest and I had a mouth call in my mouth. And a box call. So I yelled really loud on that box call.

WILHELM: Just to see if you could get results.

RORRER: Holding that mouth call—he was right there. He'd come right up this ravine and he almost busted me. By the time I get my knee to the ground and my gun across the other knee, he was there. And I started calling on that mouth call and finally calmed him down a little bit so he wouldn't just go airborne and go out of there and I killed that turkey by just doing that combination.

WILHELM: Well, you never know, like you said. I was hunting the ridge one time at home. And I was walking down the ridge. And I think the turkey was coming up the other side. And there was a few rocks in between us. And, all of a sudden, I heard that turkey start to putting. And going away. So all I did was—luckily I had my mouth call in—I just putted back at him. He come back. I mean, hens do that. He didn't know what had spooked him. He just knew there was something there and you just told him it was another turkey.

RORRER: He seen the movement or something.

WILHELM: Right. So, I mean, you don't ever know how they will react. It depends on what they saying and whatever.

What single piece of advice would you give a beginner?

RORRER: Watch videos, learn some about turkeys, talk to people—experienced turkey hunters. And let them give you some good advice. And just don't over-call or call out. Know that call before you go out there to hunt. I think, sometimes, people, they go out and don't know what they're doing. They educate the turkeys.

WILHELM: You can hear them in the woods. Okay, you'll know right off the bat. There's a guy—I'd be over there and you're hunting—and he'd go [making strange calling sounds]. I mean, turkeys don't do that.

RORRER: They know that's unnatural.

WILHELM: [laughing] And, yeah, they over-call. I mean, there's a lot but the first thing would be not to over-call. But, like he says, you gotta watch what you can. All the videos. Of course, most is gonna show you, most of them are successes. But it gives them a general idea what turkeys are about. You're not gonna be successful every time.

RORRER: Not every time.

WILHELM: I had a boy at work. He was a rookie. He wanted to go. He went above his house on a ridge. He called up a jake. First morning. Okay, killed it: *This ain't nothing.* Three years later, he ain't killed another one. [laughing]

RORRER: That's right.

WILHELM: But he learned real quick that it ain't as easy as it looked to start with.

RORRER: Exactly.

Have you kept track of how many turkeys you've killed over the years?

RORRER: I haven't.

WILHELM: I have no idea. That wasn't the point to start with.

RORRER: It's the furthest thing from my mind.

WILHELM: I can think back and probably try to add this, that and the other. I'm not sure. I probably couldn't get them all. I could probably come close cuz I got memories of most turkeys I've taken. But especially before I started the quest, I killed a lot of birds before that.

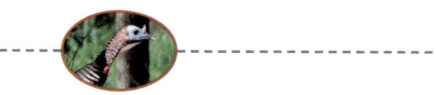

Do you recall the moment when you actually started thinking about the quest? You had killed a lot of birds before, as you've said, and you'd hunted numerous states. But at what point did you say, *Hmmm—maybe I'll try to get a wild turkey in all 49 states?*

RORRER: I do. Mark Taylor at *Roanoke Times* found out I had completed the World Slam. So Mark contacted me and he's wanting to do a spring article in the paper, and he wanted to know if he could come and talk with me. And I said "sure." So he came out and we sat in there at that bar, and talked for an hour or so. He brought his photographer with him, and had taken pictures of some of the turkeys that I had killed in the past. And he said, "Daniel, now that you've completed this feat, what is your next goal?" I hadn't thought about it. So I sat there and pondered on it for a little while.

WILHELM: It didn't take long, did it! [laughing]

RORRER: And then I said, "Mark, I wanna take a turkey and every state that has huntable turkeys." In 2001 was when that he came and talked with me and interviewed me, but with already having some of the states behind me in doing these slams, then I started in 2002 planning other states, and I give it everything I had. I just got so wrapped up in it I was like a drug addict. [laughing]

How about you, Jimmy? Do you remember a similar sort of epiphany when you said, "I'm gonna go do this?"

WILHELM: Yeah, mine was after I had a Grand Slam. It was in '98. I almost had two. I went hunting in '97 in West Virginia. It's the first out-of-state bird I hunted. And it was with my son; he lived over there. So I registered that bird. And when I did a slam, of course, I registered those birds and it was kinda like him. I got to the end of the year and I said: *You know something? I just wanna be able to say that I did this.* And I knew other people had

done it or was in the process: Rob Keck and stuff and everybody knew. I didn't really pay attention to who was doing it or when. It was just kinda a personal thing. This is something that an old working boy stiff that's been able to achieve this.

So it was relatively early on.

WILHELM: Yeah.

And it wasn't like you had been to 30 states or anything close.

WILHELM: No. Like I said. I had the one and I'll tell you the truth, why I registered for that bird I really don't remember. I know I was with my son. But when they did the slam, I said these birds are registered. I said now that's four more states. I went to Florida, got one down there. Then I went to Texas, we got two in Texas, me and the boy. Went to Nebraska, I got two there. And I had a friend wanted us to hunt in Missouri with him and I come back through and got a bird there. Then I killed one in Virginia. If I'd a had that other Florida bird, I'd a had two slams in one year. And, course, that's where I started so I really wasn't pushing for two birds. But after I looked back I said "damn." [laughing]

RORRER: Yeah, when I completed this U. S. Super Slam, they didn't actually have a name for that slam. So I called to force the N.W.T.F., force their hand, in coming up with a title for that slam.

WILHELM: They had to have something.

RORRER: They just didn't have it and they actually put out online, on the web, for people's suggestions to come up with a name for it. And some guy made a remark of, tell that rich dude to go back to golfing. This turkey hunting's for us poor folks. [laughing]

WILHELM: Yeah, right!

In which year did each of you start and then accomplish the Super Slam?

FACING PAGE: Awash in memories: Daniel Rorrer took this turkey on May 12, 2017 using his late father's old H & R single-shot 16-gauge—the very first wild turkey the gun had ever taken. Daniel's dad hunted squirrels, rabbits and sometimes crows when they were pulling up his corn after planting. Dad was born in 1911 and died in 1995. Over the winter his son had the gun expertly restored and re-blued in his father's honor.

James Wilhelm with the 21-pound Rio he took on March 11, 1999 on the Big Island of Hawaii. It took him two hours.

RORRER: I started in 1997, March of 1997, and completed it May the 5th 2011.
WILHELM: Well, my first one was registered in 1997 in West Virginia, and I finished it in 2012.

What was your first state?
RORRER: Florida.
WILHELM: West Virginia.
And your last?
RORRER: Rhode Island.
WILHELM: Arizona.

As you were making your way to 49, was there any particular strategy, any rhyme or reason, to the order of the states?
RORRER: I tried to do the far-away states while I was younger. At that time my knees had begun to bother me somewhat. And they just gradually got worse, but that's what I concentrated on is the far-away states and then I started closing in to the ones closer. I hunted as many, as seven states in one spring and harvested turkeys in seven states in one spring.

Did you fly to most of those states?
RORRER: I did. Later down the road, some of the folks that I hunted with, some friends, some of them didn't like flying, they wanted to drive. But I like getting there, getting a rental car, and getting in the woods and scout some.

You took the opposite approach, Jimmy. You drove every place.
WILHELM: Yeah, mine was the opposite of what he did. I started locally, more on the eastern side of the Mississippi. For one thing, it was vacation time. I worked a job and had like three weeks. So that's what kinda set those. Mine was set kinda like

he was talking. Mine was three-day hunts, I limited it to three days and then, of course, I had a travel day or something. It depends on where I was going. But I lined the states up by the season openers. In other words, I started in the South, I did some of them in March or whatever. But the earliest state was where I started and then three days there a day and then this state here opened. It's kinda how mine and it went from south to north. The western states, I tried to get them in there as soon as I could.

And you said that you essentially budgeted yourself three days in each state.

When you finally pulled the trigger on the bird in your 49th state, what were your feelings?
RORRER: It was kind of a sad moment that it was over, but it was a rejoicing time. I had accomplished the thing that I set out to do. And the good Lord blessed me with health and the ability to do what I did. I was just totally overwhelmed.

WILHELM: When I pulled the trigger on the last, it was right at daylight in Arizona. And it was two or three gobblers coming in. Had a buddy sitting up in the truck waiting on them. He didn't kill them. And I just sat there. It just took me probably 10 minutes to decide I'm gonna get up and go over. You just didn't want to lay a hand on that

> It was kind of a sad moment that it was over, but it was a rejoicing time. I had accomplished the thing that I set out to do. And the good Lord blessed me with health and the ability to do what I did. I was just totally overwhelmed.

WILHELM: Three days was it, right.

What if you didn't get your bird?
WILHELM: If I didn't get it, I had to go back. And, believe it or not, South Carolina I didn't get. Yeah, I mean, South Carolina's got plenty of turkeys. But I had one walk by me one morning in the swamp, him and about six hens. I could see the birds. I couldn't tell which one he was, that's how early that was and I didn't get one that year.
RORRER: I hunted in South Carolina with my three trips.
WILHELM: Well, that's what I'm saying. California was that with me. I mean, I passed up some jakes, some places that I probably shouldn't have back then when I was doing the planning. But I did kill a few. But they were usually the last day result. Mine was kind of the opposite of what he was. Mine was more dependent on I was working two jobs, counting the farming when I first started. Didn't have but so much time.

bird but I wanted to be sure it was dead to start with, I mean. [laughing] But relief and pride more. I mean, there's some pride in it. You finished what you started. It's just it was the end, the end of the quest.
RORRER: I was blessed to have my good friend Scott Culpepper with me and Brian Teff from DNR in Rhode Island and there was five birds came in. And Scott was sitting to the right of me. And I was sitting over here and I was telling Scott there's five turkeys. And I said I want us to get a double. As the turkeys continued to come in, they started getting a little nervous like. So Scott told me to shoot and I said, "No, I wanna get a double." So he was actually turned wrong. If he'd a moved his gun he'd have spooked the birds. So I waited until the last bird was almost out of range before I shot that bird because I wanted to give him an opportunity.
WILHELM: Good thing you didn't. Last bird— that's tough.

RORRER: Yeah, we went to a different area on another tract of public land, and stopped cold and I backed off. The turkeys was in a green field. It was like they just wanted to hang out there and I backed off and called. They about ran over me. Yes, so he killed his bird in the same trip. But we had made, that was the fourth trip to Rhode Island to hunt turkeys.

WILHELM: Yeah, public land up there, it's *tough*. I mean, tough. Wildlife management areas and stuff. You've got some traffic for one thing.

RORRER: Right.

WILHELM: I've seen a lot of hunters in there, but it's tough.

RORRER: Yep. Nevada's another one because out there the turkeys when if you was out scouting, riding around in the afternoon before the hunt, and you could see a turkey 500 or 600 yards out in the field and you stopped that vehicle. It's like he had a jet motor in his rear. He was *out of there*, telling me that people were shooting at them from vehicles with rifles.

WILHELM: A lot of states out there, Wyoming is one of them, that you can shoot a bird with a rifle. You can in Virginia, but I've never done it. I did do it during deer season. But I quit that, too. It's a law, but, yeah, them boys out there, that's their thing. I was in Pennsylvania this spring. It wasn't no rifle hunting, but I was hunting a wildlife management area. And I was setting just off the road, a couple hundred yards, with four or five vehicles going by before daylight, going on back into the area. I was out front. And it was probably 15 or 20 minutes after, here come a car or truck pull up, get out and call, sit there a little bit, call again, get back the truck and go on. Slam the doors. And then, another guy it was probably 10 o'clock, here come another one doing the same thing. Course, at 6:30, I killed my bird and I was setting there watching all this. But, yeah, I mean the old boy got a friend up there, and he took me out to this wildlife management area and said you can hunt this ridge down, there's a big valley. I went down, there was a field there, old strip mine was what it was. And I was on an old road going in, I just went to the nearest tree and sat down before daylight. And right after daylight, well right as daylight was starting, right across the road from me, five gobblers opened up. This is public land. On up the ridge there was three more gobblers. Round behind this guy's house there was three more gobblers. And they were all back in there hunting deep. I said that's fine, you all go on by. [laughing] But I set there and made a few calls. Didn't do much, just a few yelps. They gobbled across the road. They was probably 200 yards, 250 yards. And after it got daylight, I heard them gobble on the ground. Two of them were gobbling going away. I made a few more calls. Never heard nothing. I was sitting there watching out that little road coming in. Here come three turkeys. So, well, okay. All of a sudden all three of them, [gobbling sound], full strut. I called a gobble, killed my bird. I mean, they came on down the road. Public land. First I missed was about the end of the first week, I mean, it'd been in for a week up there. And I'm sitting there waiting on a boy to come back and pick me up. He'd dropped me off and he wasn't gonna pick me up till 11:30. So I just sat there—wasn't nothing I could do. Well, I heard a bird gobbled down the valley. This was about 9:30. A little bit later he gobbled closer. Hmmm. So I am sitting there. After a while didn't hear nothing else and right down in the woods below I hear some [sound] heavy clucks. I kept looking and looking. Couldn't see nothing. Another about 15 minutes here comes a turkey on the edge of the woods right at me. Couldn't tell what it was until I stood up and it had about a 10-inch beard. He got within about 25 yards and he stood there and looked at me real funny, you know how they do. I said, *there's something wrong here*. Another truck's coming in. Pulled up there at 10 o'clock and the bird run down there to the woods and stopped. He was just standing there watching him. [laughing] Probably knew the license plate. So I went back the next morning. I wanted to go back the same place. There were plenty of birds there. Boy took me and dropped me off again. I went in there and actually took a pop-up blind with me this time. And I put

On April 26, 2010, Scott Culpepper (left) from Georgia and his hunting partner, Daniel Rorrer, harvested this eastern double on state land in Great Barrington, Massachusetts, in the Berkshires.

it up, got in it and put out a decoy and I was waiting on that 10-o'clock bird. Well, I didn't have to wait long. There was one over where he was the day before. Well, he flew down in the car parking area. He strutted there for an hour. He gobbled and answered me but he wouldn't come. About 8 o'clock, I called a few times and he done crossed the road. He was on my side. I said, *hmmm*. Here come a couple hens up by me and went on up over the hill. And the reason why I use a pop-up now, sometimes, is you can't sit still for hours. I don't care who you are. But I look at the road and here come that gobbler strutting down the road and there was a hen up on the bank, right above him, and she was coming my way. And he got there about 70 yards and I wasn't calling no more because he could see. And all of a sudden here come

a truck again. When he started in over there, the turkey, of course, he ran toward me, thank God, instead of flushing. He ran up to me and the truck stopped up there and the turkey turned at about 40 yards and stuck his head out like that and I killed him. The guy was standing up there. Two days, two birds on public land. [laughing] That's why some people say I got the horse shoe. And the boy I was hunting with he didn't kill nothing.

RORRER: That's like in Utah, I was hunting private land there, but I couldn't get a tag so I paid $600 for a landowner's tag to be able to hunt there. They give the owners so many tags to kill turkeys on your property. And they are allowed to sell them. It helps them pay the taxes on the land. So I had decoys sitting out and turkeys are gobbling all around. I had to get up real early in the morning

cuz I had a long ways to walk. And I had hens out around the decoys feeding around the decoys. And all at once, I hear this noise—it was a four-wheeler. It was coming in and there was an open field in behind me but the gobblers was up in the ridges. They could hear all the sound they're carrying right up above them seeing them and they shut up. And these two guys get off that four-wheeler and starts walking up through the middle of an open field with box calls, rapping on them things. [laughing] And they spooked the turkeys; they wouldn't say another word. It's impossible to hunt. So I just went away, come back later on that day, and killed my turkey. But people like that just they don't have a clue what they are doing.

Oregon, for instance. There was an outfitter that hunted everything else. He did turkeys a little bit. He took me out and said, "Go this way." That's it.
RORRER: You found the birds.

For this conversation, let's define a guided hunt as when a hired professional guide is at the shooter's side, as opposed to an outfitter who provides hunting access.
WILHELM: Okay, well, I've had probably about 10 different situations where either the landowner or a boy took me out the same way in Hawaii the first time when I was over there. The boy that took me up on the ranch to hunt, he sat in the truck.
RORRER: Well, Hawaii, when I hunted there on

> And these two guys get off that four-wheeler and starts walking up through the middle of an open field with box calls rapping on them things. [laughing] And they spooked the turkeys … people like that just they don't have a clue what they are doing.

WILHELM: And if they paid attention, like you said, and just read or watched some videos or whatever, they would know not to do that.
RORRER: Sure.

Were all your Super Slam gobblers taken in the spring?
RORRER: Yes, yes.
WILHELM: Mine, too.

How many did you take with a guide and how many hunting alone?
RORRER: I think it was four or five states. Just a few. I made a note here and I counted them up.
WILHELM: My question to you is gonna be, what do you mean by a guide? I had people take me and drop me off where the birds are. Let's just take

that Parker Ranch, one of the guys that took me out, he wasn't turkey hunter. Didn't know beans about it.
WILHELM: That, to me, that's not a guide.
RORRER: There was a limited amount of trees that the turkeys could roost in where I was hunting. And there was a long trench or gully that went toward the ocean, and he wanted me to set up down inside that gully and peek over the top and more or less stalk a turkey. I looked and I seen one tree on the back side of that gully. I refused to get down in it. I said: "I'm gonna sit with my back in this tree. If you want you can get behind me and video." I started calling and two gobblers came in with a hen. This hen, she went all to pieces. She was a dominant hen. I mean, she was fussing with me, we was cutting one another off, back and

FACING PAGE: Tax day bingo! On April 15, 2005, James set up in a field in northeastern Oregon and 20 minutes later called in this Rio Grande off a ridge on the other side of a creek.

After harvesting typical wild turkeys in 49 states, on May 5, 2016, Daniel took his first non-typical bird in Virginia.

forth. She came into the decoys and the two gobblers came strutting in behind her. So I was getting ready to pull the trigger on one of them. And just before I did, to my left, out of my side vision, I seen this turkey coming running just as hard as he could run. He was the dominant bird. He came down, ran the other two turkeys off, and they all disappeared up over the break. Well, this hen, she just stood there. And I mean didn't move a feather. She just stood there, planted there, and after things settled down then she started calling. And I thought to myself: *Well, it just don't get better than this. She's gonna be my caller.*

Did she perform?

RORRER: She called that dominate bird back in and I killed him, but I could take another bird, and the wind had got up real bad then. It was down in an area where there's some of this brushy looking stuff that don't grow very high, you know, and the turkey come in and he got in behind that. I couldn't get him to budge. So I told this guy that took me out, I said: "I been watching that bush. The wind catches it and takes it over." I said, "The next time this happens I'm gonna shoot that turkey." It was too thick to try to shoot through and kill him. When a big gust of wind hit that bush and took it over, I killed that turkey. The guy couldn't believe his eyes. He about freaked out. [laughing] But it was snow on the mountain. And you could see the Pacific Ocean. I flew into the island of Kona and that was 17,500-acre ranch and they ran 40-some-thousand head of cattle on it at one time. Patrick Fisher was the manager of the ranch. You don't think of Hawaii being one of the largest cattle states; you think maybe Florida or something.

WILHELM: Where I hunt, at Kalena Ranch, it's a working ranch, and back then when I first went in there it was just kinda me. I was the first one on there that actually paid to go hunting, the year I went. Then I went back last year and they actually changed the rules. They just hunted weekends so that the ranch actions could go on. It used to be a real big ranch. But what the boy told me, where we was, it was a pretty good size, but they, the family, had split it up in three different sections. I was only on one of them.

RORRER: Parker was still one of the largest working cattle ranches in the U. S. But while I was there, this gentleman by the name of Mike Curley, was coming in to guide for Patrick Fisher. So he actually owned a ranch in San Jose, California. So he got to talking with me and we were discussing about what I was trying to accomplish and he said, "Well, you just come out to California and hunt my ranch."

WILHELM: You learn there's connections everywhere.

RORRER: I went out there and he had one of the ranch hands take me out. I said, "I don't need a caller—just take me." So I started calling and he

FACING PAGE: A corner of the Rorrer trophy room. Top: ocellated wild turkey, April 5, 2001 in Campeche Mexico and the border of Guatemala. Bottom left: April 18, 2011, Clairborne, Tennessee. Bottom right: April 21, 2010, Petersburg, Indiana.

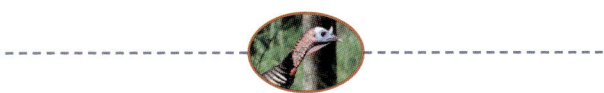

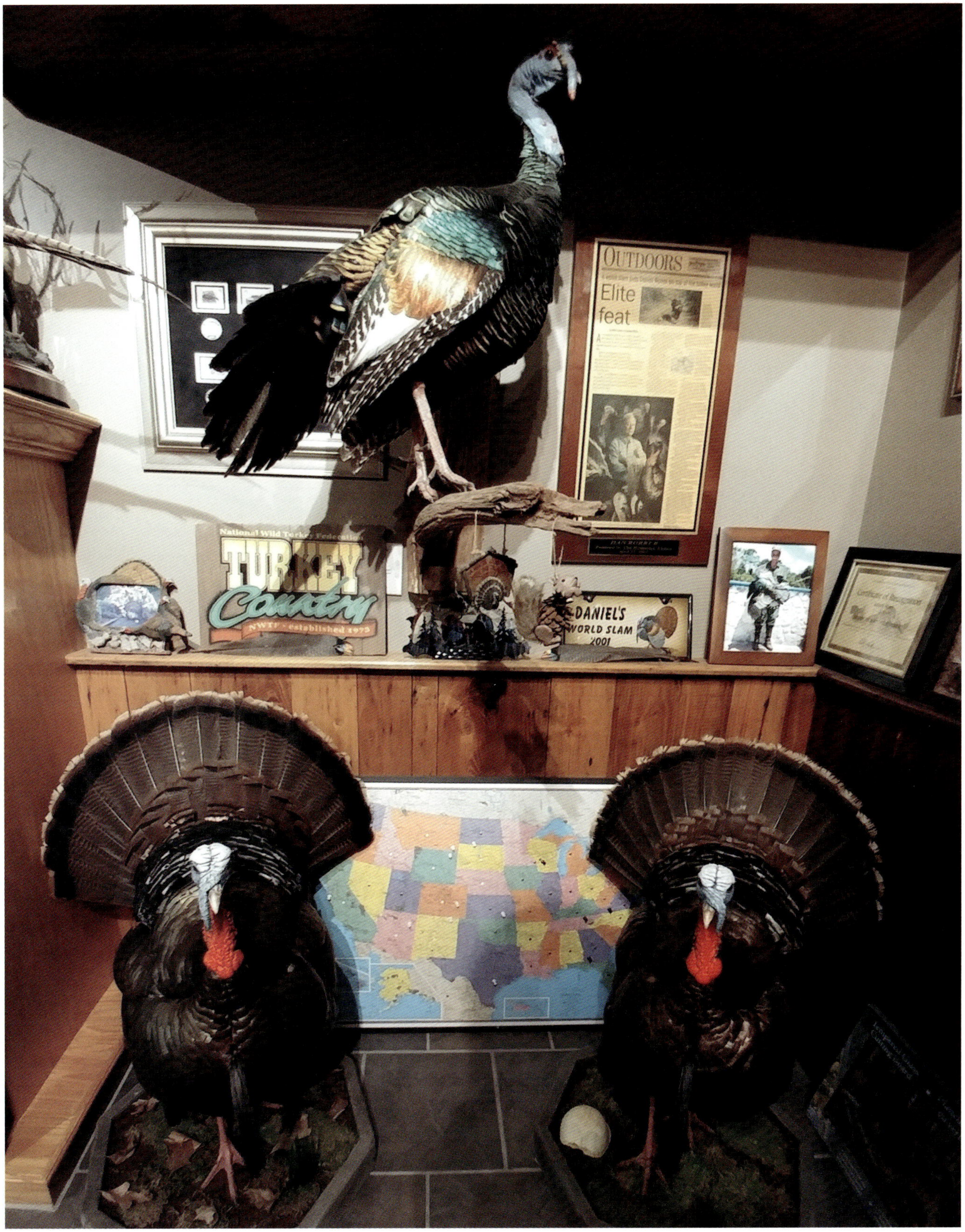
OUTDOORS
Elite feat
National Wild Turkey Federation
TURKEY Country
NWTF · established 1973
DANIEL'S
WORLD SLAM
2001

James with a Virginia bird from "a friend's place" in the Blue Ridge Mountains, May 19, 2012.

said, "That turkey is over a mile away." He said, "He's on another ranch and we can't hunt it." But I couldn't hear the turkey. So I waited about 15, 20 minutes and I called again and the turkey gobbled again. And he said he's closer but I still couldn't hear it so I waited 15 minutes more. So I called again and I could hear him by that time. We went back and forth for I'm not sure how long. But anyway he came in, crossed the road between the ranches, come under a barbed-wire fence, come up to my decoy and I shot it and brought five hens in with him. And the dominant hen that was fussing with me, she would not leave when I shot that turkey. I got up and tried to shoo her away. I'm doing this, and she's just running around with her tail fanned out and her wings.
WILHELM: Peeved.

RORRER: And she was so upset with me and I'll never forget what I said: "Sorry, honey, you'll have to find you another lover." [laughing] That's the words that I used.

Throughout your quest, did you ever get discouraged to the point where you wanted. . . .
WILHELM: To quit? No. Never. Never. Even, like I said, even when I broke my back, I still had Arizona to go—I was going some way or the other! And I still go. I've always been a very strong-willed and determined person.
RORRER: If I set a goal to do something, I'm gonna accomplish it one way or another.

Did that commitment ever put any strain on your family relationship?

RORRER: Absolutely not.

WILHELM: No, not once.

RORRER: My wife and family encourage me to do what I set out to do. And she sacrificed a lot for me.

WILHELM: People wanting to do it better have a good wife and mine is great. I mean, we do our things and we're individuals and she knows that. She does her stuff too.

When you were aiming to get a bird in a particular state or a group of states, what was your planning process? How did you sort of figure out, *Okay, next spring I'm going to do this?*

WILHELM: My planning was, of course, how much can I afford to do, okay? But it was mainly just what can I fit between that date and this date. What opens when and where, you know? I sacrificed a lot of hunting time in Virginia, because all the other states, a lot of them, are the same as ours. But when I got back from up North I had one week of the season left in Virginia. I killed three birds in seven days. Two days later, I got my granddaughter one. The last day of the season. She killed one using my gun. You don't know how proud that is, baby.

Jessie, the 14-year-old.

WILHELM: Jessie, that's right. That was actually her third turkey. She was 10 when she killed her first one. It was a fall bird, a 21-pound gobbler. One week later she took her second bird. It was a 12-pound hen with an eight-inch beard. She wanted to shoot a jake, but I wouldn't let her. I told her, "No, you're not gonna." I could have slammed, I could have had a slam if you wanna call it in hens. All the years I've hunted and I've never shot one, because I've never been interested in doing that. But for her, that bird was something she might never do again. And so she did take the hen. Then, she actually killed her first spring gobbler with my son a year after that. And then this spring, I got back and, of course, she was in school. And I took three days to get my first bird. Two days later, I got another one, and two days later I got another one. So that was on a Thursday. I was done. And I went out Friday, scouted a little bit, cuz I started thinking. He took one daughter and I took Jessie. And I got a younger one, she's starting now. And I had a bird for each one of them. I knew where there was one at. Seen them, knew they were there. And so the one I picked out for Jessie was on some distant kin of mine's property. And I had never asked him before. I called him up, and I said: "I got a granddaughter I wanna take down here. Is it all right if I take her?" He said, "Yeah, man, go on—no big deal." And so we went in that morning before daylight, set up a pop-up, got in it. Sure enough, right off ridge, right down in front of us, gobblers. I said, *okay, he had been working the creek bottom*. And so I called a few times and the same two or three more hens fly out. It was in an old pasture field, and they kind of went away a little bit. We were sitting there. I called again. Finally, they were starting to come back up the creek. Up the edge of the woods, there in the pasture. And the gobbler got within 60 yards, and he was right down over the back. All you could see was his head pop up once in a while. Well, one of the hens come way out in front of everybody else. She come on by the blind, and I think she was standing back here, looking in the back hole of the blind because something spooked her, okay? She didn't run, but kind of a fast walk. She went back and it took all the birds away. I said, *man, what the heck?* And so we sit there a little bit, probably 15, 20 minutes, I made a couple calls. Bird gobbled down the creek again, okay? So coming along and I called again, and he gobbled. He wasn't really 60 yards just out of sight. So he was coming out, and he was coming 40 yards. And she'd been shooting a lot of skeet and trap in a 4-H shooting team. She's pretty good, and she'd been using the 20-gauge that I got her, an over and under. And she was shooting three-and-a-half inch Hevi-Shot. And I said, "Now, it's going to kick you a little bit more than what you've been doing." So she thought maybe it was gonna be pretty bad. I said, "You know how to hold it, right?" I said, "If you hold it right, it's gonna kick you, but it's not gonna

hurt you." You know it ain't. So anyway, the bird came along, and I was hoping he was gonna get closer, but he started walking kind of sideways to the blind up to the field. He got there about, like I said, about even with us, about 40 yards, I said, "Kill him!" And she pulled the trigger, and she got him. I mean she nailed him good. She looked at me and said, "I ain't bad." [laughing]

RORRER: But in Kansas, when I hunted out there, they had some long cornfields out there.

WILHELM: They got them everywhere. [laughing]

RORRER: The thing about it, I had worked these two birds all the way across one of them long cornfields, and I had a decoy sitting out. And they had to come under a little fence, just a place where the deer had a good trail there, and a little brushy area down through the side of the fence. So I was setting up at the end at one of the openings there right against the brush, and the turkeys came under there, come over it and the back turkeys seen them decoys over here. They went airborne. I hadn't moved nothing. If I had another five feet, I could have killed him.

WILHELM: Some of them like decoys.

RORRER: Then the next day, I went out, and I called a hen in. She'd seen that decoy, and she was out of there. I said, *no more decoys.*

WILHELM: We didn't use it with my granddaughter either. I mean, I use them once in a while. But a lot of places, if you talk to the locals, you're hunting with this guy, and he says: "Would you all ever use decoys? Well, they don't really react too good to decoys." Unless I'm setting up a pop-up, and I know where I'm at in the field, usually field hunting or something, I'll use them a little bit them. But I'd never carry one in the woods.

RORRER: I don't either. But the thing about a field, if you don't have something out there. . . .

WILHELM: They can't see it.

RORRER: Everyone wants to see something when they come out there and, if he don't, he's out of there. He loses interest.

When you do use decoys, do you have a favorite?

WILHELM: I use Avian-X.

RORRER: That's what I use. I think they have the most realistic colors. They've got some others out there.

WILHELM: There's some new ones. I've seen them. They're real good-looking, but they're expensive as a dog. It's bad enough with an Avian-X. [laughing]

RORRER: Well, I paid almost $100 for these [pointing at decoys].

WILHELM: I know—that's what I'm saying.

When you show up in a new area to hunt, how do you go about locating the birds?

RORRER: What I did, I was flying to Window Rock, Arizona. And on the plane, I was seated beside this lady from Michigan. And I needed Michigan. So she asked me where I was heading, where I was going, what I was gonna do. And I told her that I was going to Window Rock for turkey hunting. And she said: Well, my son's a state trooper. He loves turkey hunting. Just come on down to Michigan when you get back. Here's my email. You email me and tell me you're home, and I'll get him to call you." Well, I went there, but didn't do any good with him. He had to go back to work. So I was on my own at a place that I knew nothing about. So I thought to myself, *Well, I got to make something happen while I'm here.* I thought, *You know, these people know a lot of farmers.* So when I got out of my car, this person was some kind of soil scientist or something. He'd been out to this protect the place. And I asked him and said, "You don't by any chance know someone that might let me turkey hunt on his property, do you?" And he said, "I just come from a place." And he said: "Here's the man's phone number. There was all kinds of turkeys out on the field, a corn field." So I called him. No answer. But I had the address and I put it in the G.P.S., and I went out to his place. Well, he was out working on some equipment is why he didn't answer the phone. And when I walked up to him, I introduced myself and explained to him what I was trying to do. And he said, "Well, we don't just let nobody hunt here." And I said, "Well, sir, you know, I've traveled a

Daniel called in this wary, early-season eastern bird from his blind near his home in Pulaski, Virginia, in April 2011.

long ways and all over the country trying to get this done." And I said, "I would really make it worth your while if you'll just let me hunt one day." So he said, "What's it worth to you?" And I said, "Is $100 enough?" So he accepted it and let me hunt. And I called in two longbeards the very next morning and was out of there. But that's something that you gotta be prepared for, if something fails with whatever source you have.

You need to think on your feet.
RORRER: Exactly.
WILHELM: They got a program for Illinois, it's Access Illinois, okay? And what you do is you join, you pay $25, send a check, and there's places in Illinois that will let you hunt. Some of them for nothing and some of them all the way up. Well, the first time I went through them, they give me a bunch of names. And I called up this boy, he actually charged for deer hunters and stuff. But I said, "What does it cost me to take a turkey on here?" "Fifty bucks." *Damn, I mean that ain't no big deal.* And actually I had a room. [laughing] He had a little farmhouse and he let me stay. My buddy in Pennsylvania, I stayed at his house on public land. That's the kinda stuff that's no problem. He's an uncle of the boy I work with and we've known each other from the first time I went up there. But, yeah, I mean, it's just like that. People ask me, how do you find these places? You

Wilhelm with three Georgia birds taken on one day during the second week of the season in 2013. Son Greg also tagged three birds on the same day.

gotta ask.

RORRER: Exactly.

WILHELM: I killed a bird in Ohio. It was on a slam, actually. But the lady had five acres. She was on the edge of a subdivision. The land behind her, they were changing into a subdivision. And she said they had turkeys in the yard. So me and my wife went up there one fall. I looked around: a lot of turkey signs all over the ridges. House over here, a house down here, one across. *Okay.* So the next spring, I went up and got in there and went out the first morning and set up on the hill, right just off of her line about 50 yards. I could see her house. A turkey gobbled right out over in the bottom. They was building a house right over on the next ridge—you could see it. He was gobbling. I could see him down there. He had two hens with him. He'd answer me every time I'd call. Would not budge. All of a sudden, behind me, about 200 yards, a turkey gobbled. I said, *I'm hunting the wrong bird,* so I got up and turned around and got on the other side of the tree. Made two more calls and killed him. I mean, there was houses everywhere. So you don't know where you gonna find

one. I mean, like I said, on five acres.

RORRER: Yeah.

WILHELM: It was out of town. It was legal. But it was right in a subdivision.

RORRER: I think the strangest thing I'd ever seen happen, this turkey was gobbling, running uphill, coming toward me, and he changes his course for some reason, and come in from a different angle. Well, here I'm sitting with my gun where I last heard him gobble [motions holding his imaginary shotgun sideways]. And you don't do none of this. Cuz he'll bust you. But I was gonna wait. What I was gonna do is wait until he went into strut or

but they don't get the pressure that the easterns get here. They're hunted heavy compared to the western birds.

RORRER: Eastern are the hardest subspecies there are to hunt. If you can kill an eastern, you can kill any of them. But I think the next one would be the Osceola in Florida.

WILHELM: Yeah, but you were talking about that Texas bird, I mean, the ones you were talking about over there in Hawaii or something. They're Rios. You can call the Rios and Merriam's and they will come for two miles.

RORRER: They were the easiest turkeys to kill that

> I think the strangest thing I'd ever seen happen, this turkey was gobbling, running uphill, coming toward me, and he changes his course for some reason, and come in from a different angle. Well, here I'm sitting with my gun where I last heard him gobble. And you don't do none of this. Cuz he'll bust you.

step behind a big tree or something, and then I was gonna move the gun. Well, he went behind this big tree. And I moved my gun. But before he stepped behind he looked over his back. He put that tree between me and him. I never seen him another time.

WILHELM: I had that happen in New York. Just straight away, never seen him again, never know where he went.

RORRER: That's the way this bird was.

WILHELM: Like a ghost. Yep, all they gotta do. The eastern is the worst. I mean, you can't move on an eastern bird at all.

RORRER: No, you can't.

WILHELM: The Merriam's are a different story.

RORRER: Yep.

WILHELM: If you're pointing this way, and a bird comes up over here, just pull the gun around and shoot it. It takes him about three seconds. . . .

RORRER: Yep, to soak in!

WILHELM: *Hey, what's that?* They're a little slower

I ever killed.

WILHELM: But they will come further than any. The easterns—you've gotta be within, I don't know, 150, 200 yards. I've seen them come 300 but they were really hot and looking.

Do you remember the single most difficult bird that you did get—one that stands out?

RORRER: *Didn't* get?

Did get. A bird you killed. Or one that eluded you.

RORRER: Yeah, there was one in Georgia—Georgia was another state I had to repeat two or three times.

What was the circumstance around getting that bird?

RORRER: That bird, he would commit and start in, but he would just hang up. He would not cross that line. My friend, he'd tried it back. I called. Nothing. Couldn't make nothing happen. But he

was just a tough bird, he was an old bird, he had been hunted before, and he was very shrewd. He didn't get that old by being dumb.

How did you eventually fool him?
RORRER: I didn't kill him. Then another time when I went down to hunt with Scott, he was in the same season. I went back down and Scott had to go back to work. He worked at Kodak and he told me where to go and down to the cabin where he was a member of the hunting club. He told me where to go and I went out there. Several turkeys were gobbling at a distance, but I called a jake in, and I didn't wanna shoot the jake. So I came back and Scott seen me and he said, "I sure hope that he got his bird." Well, I didn't. And I remember telling Scott, he asked me, he said, "Well, did you see anything?" I said, "Yeah, I could've killed a jake, Scott, but I just guess it's just the good Lord's way of us being able to hunt more together."
WILHELM: What happened to me in California, I passed up jakes. But the second time I was there, I had four jakes, maybe five. I was trying pick out one—I wasn't sure about him. He had a full fan but not a hell of a lot of beard. Last day hunting. I've gotten a lot of bearded birds since in the same place. But for the slam itself there was at least four out of the 48 that I took jakes. And I could've done it quicker if I'd have shot some other jakes.

How about an individual bird that was so difficult that you never did kill him?
WILHELM: Kinda the same situation. I worked one for like three years, the same bird on the same ridge. And he just, like you said, he had the mentality that I never did kill him. Somebody else must have. It was on public land but I don't think so. I walked in on guys that was calling him and I'd back off and leave. He was still there the next year. [laughing]

How do you know it was the same bird?
WILHELM: Same tree. [laughing] I've done that twice. I did kill one. Took me four years to kill him. And I finally did. That was when I first

started hunting; it wasn't part of the slam. It was one of my first birds, I'd say it was probably in the first dozen that I ever shot. I couldn't tell you what year it was now. But it was on the same property, same place I'd missed that one when I was laying prone. He was on the other end of the ridge in a deep hollow and I walked by him in the dark going up the side of the mountain. It was about 75, 80 yards off that old logging road that I used. He was roosting right there. Well, I got up on there one day. He gobbled back down there. Before daylight he was gobbling. So I go down, get set up, get close to daylight, he gobbled, I could lean over and see him sitting in a tree. *All right.* I even had him triple gobble. He'd fly down, he'd answer me. I'd call. He was on the next ridge over. So I get up, go around, set up on him again, call him. He'd answer me. Next time I heard him, he was on the next ridge over. He would not come, all right? Never did come. I did that for like three years and all I was using was a box call cuz that's all at the time that I knew how to use. I hadn't started the mouth call much. And that start of the fourth year I said, *I am not gonna call that bird again.* And the reason I knew it was the same bird, he was in the same tree. Every time I heard him, he was in that same tree. Well, I got up there one morning, he started up. And like I said, I had done decided I wasn't gonna call him. I took my box call. There was a stump there beside the road. I laid it on that stump so I'd know where to find it. And I knew if I took it with me, I was gonna use it. [laughing] Okay, now, I got back down there and got over in front of him there about 80 yards. It was still dark. That bird would gobble in the dark. I got down prone like I did the first time but this time it was an army crawl. I got within 40 yards of that tree before it got daylight—enough to where I was afraid to move anymore. Of course, now, there's rattlesnakes in this hay! [laughing] But I got the gun up. It was the best I could just kind of down over the ridge from a tree. I could see him, sitting on a limb, gobbling. And, I mean, it was peeving me off. And I said, *when that bird touches the ground, he's dead.* [laughing]. And when he hit the

Daniel with an early-season Georgia turkey, March 30, 2010.

ground, he didn't take one step. He got shot. I owed him one. [laughing]

RORRER: Most of the time them birds were like that. When he gobbles, all the other turkeys know better than to gobble.

WILHELM: They shut up.

RORRER: They will not gobble.

WILHELM: Me and my brother-in-law killed one like that.

Have you ever purposely passed up a bird that you could have killed easily?

RORRER: I have.

Why?

RORRER: Because I wanted a better bird. [laughing] I was culling him out with spurs and beards. I just wanted a better bird.

WILHELM: I'm with him. I've passed up a lot of jakes. And I passed up a lot of bearded hens.

RORRER: I have, too.

WILHELM: I know a buddy of mine, a friend, young dude, he's got a slam with hens. But it's just something that I have never even thought about doing. But my granddaughter that day in the fall, yeah. I got no problem with it. I mean, to me, when I got my son his first bird, or when I got my granddaughter her first bird, that was actually as exciting to me as anything I've ever done.

RORRER: Yeah. I have never been able to hunt turkeys with dogs. Gerald Austin down Buckhannon, Gerald has two good dogs, turkey dogs. Well, Gerald invited me to come down and hunt with him and this was in the fall.

WILHELM: Yeah, he's in our club. Makes calls, too.

RORRER: So the dogs knew where the turkeys

Wilhelm's elusive "Little Rhody" turkey killed from 10 feet way on a diary farm in the Ocean State, April 29, 2010.

were. They ran in there and busted them turkeys up. And they came back and Gerald and I were sitting here like this with a little blind like there. And those dogs laid down right beside us. Never moved a muscle. And those turkeys wait until one starts calling and then you start calling. And that flock is trying to regroup. You can call the whole flock in. But it was an experience being able to hunt with them dogs like that.

What's the strangest place you ever killed a gobbler?
WILHELM: You got mine: in the backyard in that subdivision.

RORRER: Well, in New Jersey, when I hunted with Jim Hascup up there. We seen these turkeys down on the road, on the main road. And him and his buddy, Bobby K.—I can't even pronounce his last name, it's a name about that long. But, anyway, we went and set up. Houses everywhere. We set up on this little place where Bobby said that we could hunt. And they had these rock walls coming around. So we started calling and Jim, he was using a slate call over to the left of me. And Jim said, "You're right-handed, aren't you, Daniel?" I

said yeah. So, I had set up and the turkeys come down and jumped up on this rock wall and three of them started walking down that rock wall. And I didn't even wanna shoot them off the wall, but if I'd moved the gun, he would have seen me or tried to turn. So, I just slipped the gun up to my left shoulder, didn't do none of this stuff. Just eased it over real slow and slipped it up in my left shoulder and shot that turkey when he hit the ground. And I thought, *My word, I ain't never seen nothing like this.*

WILHELM: That's not the craziest story, if that's what you wanna know. I tried to find a place in Vermont. I actually called a game warden up there. I called the guy. I said, "Do you know anybody up there that allows turkey hunting?" He said, "Well, I don't turkey hunt, but I got a guy that works for me that does." He gave me his phone number. I called him up. This is a game warden, now. They ain't all bad. [laughing] Some of them are butts, but a lot of them ain't. They do their job and it's fine. But this boy actually said he knew a farmer. Used to be a dairy farmer. He's running cows. And you can hunt, actually, you can hunt up there any-where. It's not posted. You don't have to ask. I don't do that. I wanna know my boundaries. I wanna know where I'm at and who I'm on. So, the boy took me in the day before I was hunting, in-troduced me to the farmer. He said, "You go." He said, "You might run up on somebody else because it's not posted." I said, okay. It actually was a farm that the game warden hunted on a regular basis. So, that morning I went up mountain ridges, and over some pastures, and all upper ridge. Got up on timber ridge. And there's daylight. And one started gobbling on a ridge right above me. There was no way of getting to him. I mean, he was on top. That was it. So I'd call, he'd answer. I'd call, he'd answer. And I was sitting there. Started down the end of the ridge out of sight, an old hen come by me, jumped up on the log beside of where I was sitting—it was probably 10 yards. She jumped up on there, and jumped down, and went her way. I said, *well, that's about the end of that deal.* And I'd been hearing, when I first started, there was two

gobblers down the ridge behind me. They were closer. Here we go. I'll get around the other side of the tree again. I did. Made a call. They were closer. Made one more call. They answered me and then they come within sight. One of them was strut-ting. The other one wasn't. They come on up there. I let them get within about 30 yards. And I picked out the strutter and I killed it. Well, the other bird run down in the woods about 80 yards and stopped. So I called again. And he just stood there for a second, then he went on. I said, okay. I got my cellphone out and called my wife. We're sitting there on the phone telling her I got my bird and I looked up and here he come back. I mean, he done left. I hadn't called no more but here he come back. It's the same bird I can tell by the beard blends and stuff. He walked right up there and I shot him so I had two birds. I don't understand why he come back, I still today haven't figured out why he came back. That was crazy.

RORRER: Yeah, I killed one in Wyoming. There was three birds gobbling. And they would gobble and it sounds like they're closer and then they'd go away. And then the cottonwoods there. And it was windy as it could be on that particular day and the turkey, he would come just almost in shotgun range and go back. Finally, I called all three of them in, and when I shot that dominant bird, I probably stuck his head way up. And when I shot him, and he hit the ground, these other two jumped on him. And they started plucking feathers. Looked like I body shot him. [laughing] I mean, there was them little old short feathers everywhere.

WILHELM: I had that happen in South Carolina.

RORRER: They thought, *Well, I guess it's time to get even with you, big boy!*

Have you ever even remotely considered what these 49 states cost you?

RORRER: Lord, I don't even wanna think about it.

WILHELM: Let's see. A condo. [laughing] No, I'm serious. I don't care. I know the boy you was talking about that had his article in a hunting magazine about doing this on the cheap. There ain't no cheap.

RORRER: There is no cheap way.

WILHELM: I don't care. There's just no cheap.

RORRER: Even if you had every hunt that you didn't pay a dime for the hunt itself.

WILHELM: By the time you pay for the rooms and the gas and the travel, and the hunting license.

RORRER: Exactly.

WILHELM: It's not cheap.

RORRER: The hunting license is very high in some of these states.

WILHELM: Yeah, it's $300 in some of them. For a turkey.

Time aside, the expense is definitely something that somebody considering pursuing a Super Slam has to seriously consider.

WILHELM: That's the first thing, baby—you don't live at all without it. [laughing]

RORRER: Yeah, Yeah.

WILHELM: That's the main thing. Another thing is it takes a lot of planning, You better do the research you have to. Like I said, I plan mine at least a year ahead. If you don't, a lot of times you can't find a place to hunt.

RORRER: A lot of these states are draw states.

WILHELM: If you don't draw it, you don't go. But, yeah, I mean, I think now a lot of the draw states are pretty well 100 percent the first bird you draw but it's like Michigan now, I think it's draw, but it's for one week.

RORRER: Right.

WILHELM: Wisconsin's the same way. You've got

> I was hunting close to the fence line and turkeys come in, I called them in several times on that side of the fence. But it was posted; I wouldn't shoot them. I could've easily have killed either one of them. But I respect the landowners enough to not do something that ain't right. I'm just not gonna do it. It ain't worth it.

WILHELM: Even with trespass fees for a Florida bird, you can't get a Florida bird now even if you hunt on your own, unless you go public, which is almost impossible. If you go down there it's a $1,000 trespass fee. That's nothing: no guide no nothing, just trespassing. That's the cheapest you can find.

RORRER: Yeah.

WILHELM: A lot of them's $2,000 and $3,000.

RORRER: There are a few for $1,800.

WILHELM: They gotcha. [laughing]

Are there any other major considerations for somebody thinking about doing what you guys have done?

RORRER: Like I told you, a good wife. If you married you better have a good wife. A good understanding wife.

five seasons. You can have one of them. Like I said, I don't really care no more. Used to be that I would try to get lined up for the first week. I've killed birds the last day.

RORRER: Yes, I have too.

WILHELM: Especially in Virginia. I've done it in other places. But it don't matter to me no more. It used to. I thought the earlier, the better. You get the dummies And you got some ones out there. There's more birds at the first of the season. They're not worked with as much. Trampled over or people calling them or whatever. But the later birds, you get bigger birds.

Better birds?

WILHELM: Yeah, they're better birds. You get the ones that had the hens, that don't have the hens no more. The last two weeks of the season here

In 2004, Rorrer was impressed with the 175,000 acres of land to hunt on the Parker Ranch in Kamuela, Hawaii.

you can hunt all day.

RORRER: Now you can.

WILHELM: Yeah, this year I didn't need that, but years past, since they started that, I come home, hunt in the evenings after work.

RORRER: I've had to unload my gun right at 12 o'clock. I'd have turkeys I was working that was committed, that was coming to me, and that was the law. And even last year, I killed two birds here on this farm, not far from here, three or four miles. And every single time, I would call two birds in. If I'd have had somebody with me, every time I went, we would've got a double. But then, I was hunting close to the fence line and turkeys come in, I called them in several times on that side of the fence. But it was posted; I wouldn't shoot them. I could've easily have killed either one of them. But I respect the landowners enough to not do something that ain't right. I'm just not gonna do it. It ain't worth it.

WILHELM: But like some states like Georgia, you kill three birds a day. You got three birds, they'll let you kill them all the same day. And me and my son done that. We had an outfitter down there and we paid to hunt, nobody showed us. He just said there's birds here and birds there. We went out that evening, listened a little bit, heard a couple gobbles, but went out the next morning. Son went one way and I went another. At 6:30 I called in three birds, killed two of them. Went back to the cabin. My son had been working one but he couldn't get him to come. So I went over at 8:30 with him, we set up 9 o'clock, I called in one from the back side. I was on the back side of the tree, he was on his side and I could see him raise his arm. But he killed him. That evening we split up again and went to some food plots. He killed two and I killed my last one, and the boy said that it had never been done before. It's luck. I don't care. The birds have got to be there for one thing.

RORRER: And when I hunted Wyoming and South Dakota, was gonna hunt Wyoming for the morning hunt, but we heard about a front that was coming in. So we decided to go to South Dakota first. So went over there and first setup, me and a guy from Georgia that owned a poultry slaughterhouse down there. He killed his turkey. I killed mine. We got a double. Come back to

May 4, 2009—an eastern beauty. James Wilhelm's first wild turkey in Maine's Androscoggin River Valley.

Wyoming that afternoon, second setup, both of us killed a bird. A little bit lower than him there and I couldn't really get a shot, but he could and I told him to go ahead and shoot. And when he did, as soon as that gun went off, I sprung up on my knee and this other turkey's trying to figure out what was going on and then I shot him. But two states in one day like that.

Do you have a least favorite state?
RORRER: Rhode Island.
WILHELM: Nah, I got a honey hole in Rhode Island. I can't say that. It's on a dairy farm.
RORRER: But when you go to the place and don't hear a single gobble. You get one gobble in three years.
WILHELM: The public land in Rhode Island, it's bad. I went there probably two years before I ever found a farm. And I never seen a bird. Seen one feather. But, yeah, Rhode Island was tough until I found a good spot. I can't say that. I say, for me, it was New Mexico because the weather, at the time, the first time I was there, and the terrain I had to cover to get that bird. And then the second time, it was the same thing. I hunted a spot. I didn't eat, for once. But the second time in New Mexico I killed a bird the first day. But it was like the Mojave Desert. It was during a drought two years ago or three years ago and it was bad. I didn't hear but one bird and I killed one bird. For the quantity of birds and the chances, New Mexico was probably my worst. Now, I had other states that it took me three years to kill a bird, South Carolina and California. Two of them was because of the turndown. Jakes was the start one time but they had the birds. It wasn't because of the birds—it was me.
RORRER: Well, you know, Delaware was a state that you had to come and take their hunter safety course and that was the biggest joke that I have ever sat in a classroom in my life.

You actually had to go there?
RORRER: Yeah.
WILHELM: Yeah, it didn't matter if you had. . . .

In order to hunt there the next spring?

WILHELM: You have to go there in the summer. And it's nothing. It's not even a hunter safety course.
RORRER: Scott and I ended up teaching the class.
WILHELM: The guy that seen me walk in that were teaching this class, he looked at me, I told him what I was trying to do. He says, "You don't need to be in here." I said, "I know, but I got to have this paper."
RORRER: Right.
WILHELM: And they teach rookies, and I understand why. They tell them what camo does, what it's for. What the birds are, what to look for. But you gotta have that little card that says you've had that course.
RORRER: It don't matter if you've got a hunter safety card in 48 more states.
WILHELM: No, you gotta have that. And it don't mean nothing.
RORRER: This guy that was teaching the class, he got a slate or a glass call, I forget what it was, and he was trying to show everybody how that call worked. And he's running that striker and it's just skipping and screeching and awful sounds you ever heard. And he said, "Well, I've gotta take this call in and get it tuned." I thought, *Well, all you need's a piece of sandpaper or Scotch-Brite.* [laughing]
RORRER: But anyway. . . .
WILHELM: Yeah, now I'm gonna say pretty well, though, the first Delaware bird I got was on private property. Come running in, I mean running. I whistled, the bird came across, the guy was watching me, he's a friend of mine now. The bird come running across the cornfield. I had a decoy out and I yelped and he would not stop.
RORRER: He was determined, wasn't he?
WILHELM: I actually shot him on the run. I didn't want it moving, but I had to kill him, I mean, he was coming. He wasn't gonna stop.
RORRER: He wanted to be killed.
WILHELM: I don't know. [laughing] But the last time I was up there—actually, last year again—and it was on a wildlife management public area and it took me two days. But there was five birds on that place and I end up getting one. There was one group of three and I killed one of them. Yeah,

you start, Delaware's hard, but there's birds there.

RORRER: I hunted in Walton, New York, on public land and the bird had committed. He was coming to me and just all at once he shuts up. And I thought, *Well, he's either gonna come in silent or he's seeing something he don't like.* So I waited a little bit, and I heard the leaves ruffling behind. Like rain. Yup, I heard the leaves ruffling behind the tree, behind my back. And I kinda turned real slow and it was a coyote stalking me, calling that bird.

WILHELM: I had a bobcat do that.

RORRER: And that turkey had done seen that coyote and I knew it done messed my hunt up. So I just wheeled around and rolled him. One time I

tore all to pieces and you're not getting anything calling, and it gets later on in the day, I just find a place and sit down. If I'm at a good place, where I can stay hidden pretty good, then I call about every 15 minutes.

What about you, Daniel, what is your key to scouting before a hunt?

RORRER: I do that, I try to get there a little bit early and kinda walk around a little bit. And talk to people, too, where I have permission to hunt and find out where they had seen turkeys.

You mean a day or two early?

> You look for scratching, any kind of turkey sign. If you find a place that's tore all to pieces and you're not getting anything calling, and it gets later on in the day, I just find a place and sit down. If I'm at a good place, where I can stay hidden pretty good, then I call about every 15 minutes.

had one come in on Draper and I wanted that gobbler so bad. I let that coyote walk right out of there and not knowing, not realizing, that he had done messed me up. That's when I first started spring hunting. And I made myself a promise then: I will never let another one walk.

WILHELM: I had a bobcat stalking me, actually thought I was a hen. Coming right up the ridge, right? I mean, he was coming.

That's flattering to the quality of your calling.

WILHELM: Well, maybe. [laughing] But I didn't wait till he got that close. I spooked him.

What's the secret to scouting a new area?

WILHELM: I don't have much time to scout. Main thing is, I usually start calling at daylight, a little bit after fly-down time. If I get an answer, okay. If I don't, I'll move. You look for scratching, any kind of turkey sign. If you find a place that's

RORRER: Yeah, sometimes I'd get there a day early. And just try to get some information and use coordinates on the G.P.S., where people had hunted there previously, to have waypoints.

WILHELM: Just somewhere to start.

RORRER: Where they killed the bird.

Do you prefer to sit and wait or to run and gun?

RORRER: I do both. If I don't get no action I'll go.

WILHELM: Well, it's more of a walk than it is a run anymore. [laughing]

RORRER: Exactly right.

WILHELM: Back in my younger days, I don't know about you, but before I started looking for the slam and whatever, if I heard one gobble two miles away, I was gone. Not always the wisest decision cuz usually, when you get to there, there's one gobbled where you were.

RORRER: Especially if you had called it.

WILHELM: Yeah, especially if you called it. There

Daniel Rorrer's daughter Kimberly in 2015 with her first wild turkey. She had never hunted before. Kim had endured a very difficult liver transplant and told Dad that she wanted to be with him in the woods doing something he loves.

James took this Maryland bird in the spring of 2015 on the first day of the season. Jimmy walked an hour into state land before first light.

was a lot of running, gunning stuff to start with. I found out you ain't gotta do that.

RORRER: No, but if you walk though and you call little bit. . . .

WILHELM: Take your time and listen, and then if you don't get no action, walk a little further and call.

RORRER: Try again. Somewhere you gonna strike a hot bird.

WILHELM: If you get no answers, no nothing, I'll find me a place and I'll sit down. And I've killed a lot of birds in the last four or five years. And not only just before the slams—doing that because they'll come in and not say nothing.

RORRER: Exactly. I've killed a lot of birds that ain't said a word.

WILHELM: Afraid to come in.

RORRER: But if you've got a turkey gobbling and you know where he's at, sometimes you can move somewhat, close that gap some.

WILHELM: Yeah, if you hear them.

RORRER: As long as you know where.

WILHELM: But if you've got one that's not gobbling, you don't know where he's at.

RORRER: He most likely's gonna bust you.

WILHELM: Or you gonna spook him and not know it.

Let's talk a little bit about gear, equipment. During the course of your quest for 49 states, what was your favorite shotgun?

RORRER: Benelli. I love the barrel action of the Benelli. I like the shorter barrel on the gun. Cuz by the time you put a choke tube in it you're gaining two or three inches. But I think, too, the shorter the gun the easier you can maneuver through the woods, instead of hanging limbs and stuff, especially if you're carrying it over your shoulder.

WILHELM: But the action on it.

RORRER: The action on it's just great.

WILHELM: I've went all the way from, when I first started, was an old 1100. Wasn't even camo. You don' have to have camo, but it helps. Used the two-and-three-quarter-inch shells but went from that to 1187. Yeah, I liked that real good. Actually, that was my first Hawaiian gun cuz you had to register it when you took it over there. I do have another 870 that I carry as a spare. Because when I go on my trips something would absolutely happen to

the one I got. I got an edge, all right. I tried it out. I killed one bird on a slam with the 870, it's a Tennessee bird. I got an aimed-out scope on it, it was a red dot. I don't like it because of the follow-up shot I've missed. I don't care. And usually, the second shot, the bird's moving. I mean, he better be moving! But I've killed more—I gotta have that open gun. It's just for reaction time and trying to pick them up. I can't pick them up in the scope.

RORRER: I can. I have depended on the scope so much because of my vision. And I hate wearing glasses turkey hunting because on cool mornings the glasses fog up.

WILHELM: They'll fog up if you don't watch.

RORRER: If you're wearing a face mask and I just went strictly to scope and I've used one so much I wouldn't even begin to hunt without one.

WILHELM: I'm the opposite. I haven't used it. Yeah, it's the same thing.

RORRER: It's what you get used to and comfortable with. But one time I was flying out of Greensboro to Window Rock, Arizona, to hunt on the Navajo Indian Reservation. And when I got out to where we were going there at the reservation, I checked my gun. And I just happened, and I don't know why I didn't notice it at this point, but I just looked. And the rod was missing out of the takedown case. And the lock was gone. When I went to check in that morning I told the flight attendant, I said: "I have got a lock, a T.S.A. lock on my gun case. Can I go on to my gate?" "No, don't lock it. Don't lock it." And I said, "Well, ma'am, that was the purpose of me putting that lock on there. The T.S.A. can get in. That particular lock, any of them." So she said, "I'm gonna take it back here right now." Well, someone during this process taken the lock off or it was never locked one, took the rod out of the case, rammed it through my scope. And here I have nothing on that reservation. At that reservation to take that scope off, I finally got a pair of pliers and just abused the base right and everything getting it off. And then I remembered that particular Benelli kinda shot to the right. But I didn't remember how much. So I had to waste some of those high-dollar loads to try to figure out where to aim—where it was going. And I killed my turkey there, beautiful Merriam's turkey. But it took me three months to get American Airlines to reimburse me for that stuff. But it's some anti-hunter tree hugger or something.

What load do you normally shoot?

RORRER: Use Nitro 4, 5, 6 and 7 shot. Three-and-a-half-inch.

WILHELM: I use three-and-a-half because all mine are 5, 6 and 7. I don't have no 4s. It's a Hevi-Shot.

RORRER: Yeah, that's what these are. But, you know, now they using 20-gauges and shoot No. 9 shot in them. And they kill them turkeys 40, 50 yards. My nephew's got a 20-gauge. It'll kill them if it's got the right shells.

WILHELM: You get the right combination, they'll work for you.

How do you carry your gear in the field?

RORRER: A hunting vest, turkey vest. Yes, yes, and I try to make sure that I got a box call, a slate call, a glass call, a diaphragm call, owl hoot, a crow call and a pileated woodpecker call. Some locating calls, you know, mid-day and turkeys ain't doing nothing. You use the owl call early in the morning before light to get that turkey to gobble and give his location away so you can close some of that gap. You stand a better chance the closer you can get to them without spooking him than you do standing where you first hear him. A lot of times and maybe he has taken him away before he gets to you or another hunter.

WILHELM: I'm the opposite. I used to use vests for stuff. I carry a crow call in one pocket, box call in the other and two diaphragms and that's it. No vest. Just in the pockets of your shirt and coat. I got to where I just depend on that mouth call so much anymore and, to tell you the truth, success is success. I don't care how you do it. But, out of 10 states, I got nine of them, 14 birds last year with a mouth call. That's all I used. And it's just kind of something I don't have to keep up with something. And but I just don't use the other calls. I just don't see no reason to carry them.

RORRER: It gets heavy and I think you don't get near as tired if you got lighter gear.

WILHELM: It's simple. I ain't gotta worry about. I don't even carry a seat a majority of the time. Every once in a while I'll carry a pad but. Cuz you gotta sit still. But usually if I know I gotta sit still for a while it's either a pop-up or something where I got a chair.

RORRER: I got one of those Breedlove Air Cushions. It's nothing but like a wheelbarrow inner tube with camo on it.

WILHELM: How are them other, the real thin ones that they've got with the vests now? They don't do me no good. [laughing]

RORRER: Well these, I'll take it and it's got a quick

RORRER: I usually use the box to locate the bird a lot of times. But when he comes in close I don't like using that box. I like to use a slate, or use a mouth call, because you cut down on movement and everything, and the bird is not as apt to see you. But I have killed them solely with boxes a lot of times. In the old days, like I told you before, the Lynch box call was it for a long time.

Over the years, what's been your single most productive turkey voice?

WILHELM: For me, it would be just a plain cluck and then right behind that maybe the yelp. I've done all the other, the cutting and stuff. It's used in a last resort. I've killed birds with that. I had one

> Nope, just practice. Just did it. Just went out and picked up a box call and listened to a tape or watch TV. Driving my wife crazy. She said, "Get the hell out the house!"

connect on it where you can hook it in the back of your belt. And you don't have to be worried about trying to get something with one hand. You can just sit down.

WILHELM: Yeah, most of the stuff, if I'm working a bird, it's going to be quicker anyway. Cuz if the bird, if he hangs up, I give him about 30 to 45 minutes after he quit gobbling to show up. And sometimes I might have walk off on a bird. But 45 minutes is a long time, you sitting still, and that's about my limit. If he's not doing anything at all, not answering me, or hadn't showed up.

Did anyone teach you to call?

WILHELM: Nope, just practice. Just did it. Just went out and picked up a box call and listened to a tape or watch TV. Driving my wife crazy. She said, "Get the hell out the house!" [laughing]

Daniel, are there circumstances when you stick pretty much with one call? Sounds as if you generally employ more calls than Jimmy does.

bird, one year was right down over a bank. I'm talking 20 yards from me—just right there. I could hear him strutting and drumming and gobbling, but he wouldn't come up over the bank. And I finally got to where it was, *I'm going to either blow this or whatever.* I just started cutting as hard as I could cut and calling just loud as I can get. There he come right up over the bank. So you don't know. But I don't do it until it's a last resort. Most of the things that I've killed birds on is three clucks. Just go [making clucking sounds] like that—or four. That's all. They know you're there. That's it.

RORRER: I've killed a lot of birds just soft purring and clucking. A lot of birds, honestly. But on that box call, if a gobbler cuts me off, I will get pretty carried away with that call and cut. And that's what he wanted to hear.

What's your chosen time of day to hunt?

RORRER: Early in the morning. I have killed more birds 7, 7:30 in the morning than any other time

To celebrate achieving the U. S. Super Slam, Daniel enjoys making handsome calls that he gives to lucky family and friends.

of day. One time I killed a bird in the afternoon in Indiana and it was about 4 o'clock in the evening. And I had no more than gotten this out of my mouth, I told Cubby [Del Culberson] I said, "If you get a bird to gobble in the evening and commit, you can kill that bird."

WILHELM: Yep, a lot of them.

RORRER: I hadn't more than got it out of my mouth and that bird is right there. And that particular bird weighed 24 pounds and had inch-and-a-half spurs on him.

WILHELM: I agree with him with the morning stuff. Main thing was just cuz it's fresh, it's early. But I have taken birds anywhere from 6:15 in the morning to 5 in the evening—6, actually, in Montana. I won't turn down any of them. If I've got legal hunting time, I'm hunting, especially on my trips. I mean, you've got three days; you don't have so much time. Even if it's raining, sleeting, I've killed them. I had a heck of a hunt in Utah. I knew it was coming. It was snowing when I got there. Opening day I was sitting in the cabin. It was two

feet of snow on the ground and snowing like a dog. I wasn't going, but there was a gobbler gobbling 200 yards from the cabin, sitting in a tree. Wasn't no use if you can't get them on the ground. But two days later, I killed my bird just like that. [laughing]

Does your strategy change as the day draws on?

RORRER: Yes, yes, definitely.

WILHELM: I start out in the morning just listening, of course, before daylight, and see if you can get close to one, if you know where there's some birds at. But as you go through the day, if you haven't gotten anything to answer you, you haven't worked on it, I go to the sit-and-wait period somewhere around 11, if I've done worked an area pretty good and all you're gonna do is bust the birds if you walk into them. Somebody asked me one time: I said, turkeys are moving, you're moving. Well, stay put! I've found that out in the last few years, and I mean I've done good with that baby. It's just find you a good spot that you know there's birds. Good cover, either a natural blind or

James Wilhelm (right) and hunting friend celebrate their eastern turkeys in Missouri on April 27, 2000 with a beautiful spring backdrop of flowering crab apple trees.

a pop-up. I'll go sit down, put out a decoy or something and just call every 15, 20 minutes. And the first two birds I killed this year in Virginia, the last week, neither bird said a word when they come in. They come in looking but they did not say nothing. The last one I shot he come running. He was gobbling but these first two wasn't. And I killed the third one at 7:30 in the morning. But the first two actually came in at around 6:30, 7. But they were quiet. Now, there wasn't nothing going on so I just went and got in the blind. I got a certain area I hunt. I don't hunt the national forests and stuff much no more.

RORRER: When it's raining real hard, that's when I like to use a pop-up.

WILHELM: Rain and windy and snow.

Is rain and wind the most difficult?

WILHELM: Yes. Most time they ain't saying nothing. I've got them to do it in the wind. Like I said, first bird I missed, he was gobbling. But most the time, if it's raining, the field birds, they don't gobble. They will some, but not much. The bird I killed two years ago in Delaware, he was gobbling. It was raining, but it wasn't much gobbling.

RORRER: That's like Alabama, when I hunted down there in peanut fields, so dry the surface of the ground actually had probably two-inch wide cracks in it where it dried up so bad. And Scott Culpepper and I spotted these turkeys out in the other end of that long peanut field. And we decided we're gonna circle them. We're gonna go around long ways through the woods. And get on the same side as they was on. So by the time we got

there, there was another turkey out in the field with them. And they were on the end that we just come from. And we was calling and the turkeys wouldn't even lift their heads. So I got a box call and I just really laid into it for everything I had. And one of them lift his head up. So Scott said: "Daniel, I believe he liked that. I believe he heard that. Give him some more of that." So I did. Two of them toms came all the way back across that field to us. And I wanted Scott to get a shot, too. And I waited until the turkey came all the way into the woods before I shoot him. And then the other turkey, trees and things in his way, the way the turkey come in and he ran back out in the field. And he was trying to figure out what was going on with him. And Scott said, "He's too far." I said,

She come down within five feet. Turned and went up to the edge of the fenced road. The same way the gobbler went. I said, *well, pretty sure I was in the wrong place.* [laughing] All of a sudden, about an hour later, here come three gobblers out that tumble-down. They were starting toward that corner, too. I said, *what?* I just started cutting. I had the decoys out there. I cut so loud and stuff and that they just stopped. But all three of them looked at her, seeing that decoy. Boom! All three of them come running. [laughing] I got the big one. But it was just pouring rain. They weren't gobbling. But I don't reckon they could hear me. I always start out as low as you can—no more calling than you can get by with. But if that don't work, what do you got to lose?

> I just started cutting. I had the decoys out there. I cut so loud and stuff and that they just stopped. But all three of them looked at her, seeing that decoy. Boom! All three of them come running. [laughing] I got the big one. But it was just pouring rain. They weren't gobbling. But I don't reckon they could hear me.

"Well, I can take him." He said, "You want to?" And I said, "Yes." [laughing] So I shot him and that's when I was using those Nitro loads too. He couldn't believe I killed him. He was probably 50, 60 yards.
WILHELM: First Missouri bird, with me, I was sitting actually, the boy showed me where to go. Just hunting a cornfield. There was an old fence right here and a fence right here, and I was sitting right here at the corner. The field here and an old cornfield and a pond back here. And I was sitting up in that fence row and it was raining like a dog. First day and an old gobbler came out down here and started across the cornfield and I called. He never even picked his head up. I called again, nothing. Kept going, went on up in the corner field. I said, *well, maybe I'm sitting in the wrong spot.* A little bit later, here come a hen down the fence, I mean the old road right in front of me.

RORRER: Exactly. You give it all you got.
WILHELM: Give it all you got.
RORRER: Me in Nebraska, when I hunted out there, it was pretty dark outside And then the next morning when we got up to go turkey hunting, had come about four and a half inches of real wet snow. It was on every fence, little blades of glass, everything. This turkey came in—I set a jake and a hen decoy out that time—and this turkey come in, strutting in that snow. He came up and he would not take his eye off that jake at all. Turned and twisted and just kept his eye right on him. And I wanted to get it all on video, if I could. So Clay Beck, he was sitting behind me, videoing. And better than 12 minutes, that turkey stood there and twisted and turned around, and watching it, just wanting that jake to do something.
WILHELM: To move.

RORRER: And finally, he just gets tired of that and he goes over and jumps on him and beats him to the ground, and starts to walk off.

What about henned-up gobblers? How do you deal with them?

RORRER: I try my best to out-do the dominant hen. Try to make that hen mad.

WILHELM: It'll work once in a while. You get an old hen mad and she starts talking to you, it'll work. But to get them to do that, what—20 percent of the time? Maybe. If you're lucky. I kind of sit there. If you can't get the bird to work and you see which direction they're going in. And if you know where you're at. Which most times we don't when you're traveling. But if you know where the bird is going. Or at least what's over that way. I get up after you get out of sight and go around and get to where they wanna be.

RORRER: Try to cut them off.

WILHELM: If you're there, they will come. I'm not gonna say calling every time helps because if you start calling too much that hen will take him somewhere else. For some reason they don't wanna associate with another broad.

RORRER: No. And, you know, there's been times when I was working a turkey and I felt like that he wanted to come in and maybe another hen just get here and you go with me and take him right out there.

WILHELM: Last thing is, you can't fight it. I don't care. It's nothing you're going to do about it. And I've had some of them come. I've had hens come in and jump on a hen decoy. I mean, they just didn't want them in the area.

RORRER: I had one this spring, strutting.

WILHELM: [Laughing]

RORRER: Again, but you don't see that often, either.

WILHELM: It's a little bit of everything.

You mentioned drumming birds—is that common behavior?

WILHELM: I was hunting in Mississippi. First time down there. It was my birthday. And I was done. Killed the one I needed. There was a two-bird limit. And I was working this one draw. And it was woods this way and woods up there under the ridge. And there was a gobbler up on top, I could see. I was down there. I had a little stick blind that I put up because of movement. And I was watching him. Had two jakes and three hens with him. I'd call. He'd go every time I hit the call. He wouldn't come off that ridge. I could not get none of them to come down to that flat, where I was sitting there. I called one more time and I heard something. [making drumming sound] I said, *my God*, and he was right there 20 yards to my left. It was the reason he wouldn't come off that hill. He got his butt kicked when he got down there. So I killed this bird. But yeah, I mean, if you got one drumming and he's close enough, you better be real. And I don't know, if you can't see him out here, you in trouble cuz unless you got something up to where you can move. Cuz that bird's close.

RORRER: I've had them come in behind and do that very same thing, and there was no way you could've moved and killed him.

WILHELM: You can't do it.

What does it take to become an exceptional turkey hunter? What characteristics do the best hunters share?

RORRER: They just got the same knack of knowing what they're doing.

They're good at turkey hunting.

WILHELM: You gotta have the knack to be a woodsman. It's not just turkey—it's any kind of hunting. I got a grandson, wouldn't kill a fly. He'll never make a hunter. My granddaughters are different thing. It's an attitude, a feeling. I mean, they just got, they just connect with it. In other words, you just can't take anybody to do that.

RORRER: Some people are such animal lovers they wouldn't harm anything.

WILHELM: Well, I love animals. I mean, I've raised birds, all right? My wife has got three parrots. She bought them. Well, two of them she bought. One of them just showed up in the driveway. [laughing] She's got an African grey.

RORRER: Those are smart birds.

This Lone Star bird was no match for Daniel Rorrer's technique with his handmade call—March 26, 2015, San Angelo, Texas.

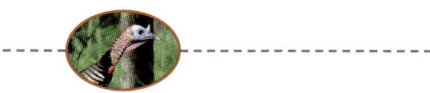

WILHELM: Well, I don't know how smart this one is! [laughing]

RORRER: Generally, they're supposed to be.

WILHELM: He is actually took up with me. They adopt one person, and I happen to be the one person. I mean, I love animals. It ain't nothing to do with that. But that don't mean I won't hunt.

RORRER: Right, but there are people that just wouldn't hunt.

WILHELM: I have no problem with that. I just don't want them cutting mine out.

What changes, in a broad sense, have you seen in hunting over the years and, in particular, turkey hunting?

RORRER:I don't know if there's any change. What worries me is there's a lack of consistency. You got a lot of part-timers. They might go one time this week, and maybe one time three weeks from now, and that's it for the season.

WILHELM: Yeah, you ain't got but a month.

RORRER: To me, that's not a turkey hunter.

So you mean lacking a degree of commitment?

RORRER: Yeah. That's the word I was looking for. In any kind of hunting, I don't care what it is—if it's duck or deer or whatever—if there's no commitment, you got a problem. And it's the long run what worries me. Part of it's because of access to property that you can hunt, of course, cuz of the population. But lot of the older guys are quitting or not hunting anymore, or this guy ain't doing it because of that. Maybe health issues.

RORRER: Well, I don't think it's a health issue as much. I better be in bed can't get up! That's what I'm saying. There's no commitment to them.

And the younger generation today is so wrapped up in the technology of everything.

RORRER: Too much. You're right.

It's up to us to teach them that there's more to life than staring at a screen. The "more to life" is

life, isn't it?

RORRER: Exactly. Now, you and I had experienced things. Looking at that screen playing video games—what is that to life?

WILHELM: It isn't. I mean, get a fishing pole, go out here.

RORRER: But I love doing all things for people that's never hunted, to help them to get their first turkey, or just whatever I can do to introduce the young people to the outdoors is my main goal.

WILHELM: You're right, getting the kids involved, not just my grandkids, but any kid that I can take, we take them.

How do you cook turkey?

RORRER: Deep fry in peanut oil.

WILHELM: It's my wife's favorite recipe, Judy Wilhelm. [laughing] Put in a little word for her there at the end.

> Take half a wild turkey breast and put in freezer long enough to stiffen up enough to slice into three-eighth- and half-inch slices. Coat each slice in seasoned flour (salt, pepper and any other seasoning desirable), then place in skillet with one or two tablespoons of olive oil. Brown on both sides until cooked through. Take meat out of an and put in enough flour (one or two tablespoons) to make a paste. Add part water, part milk—you can also use chicken broth—and stir until thickened. In the meantime, boil water and cook egg noodles until tender. Drain, pour gravy over noddles and turkey on individual plates, and serve.

James tagged this Rio turkey in the southern California chaparral on April 5, 2011. The next day he headed north, where he pulled the trigger on another Golden State bird in the live oaks north from San Francisco.

INDEX

Page numbers in **bold** indicate photograph

PHOTO CREDITS

Chris Ellis
Front cover image of hunters

Timothy C. Flanigan
Front cover image of strutting gobbler, back cover, all images of live turkeys and feathers throughout book used as decorative graphics

James F. Hascup Jr.
84, 88, 94, 97, 101, 102, 107, 111–12

Dave Owens
7, 8, 12, 13, 16, 17, 18, 20, 21, 22, 23

Thomas R. Pero
3–4, 25–26, 42, 78, 82, 91, 104, 109, 116, 147–48, 149, 168, 188

Jon D. Pries
117, 122, 123, 126, 127, 130, 131, 134, 135, 138, 139, 142

Daniel Rorrer
154, 160, 164, 167, 172, 176, 180, 184, 192

Tom "Doc" Weddle
5, 9–10, 27, 30, 31–32, 33, 34, 35, 38, 39, 43, 45, 48, 49, 52, 53, 57, 61, 66, 69, 72, 76

James Wilhelm
152, 155, 161, 165, 169, 173, 177, 181, 185, 189, 193

Own a Special Collector's Edition

A leather-bound limited edition of this book is available from Wild River Press at $149.95. The cover features a handsome copper-embossed image of a strutting tom turkey on rich brown leather. These books are signed by the author and numbered one through 49, in honor of the U. S. Super Slam. It's the perfect gift for your favorite turkey hunter—or a wonderful addition to your own sporting library. Order by telephone at 425-486-3638 or send inquiries to tom@wildriverpress.com.